Metamodern Vision *of* Tola Wewe

MOYO OKEDIJI

Metamodern Vision *of* Tola Wewe

MOYO OKEDIJI

ISBN 979-8-218-07676-4
Published by Onàism University Press, Ilé Ifè, Nigeria.
Printed by Northline Printing Company LLC

Cover painting: House of Yemoja.

Contents

Introduction

The casualties are not only those who are dead;
They are well out of it.
The casualties are not only those who are wounded,
Though they await burial by instalment.
The casualties are not only those who started
A fire and now cannot put it out. Thousands
Are burning that have no say in the matter.
The casualties are many, and a good number as well
Outside the scenes of ravage and wreck;
They are the emissaries of rift,
So smug in smoke-rooms they haunt abroad,
They do not see the funeral piles
At home eating up the forests
Caught in the clash of counter claims and charges
When not in the niche others have left,
We fall,
All casualties of the war,

Because we cannot hear each other speak,
Because eyes have ceased to see the face from the crowd,
Because whether we know or
Do not know the extent of wrongs on all sides,
We are characters now other than before
We are all casualties,
All sagging as are
The cases celebrated for kwashiorkor,

The Casualties (To Chinua Achebe)
- John Pepper Clark.

This book, *The Metamodern Vision of Tola Wewe* is written as part of a larger curatorial project on the work of the prolific Nigerian artist, Adetola Wewe, whose career, it is clear, deserves a retrospective.

I have known Wewe since 1979, when he gained admission into the University of Ife, where I was a young teacher, after my own graduation from the same university. Wewe was a promising student and I became interested in his work quite early.

We were all young in those days, and quite serious – perhaps too serious – about art. Our sincerity was built on passion, not knowledge; we were driven to rethink art more out of a feeling that something was wrong with what we were doing than out of any experience of what art was or could be. We did not like the art we were doing. We did not like the art anybody was doing. We wanted to do things differently, but we didn't know exactly what we wanted. But since we were young, we didn't realize exactly how tall our ambitions were, nor did we ever consider them formidable.

We questioned everything and everyone, but didn't know what questions to pose to ourselves. This innocence, if one may call it that, made our task all the more difficult, probably even romantic.

If we knew then what we now know, we probably wouldn't have embarked on the journey that we did. But we were exuberant, driven and relentless. We didn't understand where we were going, or how to get there, but we knew we were not satisfied with where we were.

Little did we realize that what really needed fixing was not so much art as real life. Our dissatisfaction emanated from the life around us more than from the making of art. The angst that drove us came from the sociological voids within which we lived, a space in which we did not find any foothold.

But it was not just us. It was an experience that enveloped the entire country. Nigeria was then experiencing a slow but certain transition into a hostile trap for the tens of millions of its citizens. It was not a condition that art could fix. But the only tool we had was what we studied at school – painting, drawing, sculpting,

“The battles of the years after the war were not physical as much as psychological. The physical battles of the war were certainly devastating.”

performance and installation. We thought that the problem was with these things and we sought the solution to life only through these avenues.

To understand the circumstances we found ourselves – and within which we attempted to make art – one must revisit the cultural landscape of Nigeria between the early 1980s and late 1990s.

Little did we realize at that time that we were war artists. Nobody spoke about the “civil” war that ended in 1970, perhaps because we called it a *civil* war, something minor, not too consequential – and certainly something that had ended and with which we had no connection.
It was actually not that simple. We just got caught up in the rhetoric of the politicians, who wanted us to imagine that the war was not important and was already behind us. But anybody who has survived a war would realize that the peace that comes after the war could be just as difficult to navigate as the war that ended.
The battles of the years after the war were not physical as much as psychological. The physical battles of the war were certainly devastating. But the pains of the peace that came after the war result from a different kind of injury that only a post-war era brings – psychological traumas that are locked up within the mind, difficult to reach; inaccessible to reason; impenetrable to light. Lurking behind every look was the unseeable specter; behind every word was the noisome silence; behind every perfume was the stench of death; behind every taste was the bitterness of hunger. It was a hunger for something different, something not available – undefinable even.

The civil war was brief; just from 1967 to 1970. Our generation, Wewe’s generation, came out of the development that led directly to that war. We were born into it, grew up in it, experienced it and are survivors – as well as victims – of it.
The thick, dense, acrid smoke of that war provided the architecture of our cribs, and we pulled into our nostrils that same acrid smoke when we first inhaled at birth. We were children of an era that was gradually falling into the precipices of a national calamity for which we were not prepared and of which we were oblivious.
The years before the war spanned only six years following the political independence of Nigeria in 1960. A year before this independence, Wewe was born in the western bayou of the Niger delta, a dense riverine foothold between the Atlantic Ocean and the vast farmlands where the fishing communities tended agricultural products on small plots of communally held land. Within this land, rich in myriads of minerals, was also crude oil, the discovery and exploitation of which was to throw the entire country into a chaotic spin, that eventually precipitated the civil war.

Though 1960 was the year that Nigeria became independent, and celebrated its freedom from its colonial occupiers, it was in 1914 that Britain created Nigeria. There was nothing by that name before then. What existed was a large number of indigenous peoples of various ethnicities, living together with varying degrees of amity, until Britain joined the various colonies and protectorates it had conquered, into one administrative unit, for greater economy. This amalgamation of the numerous ethnic groups did not prove happy, and by 1960 when Britain gave Nigeria political independence, the tension among its peoples was already so taut that only six years later, the inevitable war erupted, tearing apart the tired seams that had until then, held them together.

It was within the years that tension started building in Nigeria toward the war that Wewe was born. While his riverine communities might have been oblivious to the beating drums of war, they were loud and clear to the inhabitants of Northern Nigeria, in whose land the bloodshed began, before spreading South-east, which now became the center stage of the theater of war.

It was a wasteful war that squandered the lives of more than 2 million men, women and children, most of them of Igbo extraction. But the aftermath of the civil war, produced even more political turmoil, as those who experienced the war, attempted to mend their lives through the design of several political and sociological experiments – of which none has worked.

Masked in emaciated, tired and broken bodies, the survivors emerged from the war zones in 1970 – filled with anger, rage, fury and sadness – and began to mingle with the rest of the country. They were received with mixed feelings of relief, that the fighting with ordnance was over, while the anxiety of a new kind of war began to mount under the surface.

The intuition that the peace after the end of the war was going to be bitter was a reality that the adults knew, and accepted, but couldn't show or explain to those of us who were young and without the experience to process the historical conditions into which we were born.

In the first decades of the peace, therefore, those of us, including Wewe, who worked as painters, sculptors, printmakers and writers were post-war artists; though our educational system was designed to hide that fact from us as much as possible. All the experiences we had after the war were sociologically defined by a political will driven to hide and un-write the history of the war theaters within which we were born and had grown.

When Wewe graduated in 1983, therefore, he joined the company of those of us who graduated within a decade before him, and who gazed more directly at the ghoulish faces and fatigued bodies of those who crawled out from the locations in which the war trapped them.

Four young artists and I came together and formed a group that we named Ọnà, in an attempt to plot a new direction for art in Nigeria. Wewe was one of these five artists.

This book tells the story of Wewe, one of the quintuplet artists who started the Ọnà group as a journey into an unknown territory – to generate a new aesthetics for artistic practice.
It was in the development of Ọnà that I mapped out metamodernism.

How did metamodernism evolve? It started auspiciously one day when I fell upon *Elements of Semiology* by Roland Barthes. One of the most striking statements that I found in the book came pretty early; Barthes, among other statements, declared that "...there is no meaning which is not designated, and the world of signifieds is none other than that of language."
In his discussion on semiotics, Barthes, from my own perspective, did not reckon with the notion that indigenous Yoruba creative perspective about language is meaningless without the other senses.

As a visual art critic and historian, I therefore coined the term "semioptics," to designate a body of visual signs from a combination of semeion and optic. It was semioptics that led to metamodernism.

As I discovered that Barthes developed his semiotic ideas from Fernand de Saussure, the scholar of linguistics regarded as a pioneering thinker on the subject, it became clear that it was not just semiotics that needed examining. It was the entire modernist project within which semiotics evolved, a system that was colonial and thus needed interrogation. The art of Africa and its diasporas were the earliest victims of this modernist onslaught, which rendered entire bodies of works invisible; and then began to determine the terms of its visibility.

With what does one reflect on that body of modernist theorizing, except with a meta theory that is capable of engaging modernity, while reflecting on the body of art that modernity obscured or rendered absolutely invisible? This was the condition that gave birth to metamodernism.

With this book, *The Metamodern Vision of Tola Wewe*, I use metamodernism to explore the work of a single artist. Readers will discover the use of analytic discussive tools, transcending modernist lenses, in the interpretation of Wewe's work. These include myths, dreams, songs, poetry and a spirituality that explore territories of the mysterious and metaphysical in the creative process and interpretive program of Wewe's work.

Particularly striking is the use of Ifá divination devices by Wewe before and after making his work. Wewe opens up the world of the unknown and the unknowable with his paintings. It is a world in which the modernist frame of man cannot traverse. It is therefore not only appropriate, but absolutely necessary to tease out meaning from Wewe's work with the archeological tools of metamodernism.

CHAPTER ONE:

The Arrival

Yesterday. Today.
Tomorrow.

Tomorrow is Yesterday's
Today.
Today is Yesterday's
Tomorrow.
Yesterday is Tomorrow's Today.

Tola Wewe gets up in the middle of the night. Soundlessly, his body works its way to the studio: to paint away the pains of humankind and rebirth the joys of new beginnings.

As he moves down the steps, he is still in the land of dreams. This is the perfect time for him to paint, a time that is truly countertime - when other human bodies and minds have been conditioned to sleep – this time when tomorrow is not yet finished and yesterday is not finished yet.

I

Time has timed out on Tola Wewe's canvas. Discarding the current concept of time, he traverses the metamodern concept of reality in which yesterday, today and tomorrow do not hang forlorn and alone by themselves like truncated tree trunks, but flow like tributaries of the same river, their confluence a timeless ferment of infinite creativity.

This zone is not simply designed to defy the frozen box of zero to twenty-four blocks that human life is currently broken into.

Time, he knows, is mere illusion – a mirage in which human beings are reduced to a hustling mass, on a perpetual treadmill, to catch that phantom train – which has always just left or is always just coming.

Only humans allow themselves to be so controlled. Not animals. Not plants. The so-called lower beings – arranged on a mental tier below that labeled as Man – do not submit to such unnaturalness. Women, too, are not biologically tied somatically or mentally to the clockwork. The cycle of the flow of blood is never the same with all women: every female body sets the tempo of her river to a different rhythm, and every moon, the rhythm shifts in directions that the clock cannot tie.

That is the Yoruba visionary clock to which Tola Wewe ties his understanding of time: it is not modern. It is metamodern.

Eons before the faintest dream of modernity existed, there was this elastic understanding of time. And it will be here well after folks stop being modern – not in a postmodern sense but in a milieu that qualifies and disqualifies the postmodernity, postcoloniality and modern sense – demanding that reality be released back into its own natural laws, freed from the lusts for insatiate acquisitions and incessant inquisitions.

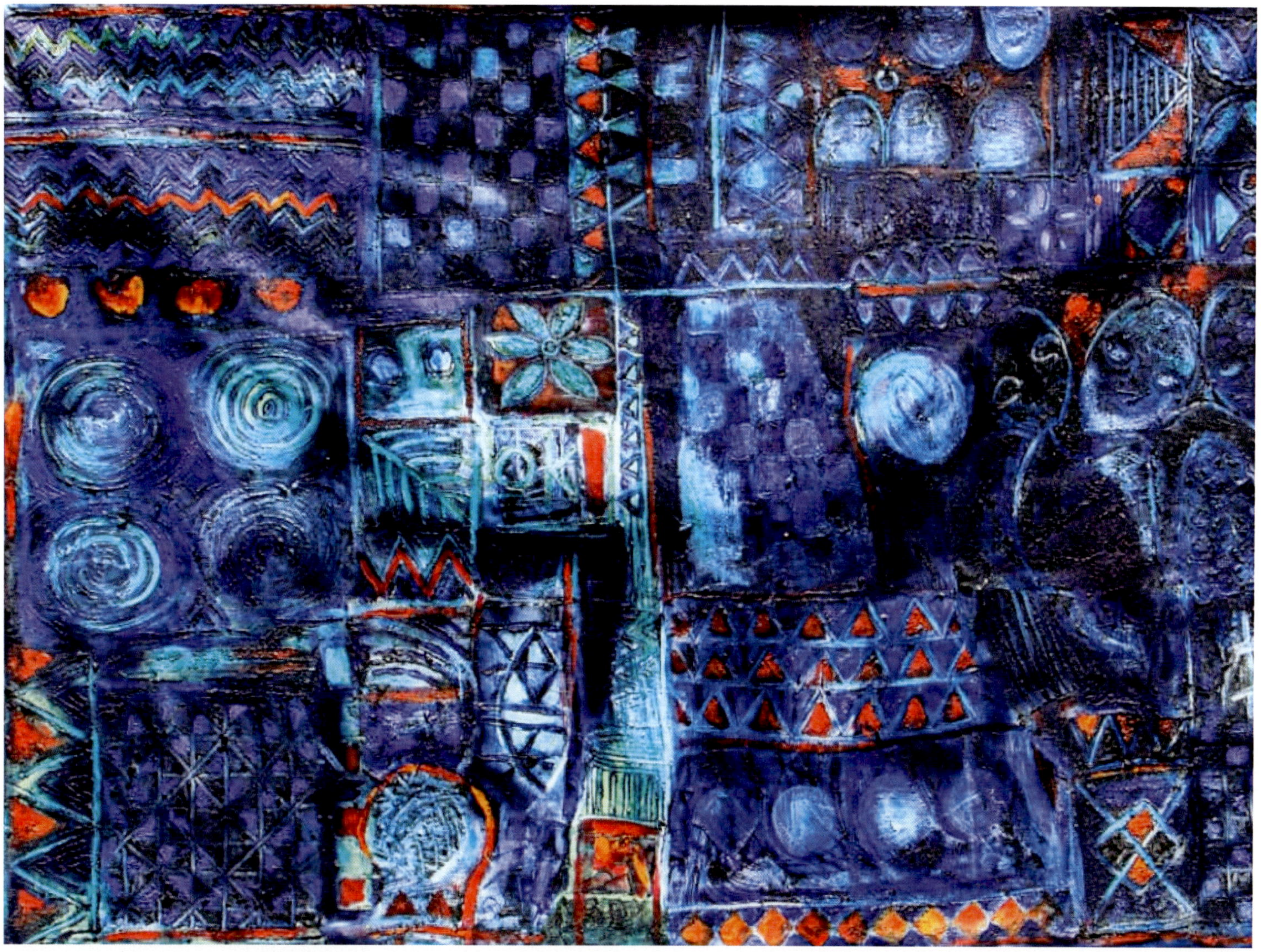

Fig. 1: *The Pluck Me Not Leaves*, acrylic on canvas, 2021.

This wakeful time fuses the body and mind together with the consciousness of everything that exists in nature. Matter does not matter now, in a reality in which there is no separation between lower and higher animals, between water and soil, between tree and stone, between air and fire, hot and cold, loud and silent, long and short, between you and me.

It is in a future that is already in the past – available, yet unknown to many and accessible to initiates only – now unveiled in the creative work that Wewe is about to reveal to the entire world.

Having surrendered his sensibilities to laws that part the curtains separating the seen from the unseeable, having tasted the soup simmered in the waters of midnight dew, cooked in the pots of The Mother – The Mothers – it is not Wewe per se unveiling these images, he is just the vehicle through which these images – that are already in the hidden corridors of reality – reveal themselves.

Our mothers who have no mothers. They are the ones who wrap their bodies with a thousand herbs, though none touches their skin.

Posing for him in this minute of hourless seconds,

"Pluck me! Pluck me! Pluck me!" They call. "The ones you plucked last night are now the roots of tomorrow!"

"I have eaten the Pluck Me Not Leaves. Leave me be," is Wewe's response.

"Hang your canvas upside down, upside down like a bat hanging only by the nails of its left foot, its right foot entangled in *Forget me Not* leaves." They commanded.

"Nobody eats the head of the Praying Mantis. It is more bitter than bile," Wewe warns.
"The night is now day, and the day is night," sings Our Mothers

"Neither night nor day contains the wings of time when the Son of the Sun flies around the moon," Wewe declares.

Walking backwards, left leg forward, like cats prowling a stage, Our Mothers enter the studio. Stretching the canvas, they prime it with the salt of the ocean, paint it midnight blue and hang it upside down like a bat from a broken egg.

At the approaching dawn, Our Mothers leave the studio, spent like the sand sickle, breathing through their fiery eyes, chanting the Song Eternal that woke up Dawn, when the first cockcrow cackled with mirth.

It was the first night of Tola Wewe's 2021 residency at my studio on Candlestick Place, Austin, Texas.

"Your home is writhing with a million and one spirits," Wewe said at breakfast the next morning. "Right in front of your studio was a bird that refused to move even after I yelled at her. She simply eyed me and hissed. I knew better than to bother her. What do you feed them?"

"Nothing," I replied. "I don't know what you are talking about, Tola. My house has no spirits; seen or unseen. It's your imagination playing tricks on you."

The previous day, I had gone downtown Austin to pick him up from the bus station. Arriving from Nigeria the week before, he had spent the whole week with his son, Oluropo, luxuriating in the sheer pleasure of babysitting his newly arrived fourth grandchild.
Being a father of only sons and after three male grandchildren, he was exceedingly thrilled to welcome his first granddaughter.

Mask-free, I hugged his Covid complaint, colorful nose masked familiarity.
"You too? I noticed people were not wearing masks on the bus from Houston," Wewe said as he climbed into my Jeep.

"Please yank off your mask," I begged him. "This is Texas. We are the perfect embodiment of the Wild West. When the rest of America is going west, we turn east."

"Yes, I read something online about Texas seceding from the United States, is that true?"

"It's just talk," I assured him. "We say that all the time just to keep the rest of the Union on their toes. Meantime, welcome to Austin, the Live Music Capital of the World!"
"Really? We will get to see some live

music performance?" His eye was alight with excitement.

"Of course," I assured him. "Every restaurant worth its salt has its resident music band. We can go and check one out tonight."

"Not tonight, maybe this weekend. I want to paint on my first night in your studio."

"What do you want to paint?"

"I don't know," he replied. "When I get into the studio, the painting will paint itself."

And the following morning, he showed me the painting - *The Pluck me Not Leaves.*

II

Tola Wewe spent the day resting. "Why is Austin so hot? The AC must always be on and I hate having it on. One must always turn on the AC.. And I hate the AC."

"That's what we go through here... but in winter, when it's really freezing elsewhere in the US, Austin doesn't experience extreme cold temperatures."

"That's better," he agreed. "I prefer hot weather to the cold. But this is rather toasty. Great weather for a cold beer. I will paint at night when the temperature goes down. I see you loaded the fridge with cold beer."

He got himself a bottle, opened it, grabbed a glass, filled it and gulped it down with a deep grunt of satisfaction.

"Good beer," he said. "Almost as good as good old Star back home. Nobody makes beers like Nigeria.

"Enjoy...What about *ẹ̀bà* and *ẹ̀gúsí* for lunch? I made some *ẹ̀gúsí* with bitter leaf and smoked fish, ready for your arrival. I know you like that. It's in the fridge. Just stick the soup in the microwave and I will make the *èbà*. Won't take five minutes."

"You warm the soup and I'll make the *ẹ̀bà*," Wewe said. "I like the *èbà* very properly done. You may not get it right."

I didn't argue with him. Food is an important art form with Wewe. He is an amazing cook.

Soon, lunch was ready and I opened a bottle of beer for myself too. I hadn't touched alcohol for months, but I knew I wouldn't be able to resist Bacchus during his visit.

"In the evening, let's go and listen to some reggae," I told him. "There's a club downtown that features reggae regularly."

"I'll nap after this lunch. It's heavy. Or did I have too much beer? Remember that crazy beer with 12 percent alcohol we used to drink when you were in Denver, Colorado?"

"Yes, you want some of that brand? There's a place here where I can get it."
"Sure," he said.
"We can get some, plus some wine and liquor, and throw a small gig to celebrate your mother's transition. We can invite some friends over this Saturday."
"Oh, my mother," he sighed. "Yes, she passed. We will do a full burial this December. You know, that her abduction really affected her. After we secured her release, she was never the same again."

"I'm sorry to hear that."

"I don't want to think about it," he said. "*Ìyá ni wúrà. Lọ́jọ ìyá kú ni wúrà bàjẹ́.*"

He got up, went to the fridge and fetched two more bottles of beer. Handing one to me, he opened the other. Swinging his legs up onto the couch, he reclined the back of the seat and was fast asleep in a matter of minutes, breathing deeply.

His sleep was restless. Very soon, I heard him murmuring in his sleep, tossing and turning, but I couldn't make out what he was saying.

He sounded upset, certainly uncomfortable. Was he feeling uncomfortable on the couch?

Soon after, he went silent, sleeping soundly, drawing deep breaths.

*

His ordeal began with a brief phone call. Strained and exhausted, Wewe took the unexpected call on his cell phone. He needed to sit down. He looked around for a seat. There was no seat near him. He rested a hand against the wall to stabilize himself.
"Hallo? Hallo? Are you there? Sad news about Mama"
"Who?" Wewe asked.
"Your mother," the voice announced. "Sad to let you know she has been abducted from her home."

A sharp pain pinched him in the middle of the chest and traveled slowly down to the bottom of his stomach.

"I think I'm going to be sick," he thought. For the past week he had been nursing an ominous feeling that something beyond his control was going to happen. Somehow his mind kept going to his mother. He had already planned to drive to the village this weekend to visit her.

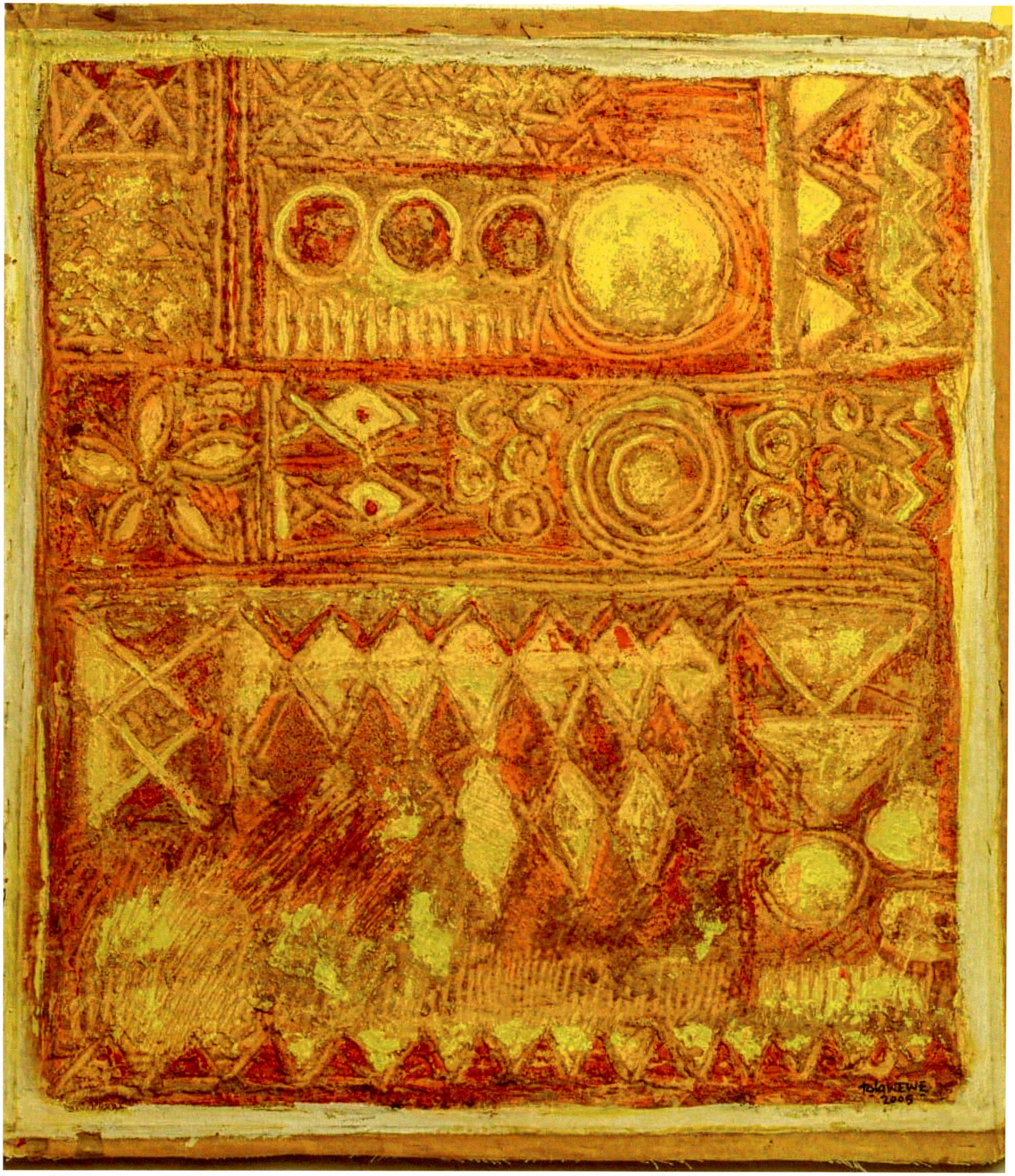

Fig. 2: *Mother Is Gold: Iya Ni Wura*, acrylic on canvas

"Hallo? Hallo? Are you still there?" the voice asked again.

"What did you say?" he wanted to be sure his ears were not deceiving him.
"Hallo? Mama has been kidnapped," the faintly familiar voice said.
He was instantly soaked in sweat.

He had been at the meeting of the Òndó State Executive Council when he felt his I-phone vibrate. He checked the number and saw that the call was from an important chief in Shabomi, his hometown in the western Niger Delta. Quickly, he left the room to take the call. The executive meeting was a particularly long session, dragging on and on, beyond midnight, into the early hours of the morning.

Having been on his seat for so long, he had been praying for a badly needed break when he got the call.

The caller did not have any details.

"Who abducted her?" He finally found his voice.
It sounded like it was not coming from inside him but from another person down the hall.
"Do you know who kidnapped her?"
"We don't know."
"What do you mean you don't know? Where was she taken?"
"Nobody knows."
"When did this happen? Today?"
"A short while ago. At about 1:30 am."
"And what time is it now?"
"I don't know. I'm not wearing a wrist watch."

Wewe, perplexed, stood alone in a corridor of the State House, his entire body shaking. He checked the time on his cell phone. It was past 2:00 am. He returned to the meeting room. He tried to control his shaking body. As he whispered into the ears of the Secretary to the State Government, it was clear to everybody that there was something seriously wrong with him.
"There is an emergency and I must leave immediately."

The secretary nodded understandingly.
"Hope you're fine," said the secretary, whispering back. The governor was in the middle of an important statement but paused as he felt the tension and fear in Wewe's shivering body.

Wewe went to the unlit parking lot.
"Everything will be alright," he whispered to himself, although he didn't believe it.
"It's probably just a mistake," he said in self-reassurance. "Must be a case of mistaken identity."

The large power generator which provided electricity to the State House clanked away in its corner – loud, irritating, invasive. Otherwise the night was still and pitch dark.

His driver was behind the wheel of his personal car, a black Jaguar, waiting for him. He slumped into the back seat "Home," he breathed.

He hardly ever used the Jaguar. His eyes scanned the dark streets, searching for any strange movement. He saw nothing. His was the only car on the road. He felt lonely and afraid.

It started to drizzle as they drove home. At that time of the year, the rainy season was slowly disappearing and the heat of the tropical dry season was beginning to sizzle. Though the car's air conditioner was fully blasting cold and dry air, Wewe was sweating. As soon as he got home, his cell phone rang again. It was his mother's number. His hand went clammy as he took the call.

"I am The Kidnapper," the anonymous voice announced. "You are the Lagos Picasso, right? You must call me back. Now, now!" The caller snapped in pidgin English.
The line went dead, as Wewe kept staring at his cell phone.
Wewe dialed his mother's number.

"Your mama is in our custody. I am using her cell phone. First thing in the morning, you must text phone credits worth twenty thousand naira to her number."

The kidnapper again ended the call abruptly.

Wewe went to bed. He lit a cigarette and poured himself a full glass of brandy. Sleep did not come. Kidnapper, he thought, as he lay in bed staring at the ceiling. A more appropriate term would be "Mamanapper."

Morning arrived slow and torturous. Wewe had not slept a wink throughout the night. He sent his driver to buy the phone credits of twenty thousand naira as he had been instructed. His driver returned within an hour and handed him the phone credit cards. He began to text them to his mother's number. The phone rang again.

"I am The Kidnapper," the voice snapped. "I asked for twenty thousand naira in phone credits. This is not twenty thousand!"

"Patience, please," Wewe pleaded. "I am still loading the credits."

"Good. When you finish loading, call me back."

Wewe completed the long process of texting the credits and called his mother's number.

"She is safe," said the kidnapper. "To obtain her release, you will deposit one hundred and fifty million naira[1] to a secure location that will later be disclosed to you. Reporting this matter to the security agents will put her life in serious jeopardy, which, as you know, may result in her death. As soon as you provide us with this modest ransom fee, your dear mother will be immediately released. Otherwise she will suffer a slow and agonizing death and the fault will entirely be yours. You have been warned." The call ended as abruptly as it started.

Wewe's ordeal is a common Nigerian tale of life imitating Nollywood, the larger-than-life Nigerian film industry. And like a bad Nollywood script, it began with incredulity. Wewe sat stunned for several minutes after receiving the call in his official residence in Akure, where he had relocated a year after he accepted the technocratic position of Commissioner for Culture and Tourism of his home state, Òndó. He slowly recovered his mind and began to rally his resources of friends, colleagues, and acquaintances.

His first and most important commitment was to bring his mother back home safe and sound. He also believed that he could outsmart the kidnappers and bring them to justice: after all he was a member of the Òndó State executive committee, with the entire security apparatus of the state at his disposal. He placed a call to the head of the state's security forces and received assurances that the abductors will be apprehended, and his mother brought home unscathed.

"*Àwon olópã fi mí jeun,*"[2] Wewe recalled later. "They kept telling me every day that they were closing in on the kidnappers. In fact they hardly raised a finger to assist me."

Wewe called a meeting of family members to announce the bad news. Relatives from his village came and confirmed the news: not only was his mother missing, his eleven-year-old niece, who was his mother's favorite house sitter, was also taken by the kidnappers.

His brothers and sisters broke down; weeping profusely throughout the family meeting. In tears, his immediate junior brother, known as Chairman, pleaded, "Don't bring in the police because they are only going to make matters worse. Let us look for the money and settle the abductors."

Someone suggested negotiating with the criminals to reduce the ransom figure. One of his sisters remarked that Wewe's fortune as a celebrity artist and state commissioner was what attracted the kidnappers. Wewe started feeling guilty and responsible for the atrocity. He left Akure, moved back to his personal house in Òndó, and kept his cell phone permanently in front of him; on the desk in his studio where he retreated.

He was unable to eat or sleep, as anxiety and depression began to unravel his characteristic calm disposition.
Only a couple of months prior to the abduction, the wife of the Commissioner of Works was kidnapped and an undisclosed

but generous ransom was paid for her release. Kidnapping had become the new strategy adopted by members of the underworld who targeted the rich and famous in their bid to get rich quick. Business tycoons, expatriate oil executives, journalists, politicians, and even religious leaders and their families were constant targets. Abduction had become a multi-billion Naira enterprise in Nigeria, and the police seemed unable to find any solution to the problem. No kidnapper had been arrested; huge sums of ransom money had been paid. Many people complained that there was evidence of collusion between the security forces and the criminals.

As he sat perplexed in his studio, Wewe's cell phone rang in the middle of the night. It was the voice of the abductor.

"Call me back. Now, now,“ the kidnapper barked. Wewe dialed his mother's number with a trembling finger.

"Picasso, I have confidential info that you have informed the police," the kidnapper said with a chilling and mocking chuckle. "What can't you understand? You are only putting your mother's life in jeopardy. We give you three days to produce the money or your niece will be decapitated and her head sent to you."

Wewe found his voice, "I want to negotiate. One million naira, and the money is yours in the morning."

"Are you kidding me? Your mother and niece are worth only one million naira to you?"

"Times are hard," Wewe begged, "I have hardly had any time to paint since I became a state commissioner. I'm making no money from art. And we have had no allocated fund released to us by the state. The governor is untangling red tapes to make funding available."

"Steal or borrow. This is not a joke. You have three days to produce the money in cash. You are a man of large resources. Your banks will gladly assist you."

"The ransom is too exorbitant. I can't possibly raise such a huge sum."

"Ok. A hundred million naira. Final."

Wewe was already in contact with the cell phone companies, who were coordinating with the state security forces. They used their satellite technology to detect the location of the caller within a radius of five hundred yards. The security forces informed Wewe that his mother's

"Wewe was already in contact with the cell phone companies, who were coordinating with the state security forces. They used their satellite technology to detect the location of the caller within a radius of five hundred yards"

kidnappers were calling from a location not far from Ore, about twenty miles from Òndó where Wewe resided.

"We are rapidly closing in on them," the security agents assured him. "Only a matter of hours now before we nab them."
But Wewe had a personal contact with the cell phone companies. She was monitoring the calls and provided him with a totally different story.

"The calls are coming from the neighborhood of the Koko Port, near Sapele," the personal contact said. "They are not coming from Ore as you have been told."
Wewe felt frustrated and helpless.

Day three. His phone rang. It was his kidnapped eleven year-old niece on the line. She appeared to be reading from a prepared statement: "Please pay them now, Papa," she pleaded in a halting and scared voice. "We don't want to die, please Papa, pay them before they kill us…."

Wewe switched the conversation from English to their local dialect.

"Where are you?"

"I don't know."

"Have you eaten?"

"No. I'm not hungry."

"You must eat when you are fed, ok?"

"Ok."

"Where is Mama?"

"She is in the creek where we were taken."

"Is she fine?"

"Yes. But she is not eating either."
The kidnapper did not understand the local dialect and cut off the conversation. "Call me back on your Mama's number. Now, now."

Wewe called, but the kidnapper did not pick the call.

Wewe lit another cigarette. He was living on nicotine and liquor. He could not eat nor sleep. His wife and children sat with him in the studio. Downstairs, friends and neighbors crowded into the sitting room. Everyone was quiet; waiting for the latest

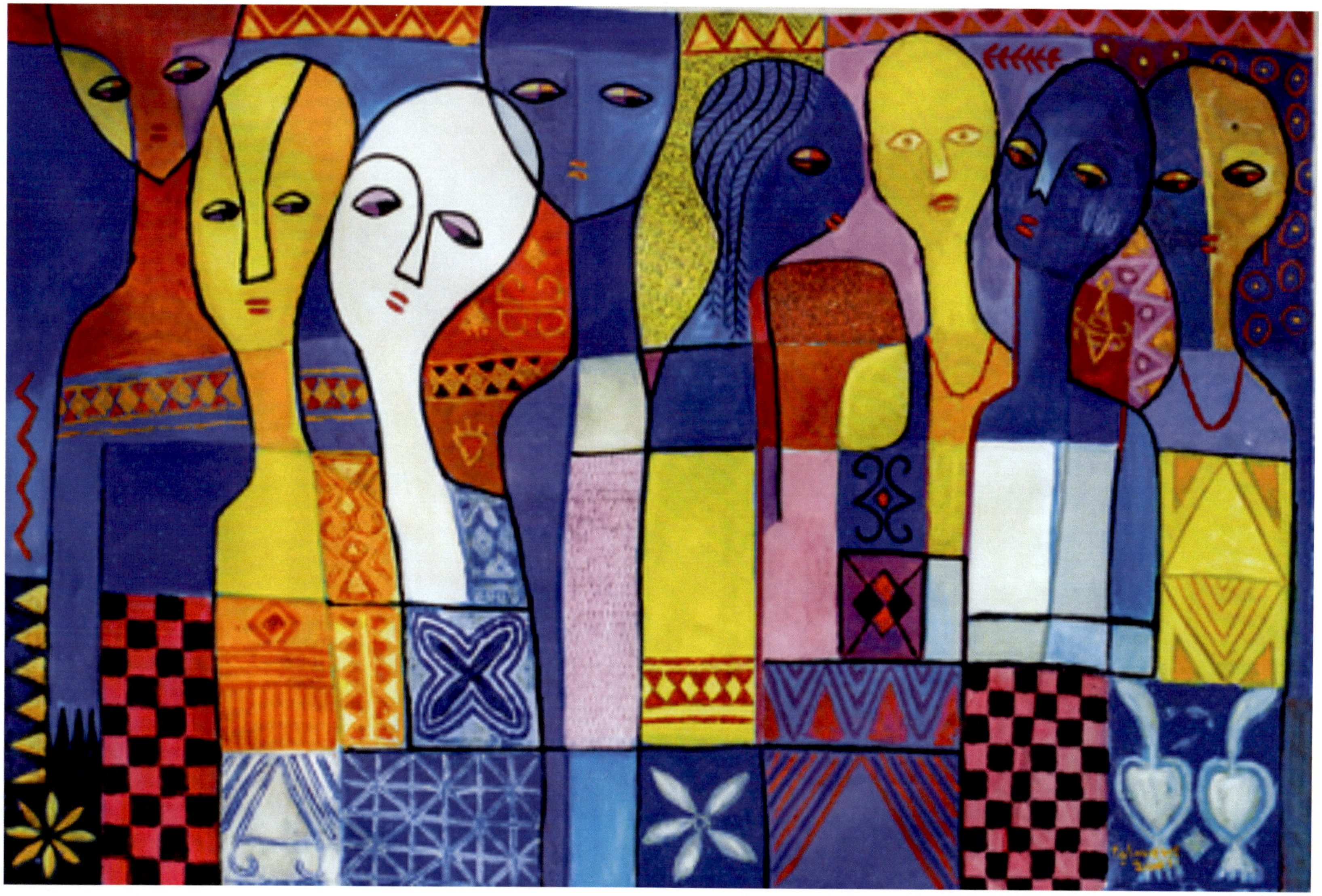

Fig. 3: *Òrìṣà Bí Ìyá Ò Sí: No Divinity is Greater Than My Mother*, acrylic on canvas, 2021.

updates. Nothing came for the rest of the day.
Day four. The phone rang just after midnight. It was his mother's number. Wewe heaved a sigh of relief as he picked up the call.
"Picasso, call me back. Now, now."
Wewe called.
"You are playing with fire, Picasso."
"The ransom is too much."
"Ok. Fifty million."
"I don't have that kind of money."
"I'll be candid with you," said the kidnapper. "We are many. But I am empowered to negotiate with you down to a minimum of thirty million."
"Still too high."
"Well, your mother is a dead woman. Farewell. If you change your mind and you want her back alive, call me back. No later than tomorrow."
*
That was when he woke up, sweating.
"I had a nightmare," he announced. "My head aches too. Do you have an aspirin or something?"

CHAPTER TWO:

Iya – Mother, Lover, Power

"Wewe seems to stand on one port as he gazes across the distant seas at the female gender, in wondrous admiration, that is simultaneously erotic, heroic and poetic"

The theme of womanhood has always fascinated Tola Wewe. The abduction of his mother both intensifies this fascination and tilts the theme in a more complex direction. The theme of womanhood, which had mostly received the handling of a lover from Wewe, now finds him complicating the female body as lover in a far more allegorical manner. The woman becomes not just the lover, but also a mother, in a manner that weaves both love and mothership together. In addition, the romantic layering of lover and mother attains a sociological coloring in which the nation also becomes a crucial aspect of the triad.

In other words, the images of woman in Wewe's work has been codified into a long journey connecting the past, present and future of his ideas into a coherent icon of love, with which he combines layers of emotions, linking personal emotions with collective desires.

Womenfolk, in Tola Wewe's paintings, have become a landscape of longings to which he reaches out with passion, but which he cannot hold on to, because whenever he thinks he has found a grip, he is weaned and dislodged.

His paintings are the vessels that he uses to reconnect and move back to the strange shores from which he is cast, after each engendered engagement.

His compositions evokes the reflections of Funso Aiyejina, in his classic *Letters to Lynda*:
I who have wandered across mountains
and across valleys in search of history,
I have recognized myself in the scars
of those who have survived the misdeeds
and the greed of our common ancestors,
ancestors who pandered to the passions
of pale gods from the Atlantic and the
Sahara,

ancestors who groveled after beads, after
mirrors and after liquid fires with which
to prop their sagging genitals, ancestors
who fashioned crude tools with which they
punctured our radiant early morning dew-
drops so that today our twin summer noons
embrace the same mad ocean of our related
pasts.

Wewe seems to stand on one port as he gazes across the distant seas at the female gender, in wondrous admiration, that is simultaneously erotic, heroic and poetic. These three elements of the erotic, heroic and poetic are applicable as a critical device for viewing the representation of femininity in Wewe's work. In some works, an element dominates the others, yet one may perceive all of the three in each composition. Some of the earliest images in Wewe's work highlight the erotic over the heroic; the more recent images are partial toward the heroic and diminish the erotic in

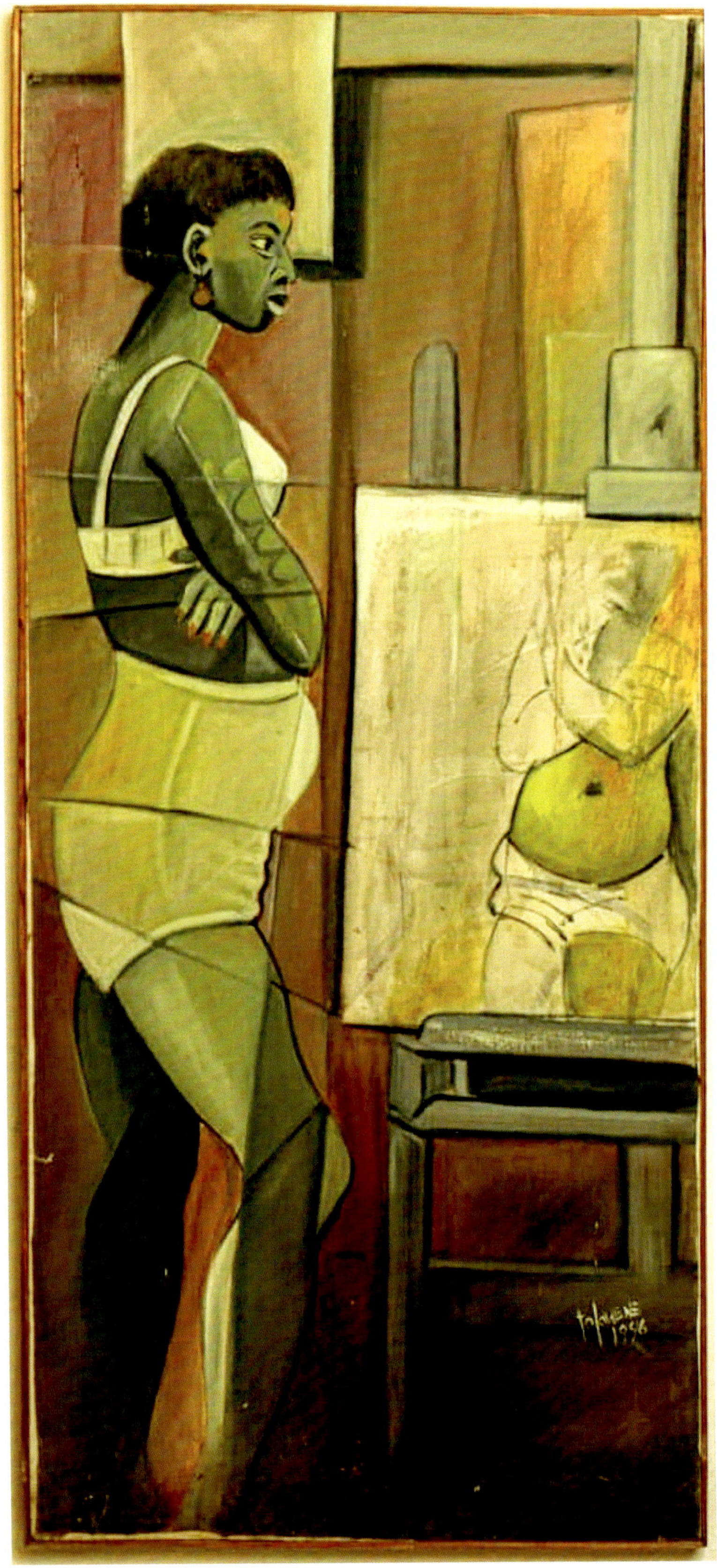
Fig. 4: *Ìbejì: Twins* acrylic on canvas, 1996

their poetic evocations.
The earliest female forms in Wewe's professional life are gazes on the female body from the piercing perspective of a perplexed observer observing a configuration that he finds not only curious but equally fascinating and intimidating. A rewarding view of Wewe's female figures may begin with his 1996 composition, *Ìbejì: Twins.*

The idea of twinning or doubling is crucial in engaging this painting at various levels of interrogation. Firstly, one must delve into the principle of *Ìbejì* in Yoruba philosophy and view the circumstances within which *Ìbejì* images are made and celebrated.

Secondly, we would then explore the specific imaging of *Ìbejì* in this painting to appreciate the cleverness with which Wewe unveils this deep philosophy, by breaking down time and space, into a discourse of fluid encounters, between reality and mythology.

In the Yoruba philosophical system, *Ìbejì* is the Spirit of Twins, celebrated as special beings who bring blessings in multiple dimensions to their parents, specifically, and to the world, in general. They are venerated as *Òrìsà* or divinities that must be handled and approached with emphatic reverence for the maximal activation of their energies, to fulfill their finer potential, in their families and through them to the wider world. The Yoruba associate *Ìbejì* with Sàngó, the Yoruba thunder and lightning Divinity. Sàngó protects *Ìbejì* children. When they are female, they are also associated with the Divine wives of Sàngó – Ọya, Ọ̀ṣun and Ọbà – who jealously assert their spirits in these female twins.

There is a large body of songs composed for the celebration of *Ìbejì*. In many instances, their mothers, at the behest of the twins, become full-time public dancers – in perpetual celebration of the fundamental principles of multiplicative increase, doubling, abundance and growth, which the twins represent. Parents of twins habitually throw weekly parties for them, to which they invite the entire neighborhood. Amidst the delicious delicacies served at these parties, *Ewa Ìbejì* – a special type of beans cooked in red palm oil – their traditional delicacy, is unfailing served to the guests, who sing for the *Ìbejì* to dance.

Despite all the divine protection and parental attention that the *Ìbejì* receive, one or both children may still transition on to the other sphere of existence, known as *Ọ̀run*— The Source. Since Yoruba philosophy fundamentally holds that there is no death per se – there is only a transition from one state to the other – therefore, the parents of the twins retain the spirit of the departed twin in a physical configuration, a process that must be supervised by a *Babaláwo*, who picks the sculptor for the job.

There are thousands of these wooden sculptures all over Yoruba communities. The sculptures are treated as surrogates for the departed twins and must be bathed, clothed, fed and kept as if they were human. If just one of the two passed, the one still here with the family assumes the duty of caring for the sculpture; talking, playing with it and carrying it around like a companion.

Wewe grew up with this rich tradition of celebrating twins. There are twins within his large extended family and he experienced, first hand, the entire process of treating twins as special beings – as divinities. He understands the principles underlying the making of surrogate images to house the spirits of departed twins. Consequently, in *Ìbejì*:

Twins, Wewe combines the ancient ideas of substitution with "modern" notions of codification, to arrive at a metamodern fusion, projecting surrogates and codes as mythographic configurations, explicating grafts and buds that defy classification as indigenous or global.

Ìbejí: Twins explores this stream of grafting in what, on the surface, appears to be a model painting in a studio. Barely clad in lingerie, a young woman stands to the left of the canvas, her gaze cast straight ahead of her, as she stares into space in profile. Just below her – in reduced dimension – is a representation of her body in what appears to be a mirror, or a canvas. It could easily pass for a mirror but the placement of the reflection on an easel suggests that it is a painting on which an artist is working. The artist, however, is missing from the composition. He is absent or invisible, in what should have been a triadic configuration of the artist-picture-model trinity.

One may think of Joseph Kosuth's *One and Three Chairs* of 1965. An analysis of the installation describes it as an inspired way of seeing reality, by a twenty-year old artist, whose view of life is not yet jaded: In *One and Three Chairs*, Joseph Kosuth represents one chair three ways: as a manufactured chair, as a photograph, and as a copy of a dictionary entry for the word "chair." The installation is thus composed of an object, an image, and words.

Kosuth didn't make the chair, take the photograph, or write the definition; he selected and assembled them together. But is this art? And which representation of the chair is most "accurate"? These open-ended questions are exactly what Kosuth wanted us to think about when he said that "art is making meaning." By assembling these three alternative representations, Kosuth turns a simple wooden chair into an object of debate and even consternation, a platform for exploring new meanings.[3]

Wewe, on the other hand, made everything in the composition, except the original model who, in fact, did not really exist beyond his imagination. He conjured up the model, the image of her standing in the painting, as well as the reflection of the image in the canvas/mirror on the painted easel. Rather than title the painting *One and Three Models*—in which the "actual" model is invisibly present outside the picture frame, just as the actual painter is invisibly present outside the frame of the composition – Wewe titles the painting *Ìbejì: Twins*. The title evokes the indigenous Yoruba concept of twinning, in which the *Ìbejì* is only sculpturally configured after transition, and hence is no longer physically available – yet present in invisibility.

Does Wewe's painting turn the body of the model "into an object of debate and consternation, a platform exploring new meanings," as in the Kosuth composition? This is not his intention. His intention rather is to evoke the complexity of the Yoruba's understanding of "deathlessness" and invisibility – in which something that is not visible or physically available is still alive in the mind of the community that retains its vital essence in image form. The model that Wewe has painted exists in Wewe's imagination; his painting of the image on canvas, standing in a profile form, is alive in the imagination of the viewer; the conversion of the image of the model from the profile into a frontal figure portraying the body of the model, is alive within the canvas.

The invocation of the Yoruba articulation of *àìkú*—immortality or deathlessness—is what differentiates Wewe's composition from Kosuth's, whose work is said to generate a *debate* or a *discussion* about *representation*. Wewe does not generate a debate; what he does instead is to metamodernizes a mental configuration of indigenous thought. Yoruba philosophy says "*Àìkú parí ìwà*—Deathlessness is the completion of being; immortality " Nothing is complete that is subject to death. And since nothing dies, everything is complete and deathless, though that thing may be invisible or physically undetectable. The effects of those things are still as palpable as the affects of the painter and the model who are absent in Wewe's *Ìbejì: Twins*. In indigenous Yoruba philosophical thought system, the *Ìbejì* sculpture comes alive to make tangible the invisibility of the *Ìbejì*, who has transitioned to the *Ọrun* beyond, as Wewe makes tangible the body of the actual model and the actual artist, who are outside the range of the visual engagement of the viewer in the painting, yet who are undeniably existent: without them the painting is impossible to make or appreciated. In symbolizing *àìkú,* Wewe invokes the "completion of being" – from deep within the wellsprings of Yoruba *Ìbejì* cosmography – in his own painting of the model, thus enacting the metamodernist fusion of the indigenous *Ìbejì* sculpture with the modernist tradition of easel painting.

Wewe raises several questions about his gendered challenges, as a male painter, to enter into the unknowable space of his female models, just as those of this world, *ayé,* face insurmountable challenges to gain access into the other sphere, the *Ọrun*, into which the *Ìbejì* passes. The only vehicle at Wewe's disposal for bridging this other sphere are his images, just as the *Ìbejì* sculpture is the vehicle that the Yoruba indigenous tradition employs for experiencing the spirit of the other world. Similarly, the medium of easel painting enables Wewe to metamodernize the indigenous mode of image making with the western tradition of imaginative composition, a twinning process that the title of the painting inscribes.

XXX

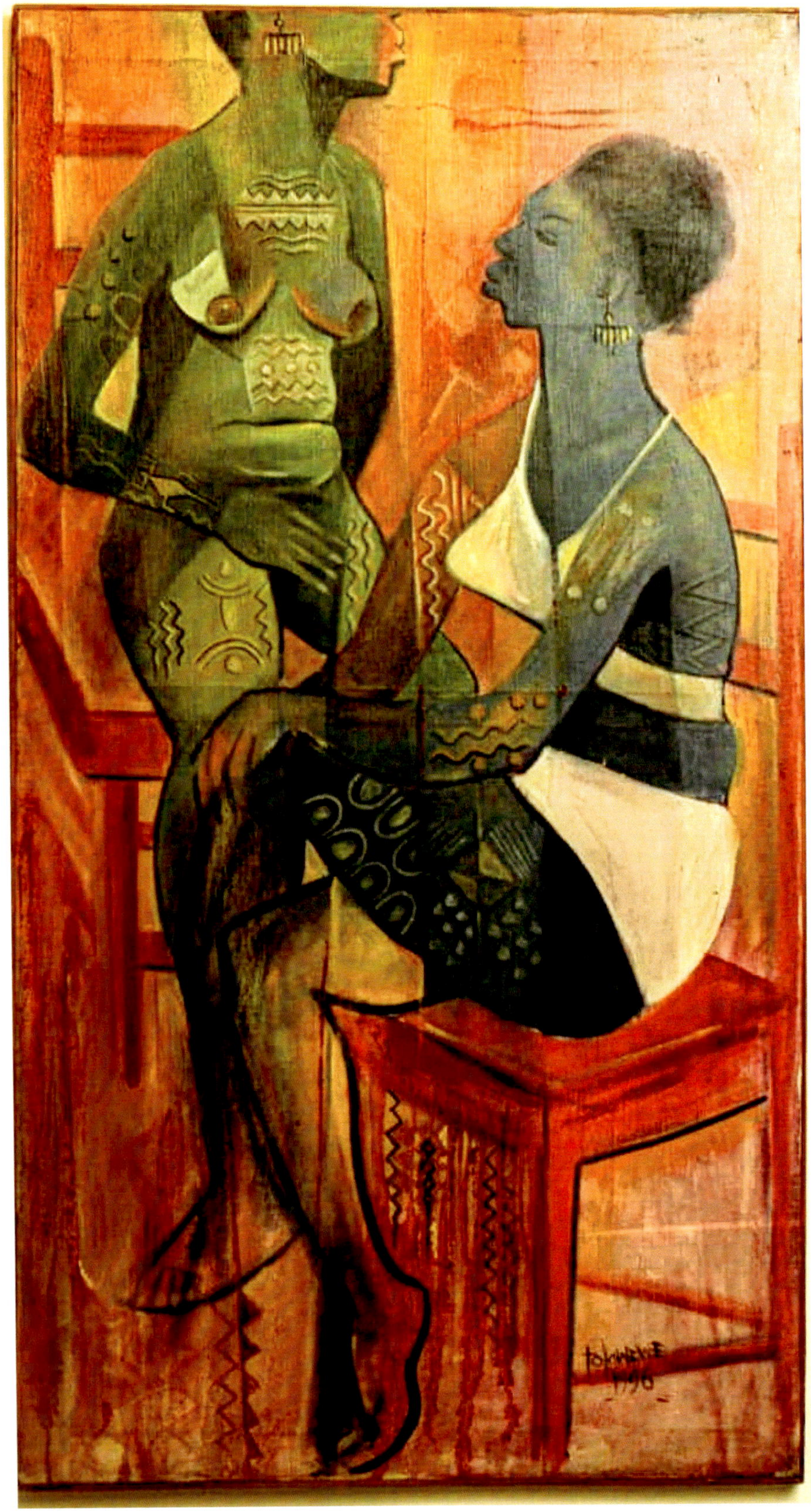

Fig. 5: *Déolá and Delilah*, acrylic on canvas, 1996.

This 1996 exploration of the female body in metamodern terms paves the way for Wewe to initiate deeper investigations into the female body. It is an exploration that journeys into various phases, and about a decade later, the female body begins to yield more sensual, even altogether erotic returns, to the viewer. But this transformation is a metamorphosis in which the studio plays a crucial role as an allegory of space, as another 1996 painting, *Déolá and Delilah,* indicates.
The studio becomes an allegory for the nation.

As the female body, in his estimation, increasingly becomes a meter for the fate of womanhood in Nigeria, Wewe begins to organize these images into patterns of sociological position in the studio. *Déolá and Delilah*, a 1996 exploration of the female body in metamodern terms, paves the way for Wewe to initiate a deeper investigation into the female body and through this, present an allegory of the nation itself. "To know the situation of a country, talk with the women," Wewe said in a recent conversation. "Watch how they dress, eat and talk about and amongst themselves. But most especially, use your eyes and watch how they walk; how they dance; how they stand on the streets."[4]

From the days before contact with alien cultures, through the colonial era and the period following independence, the role of the woman has continued to mutate, even as the country changed and journeyed from an exclusively indigenous society in which everybody practiced an indigenous spirituality, to a colonial enclave with the introduction of two foreign religions; Christianity and Islam. Wewe seems to focus predominantly on the southern part of Nigeria and the influence of the Christian faith.

Wewe sets the stage for this transition with a representation of the era before the contact with alien cultures, when the indigenous civilizations of Nigeria were intricately connected to Nature and its rhythms. Among the Yoruba people, the *Òrìsà* controlled this system. What unifies these indigenous philosophies is their unification of all forms of life as living – on a horizontal platform in which all beings are activated on all levels of the senses. The trees, humans, animals, hills, waters, and air are all natural beings, that see, speak, eat and feel – a completely different world view from that of the western culture which was introduced with colonial contact.

In the painting titled *Orita: Crossroads*, Wewe depicts the transitional moment between the indigenous era and the colonial – highlighting the violence that attended the cultural crisis, while conveying the connection between all the players (humans, animals, plants, water, air) as an organic wholeness. *Orita: Crossroads* is a ritual transpiring in a timeless zone; it is both dusk and dawn, night and day, light and dark. At the center of the ritual is a group of figures standing knee-deep in a pond of blood. The three figures on the left are female, all facing the viewer, consciously covering their genitalia with their hands. Balancing these figures are three male figures, their hands raised above their heads, their backs turned away from the viewer as they file away from the center, one figure slightly overlapping the other.

All six figures are contained in an enclosure resembling a transparent upside-down gourd, enabling the viewer to experience the rituals transpiring within the arena.

This enclosure, at the same time, appears to be the utterance of a head at the very top of the composition, from whose mouth the entire drama appears to unfold like a trickle of spittle mixed with blood, flowing vertically down the body of the canvas, dividing it into two like an equator. The central figure also bares protruding fangs in a diabolic grimace, exuding power, anger and utter disgust.

This omnipotent figure – with the largest body in the canvas – hovers above the human figures, casting its twilight illumination like a viral shadow on the sanguine ritual unfolding below it. Within the dim parts of the composition are several figures hovering in what seems to be the background; grotesque, diabolic and otherworldly, with features designed to shock viewers. Some have their tongues hanging out, their bodies twisted in tortured positions and angles. At the far right of the composition in the dark section is the representation of the hornbill, known in Yoruba mythology as the *Àgbìgbò Nìwọ̀nràn*.

In her writing, Sandra Grayson has described the *Àgbìgbò* as an ominous bird, associated with slavery in the Black Atlantic culture. Reviewing a short story, *The Yellow Crane,* a narrative about the slave trade which is part of a volume compiled by E.C.L. Adams, Grayson expatiates on her view using Professor Wande Abimbola's translations:
"In [the] ese Ifá, [*Ọ̀bàrà Méjì*] the *Àgbìgbò* bird is portrayed as evil and "regarded as a treacherous and dangerous bird who acts as an agent for death and other supernatural powers" (Abimbola, *Ifá* 211).

If *Àgbìgbò* places a coffin in front of someone's house, that person will die. *Àgbìgbò* is also regarded as a negative Ifá priest who deceives and cheats clients. "The *Àgbìgbò* bird is therefore the symbol of unfaithfulness in Ifá priests, a negation of the strict sanction of the Ifá divination system" (Abimbola, *Sixteen Great Poems of Ifá* 210).... *Àgbìgbò* carried a load of evil on his head...an evil spirit [gazing] through the side of his head.[5]
Grayson's characterization of the *Àgbìgbò* symbolism demonstrates a transitional moment in Yoruba culture, which at this point had become tainted with the Transatlantic slave trade.

This transitional moment – associated with cultural decadence and slavery – is portrayed in Yambo Ouloguem's classic novel, *Bound to Violence*:
"In almost every part of the Empire and its dependencies, an unprecedented orgy of violence ensued. The capture of rebel tribes, of free men, of defeated warriors, the sacrifice of their chief and feasting on his flesh, became ritual acts, which entered into the customs of those jittery jigs, whose barbarity fell in with the plans of the emperor and his notables....Through intermediaries, [they] encouraged the raiders to bless the wounded captives with a stroke of the saber, to carry their skulls spitted on lances and assegais to the door of the victor who – God will it – was feasted as a hero. AND AS THOUGH A BLACK REALLY HAD THE SOUL OF A MAN, THE CHIEF OF THE PRISONERS AND HIS FAMILY WERE FIRST GIVEN OVER TO THE

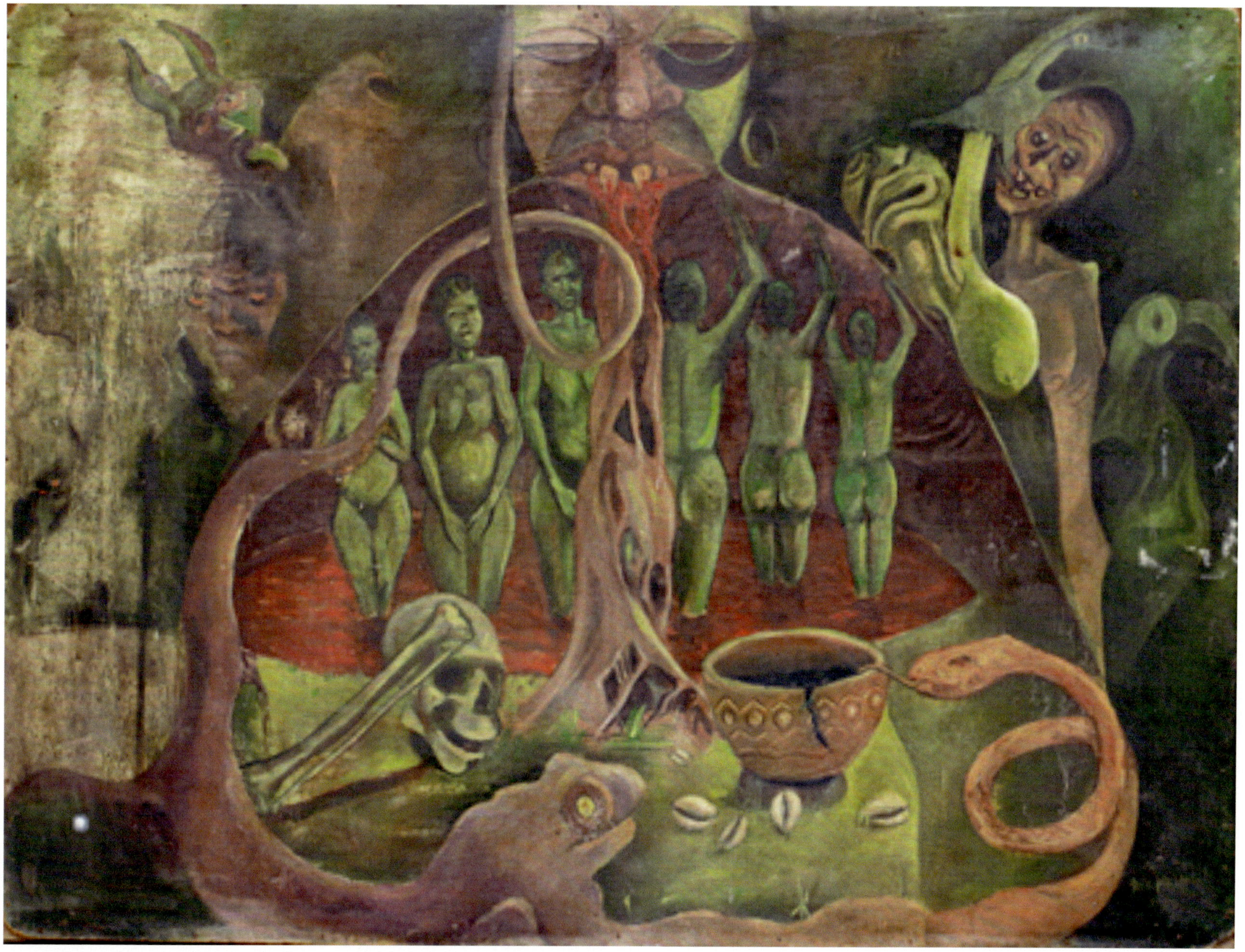

Fig. 6: *Orita: Crossroads*, acrylic on canvas, 1983

MERCIES OF THE VILLAGE WOMEN AND CHILDREN WHO WHIRLED AROUND THEM, LEAPING, DANCING, SINGING, SHOUTING INSULTS, AND SPITTING ON THEM IN ORDER, SO THEY SWORE, TO CLEANSE THEIR SOULS OF SATAN'S BLACKNESS. On the third day of their captivity, the sorcerer, his eyes aflame with pride and avenging hate, skinned more than shaved their skulls, then rubbed with karite butter….

Ordained by hatred, innate evil, blood lust, thirst for vengeance, or perhaps by a desire to inherit the qualities of the devoured victims, the ghoulish feast ended in an orgy of drinking. Cannibalism was one of the darkest features of that spectral Africa over which hung the malefic shadow of [their leader]. A sob for her."[6]

Granted that Wewe's painting is more solemn, the symbolisms of the human skull and other human bones, the pond of blood, serpents, frogs and the scattered cowry shells – the ubiquitous symbol of slave trade – are in the foreground of the painting. They highlight the era in which the indigenous tradition of spirituality became intertwined with the mercantile violence of trading in the human body; a development that has become indelibly engraved in the collective memory of the people. Once the imagination of the people crossed this *Oríta* or crossroads, a permanent permutation occurred; thereby transporting this imagination onto a cultural point of no return.

It was also a stylistic point of departure for Wewe – from the fluid transition of figures that characterizes *Orita: Crossroads*, to a fractured format. These 1996 compositions of *Ìbejì* increasingly display formal designs, elements of lines, invented colors, poetic textures and figures with angular forms and dissected frames. It is this compositional approach that defines his work, *Déolá and Delilah*, another 1996 painting. The title of the painting presents two names, the first of which is Yoruba while the second, Biblical. The figure named Déolá – as one can imagine – is placed in the background, on a slightly higher plane, with Delilah somewhat lower; nearer the viewer. Déolá is nude, her body intricately decorated with Yoruba body art called *ìlà*.

In an essay titled "Beauty and the Being: Aesthetics and Ontology in Yoruba Body Art," Henry Drewal discusses the processes and principles of these body marks among the Yoruba people, well before the advent of Europeans.[7] These same marks are found on Yoruba sculpture, as Cornelius Adepegba indicates, and they are replete on the textiles, pottery, calabash and other inscriptions of the Yoruba people.[8] Wewe uses the body art to break down the time and cultural distance between Déolá and Delilah who is clad in western underwear to conceal her nudity. Déolá, on the other hand, does not appear to be particularly bothered by her nakedness; thus representing a period when Yoruba women lived in a different ontological culture – one in which they were not ashamed of their bodies. Their attitude to nudity was to consider it a normal state of being, notwithstanding their wide array of textiles and fashionable attires – the formal *gèlè*, *ìró*, *bùbá*, *ìlépá*, *ìborùn* as well as their informal *yẹ̀rì*, *tòbí*, *àgbékọ*. Western European colonization brought with it a different attitude towards the nude body – one in which people were expected to subdue and conceal themselves or be regarded as uncivilized, heathen, sinful: damned to hell.

The change in naming traditions from the Yoruba Déolá to the Biblical Delilah references the increasing personal and collective alienation whereby the Yoruba began to distance themselves from their ontological values; stripping themselves of things associated with their ancestral heritage. They began to cast aspersions on values related to their land, refusing to wear their "native" clothes, denying their Òrìsà philosophical traditions and even rejecting their language as "vernacular" – unfit for communication. In addition, they began to reject their age old and time-tested indigenous healthcare systems, fundamentally based on millennia of scientific medical expertise, rooted in Nature's deep, prolific, fecund and renewable abundance.

They turned their backs on their environmentally friendly adobe architecture, moved from rural places to urban centers, abandoning traditional agricultural processes, organic food, natural drinks and beverages and became ashamed of enjoying healthy condiments such as *irú, ògìrì* and *òbu*. They began to look down upon their ancestral philosophical logic systems as superstition and actively began to unlearn the songs, proverbs, folktales, ethics, mores and spirituality handed down for generations by their ancestors.

Delilah and other names taken from the Bible demonstrates the moment they began to individually and collectively embrace the values of their colonizers – as they started cherishing the ideological systems of western societies – by associating themselves with the institutions and conventions of the foreigners who invaded their lands and conquered them.

A subdued people, they began to look outside their lands – to western values – for solutions to their problems, rather than inwards. They started wearing western clothes, unmindful of the fact these modes of dressing might be unsuited for the tropical environment in which they live. They started going to church to learn about Christianity, submitting to conversions, baptism, and in many cases, even becoming evangelists of the various Christian doctrines among their people. They began to learn English, French and other European languages, considering these foreign languages as by far superior to their own indigenous languages.

"They learned and imbibed western modes of thoughts, ideology, politics and economics, considering these as denoting "modernity and progress".

They began to learn western medical and healthcare systems, trusting the use of chemicals and artificial drugs to stay healthy and battle sickness. They started constructing houses with the use of materials imported from western countries and to build houses with architectural drawings adapted from foreign cities, though these might not be suited to their natural ecology.

In search of jobs, they looked for government employment as teachers, secretaries and administrators wherever they could find positions, no matter how far away these may take them from their places of birth or area of origin. They increasingly addicted their taste to processed foods and drinks – sugar, salt, fast foods, canned items and bottled beverages – trying cuisines imported from the lands of their conquerors, assuming them to be marks of sophistication to be seen to enjoy these alien tastes. They learned and imbibed western modes of thoughts, ideology, politics and economics, considering these as denoting "modernity and progress". They studied western literature, music, sports and entertainment as signs of "progress" and a demonstration of "sophistication".

Delilah, in Wewe's composition, therefore occupies the front of the composition while Déolá is pushed to the back, the top of her head cropped from the picture place as if she is disappearing or fading away from the viewer. Wewe, nevertheless, places Déolá above Delilah, in a way that might betray his personal taste and desire for that past – a form of nostalgia for an era that is being erased right before his eyes.

The body of Delilah, despite her preference for western garb, is not totally rid of the traditional influences that her change of name appears to convey. Wewe colors Delilah's body with the same indigo blue that traditional Yoruba sculptors use as pigment to cool down the high energies of their angular wooden compositions. In addition, the uncovered parts of Delilah's body still carry the same decorative patterns of the traditional Yoruba body art, that Drewal and Adepegba so eloquently describe in their writings.

In other words, Wewe shows in *Déolá and Delilah* that as much as the people attempt to push their ancestral presence behind them to embrace new traditions and alien ways, these inherited ways are so integrated into their ecology that it is impossible to banish them into some forgotten past.

The more the people attempt to forget these indigenous pathways, the more their struggles and failures surface in the contradictions that play out in their daily activities. It is therefore not unusual to find that several people who are devoted churchgoers and who espouse Christian values are also not unknown to Òrìsà priests and visit diviners as a backup to their western belief systems. The priests and pastors of the Christian churches are also believed to be surreptitious devotees of indigenous divinities, while preaching against these indigenous belief systems publicly. They do one thing openly and the opposite privately – creating a cultural hybridity that Wewe's *Déolá and Delilah* so visually captures.

The painting shows the past and the present as traditional and "modern" references. In addition, Wewe depicts a metamodern space of in-between interstices as a space of questions, contradictions and speculations that unsettles the appearance of a separate identity for the two protagonists in the studio. In theory, they are different. In practice, however, they are intricately and densely intertwined as a singular yet complex cultural experience that Wewe neither castigates nor instigates – but simply interrogates.

Wewe pushes this idea of the layered cultural palimpsest in African society further in Figure 7, titled *Ààrò Mẹ́ta: The Tripod.* Three female figures overlap in a carefully orchestrated progression from the foreground to the background. They also serve as an allegory of the impossibility of separating time into three distinctive experiences – present, past and future – despite the temptation to do so in real life, just because the clock apparently and supposedly ticks to time.

In the deepest space of the painting, at the extreme right, Wewe places the darkest figure, totally nude except for a short *bàǹtẹ́* (skirt) wrapped around her waist, extending to her knees. In the mid-ground is the second figure, clad in skimpy western garb, her body of a medium tone within the melanin palette of the composition.

The third figure, the one nearest to the viewer, has the lightest skin tone. It is also striking that this figure is stark naked, without a stitch on her luminous skin. It is clear to the viewer, however, that this figure is African, obvious in her facial features and hair texture. Her parted lips suggests that she is addressing the other

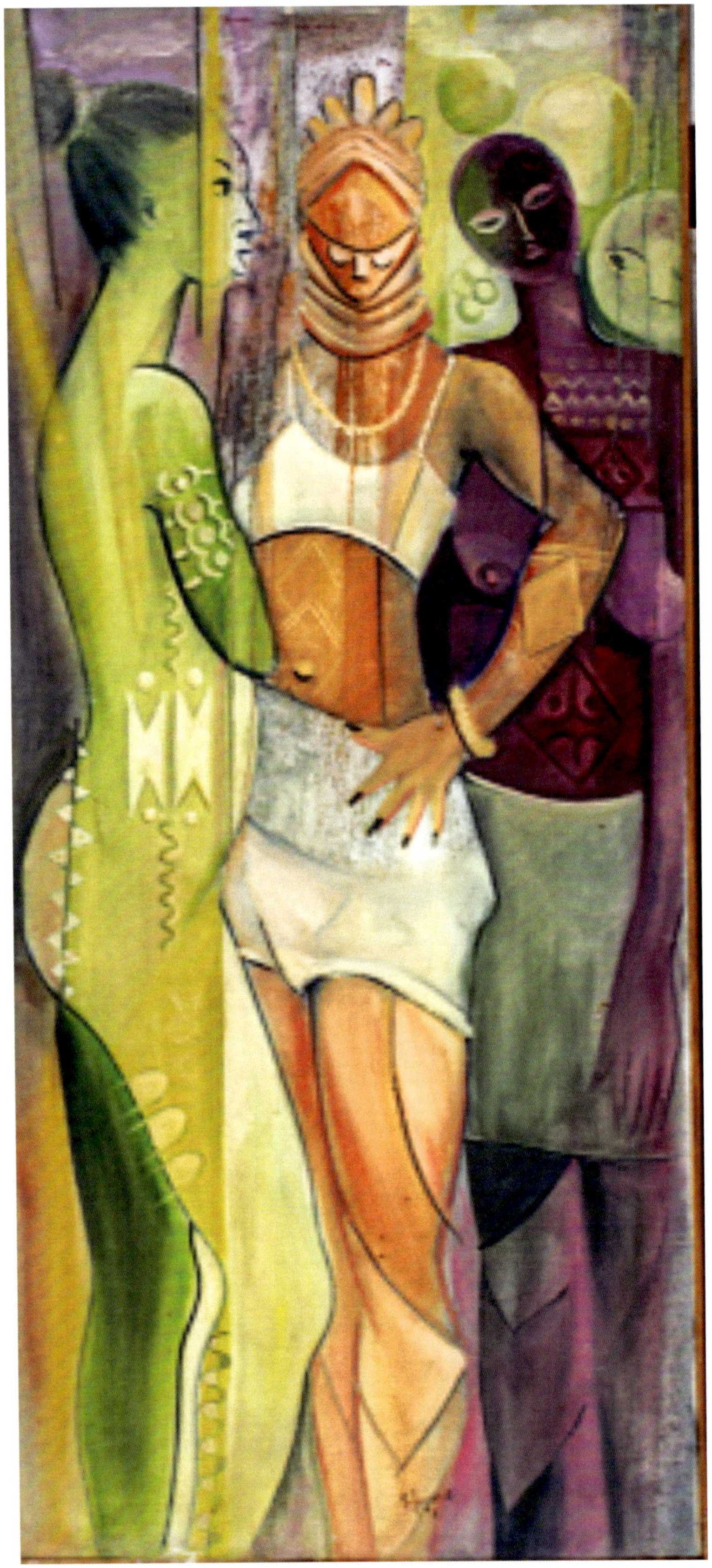

Fig. 7: *Àarò Mẹ́ta: The Tripod*, acrylic on canvas, 1996.

two with her body positioned in profile, a frame for the other two, who are both frontal, fully facing the viewer.

As codes for telling time, the darkest figure, receding the most as she is, into the back of the composition, is the embodiment of the past. Her body portrayed in geometric gestures is suggestive of indigenous African two-dimensional art – especially indigenous painting traditions found in several Yoruba towns and cities, on the walls of scared spaces. She is watching the viewer directly – deliberately turning and inclining her head to impress on the audience that her eyes are set on them. Though it is clear that she is watching the viewer, her eyes are obtuse and impossible to catch because they are represented as dark space, set deep inside a schematic pattern.

The middle figure is especially striking – she is right in the center of the composition and is wearing a sculptural covering for the face.

This cranium sculpture, known as the Sowei, is an initiation headpiece among the Sande, spread across Sierra Leone, Liberia and Guinea. The sculpture is used in initiation performances, funerary rituals and other ceremonies involving young women of Sande society. The Sowei is the representation of young female beauty – with its intricate coiffure, ebony dark and lustrous skin, glistening as it reflects the radiant sun at noon.

The Sowei sculpture is described as the only form of headpiece worn by women for public parade in Africa, asserting the power of women among the Sande as crown-wearers whose parades dominate community centers.

Wewe gives the sculpture a golden ocher glint that blends with the rest of the female body, turning it into a pillar of light in the center of the composition. Because the Sowei conceals most of her face, she is present and inscrutable, like an unfolding verb, representing the ongoing moment or *Òní*.

The contradiction of the ongoing era, in which the indigenous head contrasts with the western street clothes, is an allegorical statement about the cultural dilemma that people in Africa negotiate now – a traditional psyche trapped in a westernized body.

The third female figure, totally nude and right in front of the canvas, is the future whose face is turned away from the viewer, while her body appears optimistically and boldly available – in open display. The future is not bashful nor modest in her appearance. It stands defiantly in contrast to the other two figures, with their partially clad semi-naked bodies. It appears to be speaking to the present and the past, instructing and guiding them from a vantage position of one that has experienced them, even though they are unable to see her. With her total nudity, she suggests a future that repeats the past by transcending the present through returning to what the present is trying to deny.

The further the present tries to move away from the past, the more it returns to what it is attempting to evade – a history helplessly repeating itself. The bright body of the forthcoming era is futuristically fluorescent with the luminous glows of a lunar landscape.

These three female bodies unite in a unit as a tripod – *Ààrò Mẹ́ta* – the three evenly spaced cooking stones of the traditional hearth. In Yoruba culture, there is a proverb, *Ààrò mẹ́ta kì í dọbẹ̀ nù*: the three cooking stones of the hearth never spill the stew – that is, the strategically arranged stones provide stability and balance to the cooking pot placed on them. Time is the cooking pot, which the past, present and the future props up like the stable tripod – unshakably steady.

CHAPTER THREE:

The Years of War and Love

Tola Wewe lives in Òndó, a city about thirty minutes from Ilé Ifè, the spiritual center of the Yoruba people. Wewe attended the university in Ilé Ifè for his first degree and he has lots of friends in the ancient city. Next to Ilé Ifè is the city of Modákéké and Wewe typically drives through Modákéké on his way to Ilé Ifè from Òndó. In the last 200 years of their co-existence, Ife and Modákéké have been bedeviled by sporadic wars. The people of Ilé Ifè are the original settlers of the land. The Modákéké people migrated to settle next to Ilé Ifè from the northern part of Yoruba country, after the fall of ancient Oyo to marauders from the north. The people of Ifè welcomed and hosted the Modákéké people but the two became engulfed in conflicts pretty soon thereafter. Since then, outright wars, including seven notable periods of armed hostilities have erupted between these two consanguine neighbors – 1835 to 1849, 1882 to 1909, 1946 to 1949, in 1981, and also 1983; from 1997 to 1998, and as late as the year 2000. From 1983, when he gained admission into the University of Ifè (now Obafemi Awolowo University) and since his graduation in 1983, the Òndó-Modákéké-Ifè route has become one that Wewe plies regularly.

Ògún is the Yoruba Divinity of war. Wewe is partial to Ògún and other Yoruba Òrìsà. But as an artist, he is particularly enamored of Ògún - Ògún is also the divinity of artists. Ògún guides creative thinkers – sculptors, painters, poets and all who use tools.

One of the tools that Wewe uses is his car, with which he drives through the country to deliver his works from his studio to collectors, galleries, and museums. Wewe shares his love of Ògún with Wole Soyinka, the Nobel Laureate, whose patron Òrìsà is Ògún and who has written copiously about this divinity. Red is for war and green is for agriculture. Ògún wears both red and green in a bold combination of colors, transforming himself into the symbol of balance; of courage; of hope.
In an epic poem, Wole Soyinka celebrates the visit of Ògún to the war camp of Shaka kaSenzangakhona, the Zulu monarch and general, "*Rògbòdìyàn! Ògún relé Shaka, ó di rògbòdìyàn,*" writes the laureate in his lyrical myth, *Ogun Abibiman.*

Inside the only moving car within miles around him, Tola Wewe is driving along the lonely road, while listening to the stutter of machine guns coming from some bushes ahead of him.

"Automatic guns sound like a bad stutterer," he thinks.

In Yoruba, the trigger of the gun is called "*okó ìbọn,*" or the phallus of the gun.

"Why do automatic guns stutter?"

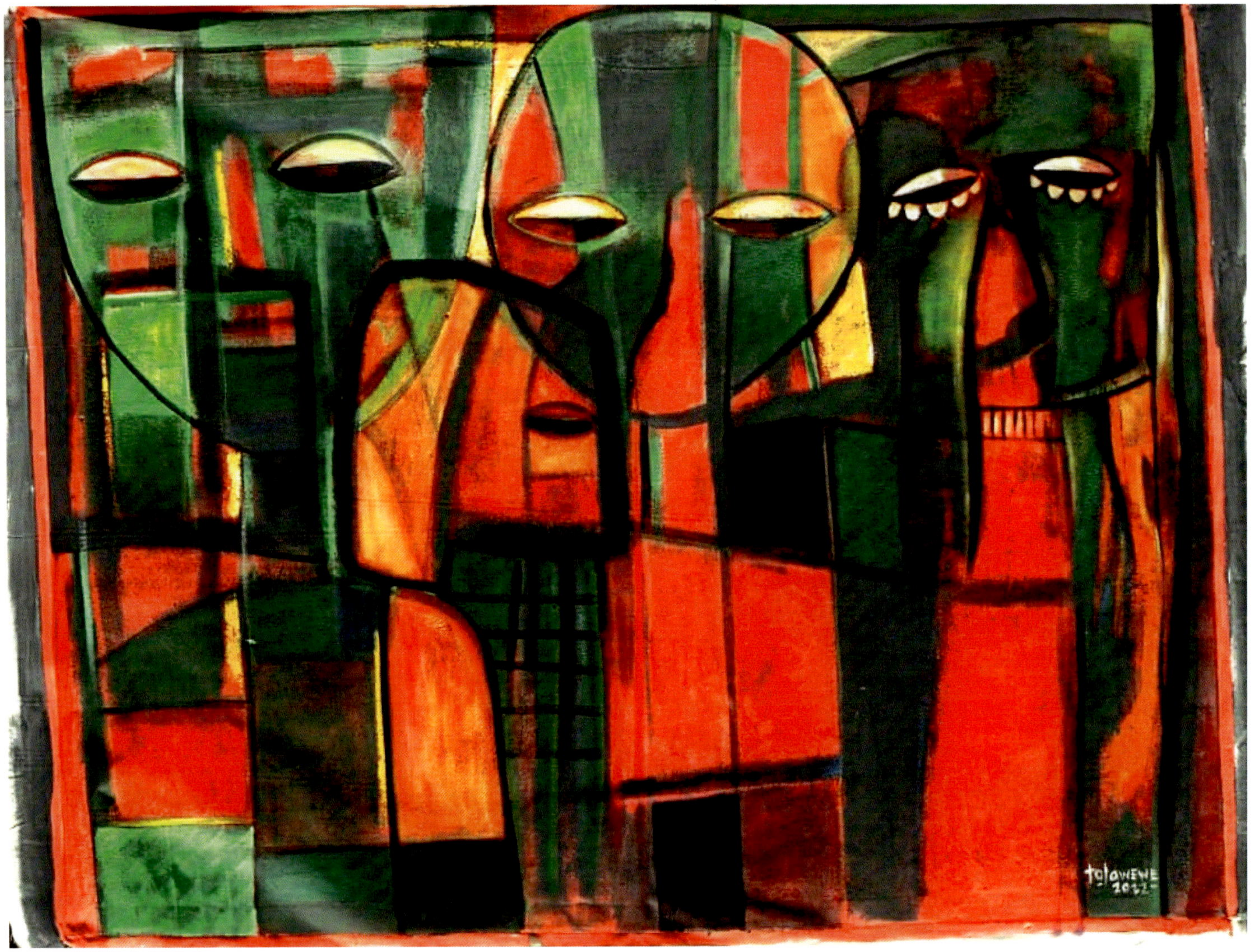

Fig. 8: *Ògún's Colors of Season of Balance*, acrylic on canvas, 2012

He knows too well the answer to his own question. The smile on his face is a mask. His mind is reeling as he grips the steering wheel harder: automatic guns stutter because people are pulling the trigger – the tiny phallus of the gun. What man would not stutter when his manhood is tugged? The gun gets mad when you touch its genitalia. Even a goat would get angry. But – however miniscule – when you tug at the manhood of a lion, you must face the consequences.

And at that moment, along the road on which Wewe was negotiating his rickety car, angry young men were yacking off the lion's manhood, playing with fire; teasing death; playing God and Devil.

It is in the late nineties, and war has broken out again between the two consanguine neighbors: Ilé Ifè and Modákéké.

But an artist must live on his art, even while others are killing each other, Wewe concludes. And as an artist, he focused his mind on conveying his goods to the market, as he drives from Òndó, the location of his studio, to Lagos where art dealers are patiently waiting for him to deliver his new paintings.

The road through Ilé Ifè and Modákéké, on route Lagos, is pocked with perilous potholes. Yet he avoids the other road from Benin to Lagos that is less raggedy. Armed robbery is rampant on that alternative highway. He has a choice between the robbers and the combatants, and he chooses the road of the warriors, with whom he could negotiate. His chances are much better with these warring young men. If he is fortunate, he will not run into them. But if – unfortunately – he runs into them, chances are that they won't shoot him on sight; chances are that they will be so shocked by his audacity – daring to drive towards them in the midst of the ongoing carnage.

They will most likely talk with him. From his dialect, they will know that he is neither from Ilé Ifè nor Modákéké. They are not interested in attacking foreigners – their feud is with one another. Chances are that, as usual, they will ask for money, and he is ready to pay his toll fees. Additionally, he had bottles of *ogogoro* (a particularly hard locally brewed liquor) to offer them – a libation these young warriors find irresistible. *Ogogoro* is a strong fuel for these kid fighters, with their permanently red, dim eyes, their drawled guttural sounds, floating on intoxicated, garbled utterances.

He knows that they need the Dutch courage to keep going. After all, these are mere boys, mostly teenagers, living in fear of death, or worse – the fear of sustaining serious injuries from guns and machete cuts, in a war without medical support.

His car is loaded with painted canvases to which these young fighters are unable to relate. He has been a full-time painter now for more than twenty years. The seasons flashed by like lightning flares.

A virgin rising from the dark bed of night, the morning sun is still yawning and sleepy. You must catch the sun before it rises, otherwise today leaves you behind, and your life is a cycle of yesterdays, he is thinking. But artists use yesterdays to build a palette of tomorrows, without which there is no future.

Lagos, to which Wewe is driving, is only two hours away, as the crow flies. But the crow does not fly any longer in this neighborhood. Only vultures pilot the brooding sky now, looking for abandoned bodies of fallen Ifè and Modákéké warriors. In this dim cultural dawn, however, it is impossible to see the vultures. But they clearly see you. They lurk under the shadow of giant trees, laying their eggs in abandoned vehicles damaged beyond repair, stained with the blood of fatal victims of road accidents, that occur with tragic regularity along these meandering narrow roads from Òndó, via Ilé Ifè and Ìbàdàn, to Lagos.

About two decades ago, he held his first show at the Alliance Francaise in Lagos. In those days only the foreign diplomatic missions had exhibition outlets for artists in Nigeria. Things have changed now. These days, there are many galleries, not only in Lagos – Nigeria's art capital – but also in Abuja, the Federal Capital, and even far way Port Harcourt – regarded as

the Garden City of art – where lots of oil technocrats and expatriate art enthusiasts reside.
Art is love and this is exactly why I make art, Wewe reminds himself as he drives reflectively, observing every movement around him. In these days of hate and mindless killing, the world needs the careful eye of the vigilant artist: the world must feed on hope; on art; on creative minds; to keep going; to reinvent itself; to rebirth its hope in humanity.
"This is why I paint. This is why I cannot stop. This is why I cannot sleep or slumber. This is why my car is always loaded with new canvases."

His work is to ease the surge of hate and seize meaning from the siege of chaos, beyond the rotes of lost roads – because without love, there is no enduring art.

I chose love always, he affirms silently, in his mind.

Wewe's work demonstrates that the highest of art procreates powerful love, despite the bed of palpable pain on which it is born. For him, his mother and all women embody love. He is not making art because it is easy: he makes art because it is difficult even at the best and worst of times. Because heat and cold are kin sensations, deep art is an ironic experience – creative art can seep from the skin of individual and communal tragedy – the conflicts of understanding failure are germane to the growth of success; the contradictions of accepting death as part of life; the complications of demanding affection from a world that is filled with crude and cruel excesses.

These are the elements pushing the principles of Wewe's art beyond the pale of decorations, without which images mock and drain reality. Wewe decorates the canvas to provoke a conversation with conflictive drives, in a world that celebrates creativity and destruction as twin sisters from the same Mother – Earth. Mother Earth is a female icon and he enjoys painting the female in provocative ways; as metaphors and allegories of creativity, innovation and imagination; stretching his mind to its fullest extent.

Sometimes he uses the composition of the female body to lure attention and focus to his work. Nobody can ignore the female figure, no matter the sexual preferences of the individual. The erotic, as the feminist scholar, Audre Lorde claims, is one of the most potent forms of visual power.

He recalls Lorde's poem, "The House of Yemanja," which is a celebration of female love and also an inspiration in compositions – with layers of meanings and dimensions,

My mother had two faces and a frying pan
where she cooked up her daughters
into girls
before she fixed our dinner.
My mother had two faces
and a broken pot
where she hid out a perfect daughter
who was not me[9]

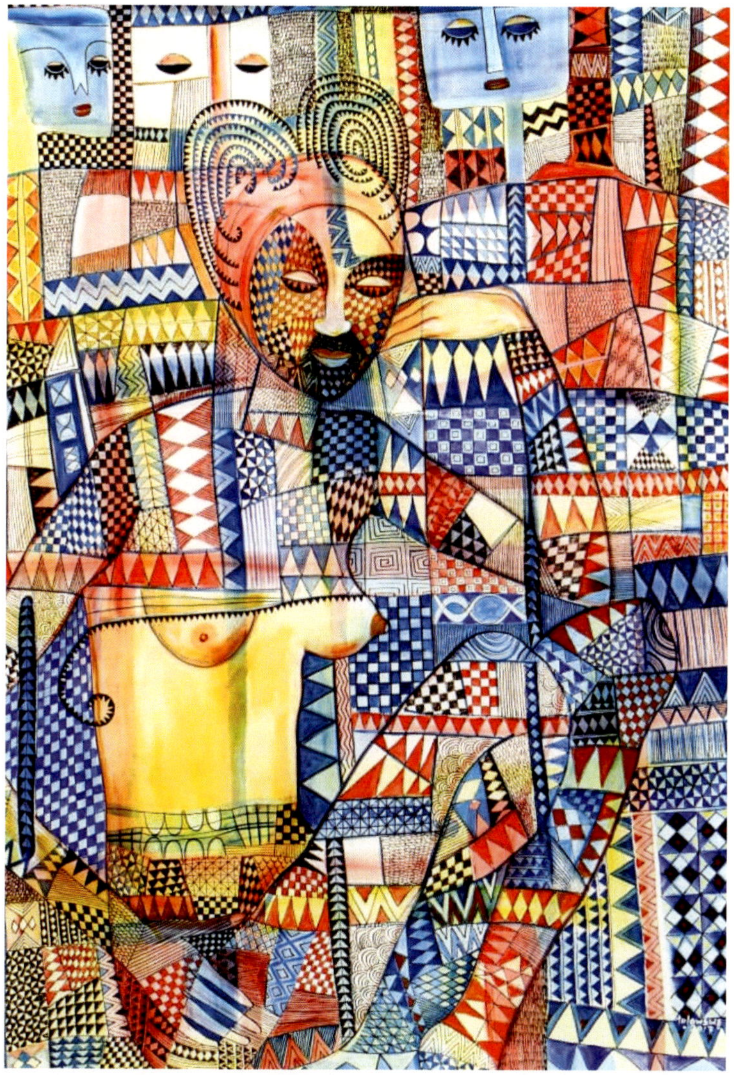

Fig. 9: *Mother With Many Faces*, acrylic on canvas.

How imaginative of her to speak of a mother with two faces! From that poetic idea, one is free to imagine a *Mother With Many Faces*, the title of this colorful painting with intricate layers of adoring patterns, celebrating the female power with the multiple faces embedded into the composition.

Is the mother the figure seated at the foreground, or is that figure one of her daughters that she is cooking up in her pots?

The composition allows for a wide range of explorations – even beyond the framework of the poem – into the divine nature of the female form as a figure of speech and articulated openness.

Wewe uses the same poetic context in the composition of his 2003 painting, *House of Yemoja*, quoting the title of the verse. Yemoja is a Yoruba Òrìsà of water, of beauty and feminine attraction, a divinity that has now crossed the Atlantic from the continent of Africa to diasporic shores, where Lorde finds it within her ancestral heritage. Wewe plays on the fluidity of Yemoja in this composition, in which he constructs several aquatic chambers to stretch the eyes from the near shores of the waterscape to the infinity of the horizon, where the sea meets the clouds; female figures morph into fishes and birds as they constantly change forms as the viewer's gaze gets drawn into them.

Lorde's treatise on the erotic is a wonderful palette on which Wewe draws inspiration as he incorporates the femininity into

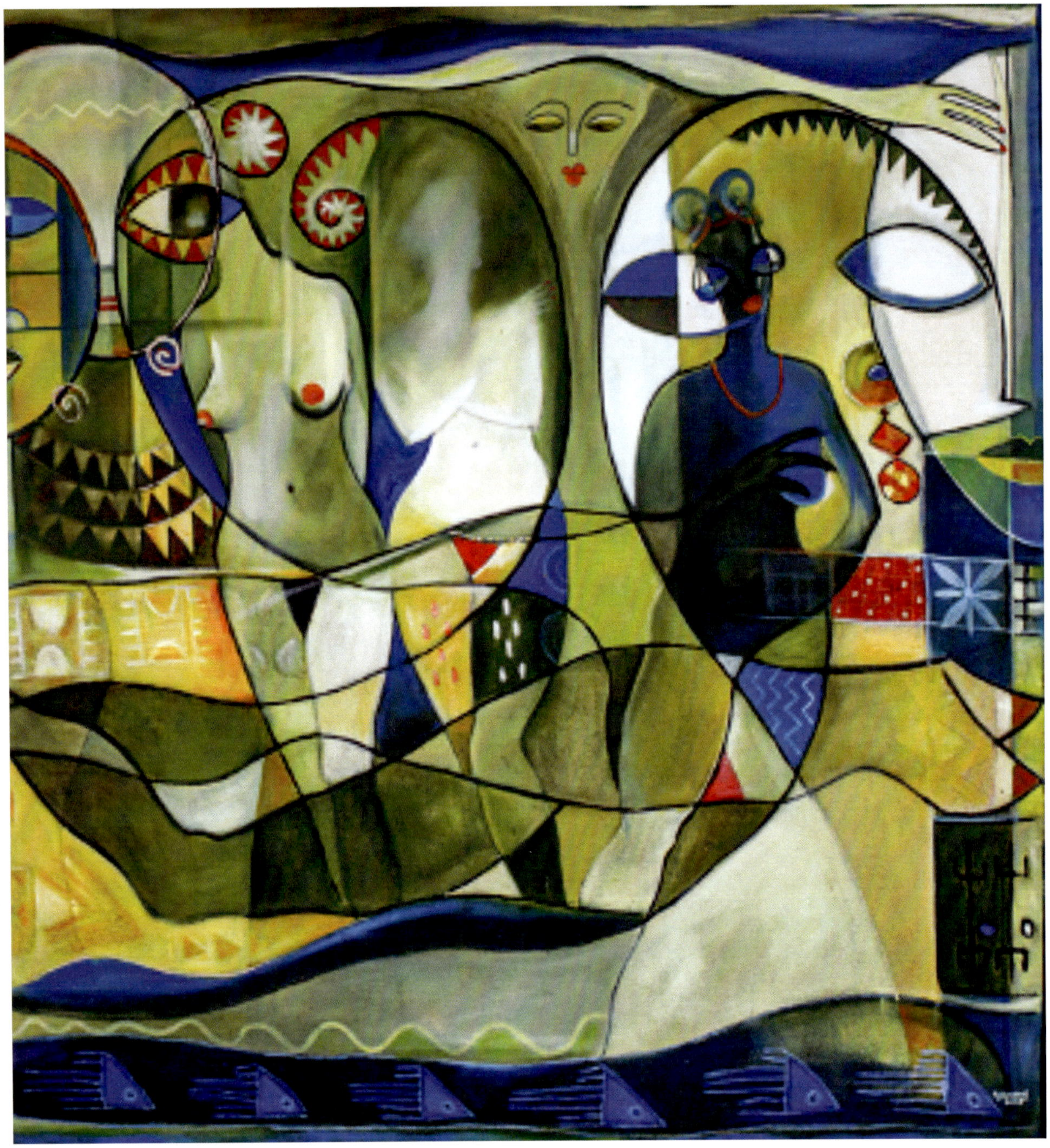

Fig. 10: *House of Yemoja*, acrylic on canvas, 2003.

his compositions. In many instances, his clients, especially women who enjoy the female form, instigate him to push the visual language of the erotic as far as possible. They ask him to be bold about it; to allow the erotic aspect of his imagination to define the scope of his investigation.

The male patrons are less articulate about their desires for the erotic female body.

"Some of the most avid collectors of my more erotic paintings are in fact women," he discloses. "It used to perplex me: while some people chastise the erotic nude female, others encourage it."

Again, Wewe recollects Lorde's reference to the power of the erotic female:
There are many kinds of power, used, unused, acknowledged or otherwise. The erotic is a resource within each of us that lies in a deeply female and spiritual plane, firmly rooted in the power of our

unexpressed or unrecognized feeling. In order to perpetuate itself, every oppression must corrupt or distort those various sources of power within the culture of the oppressed that can provide energy for change. For women, this has meant a suppression of the erotic as a considered source of power and information within ourselves.

We have been taught to suspect this resource, vilified, abused, and devalued within western society. On the one hand, the superficially erotic has been encouraged as a sign of female inferiority; on the other hand, women have been made to suffer and to feel both contemptible and suspect by virtue of its existence.[10]

Emboldened by similar sentiments on the erotic by female collectors, Wewe has allowed himself to go beyond the framework of the prudish critiques of his

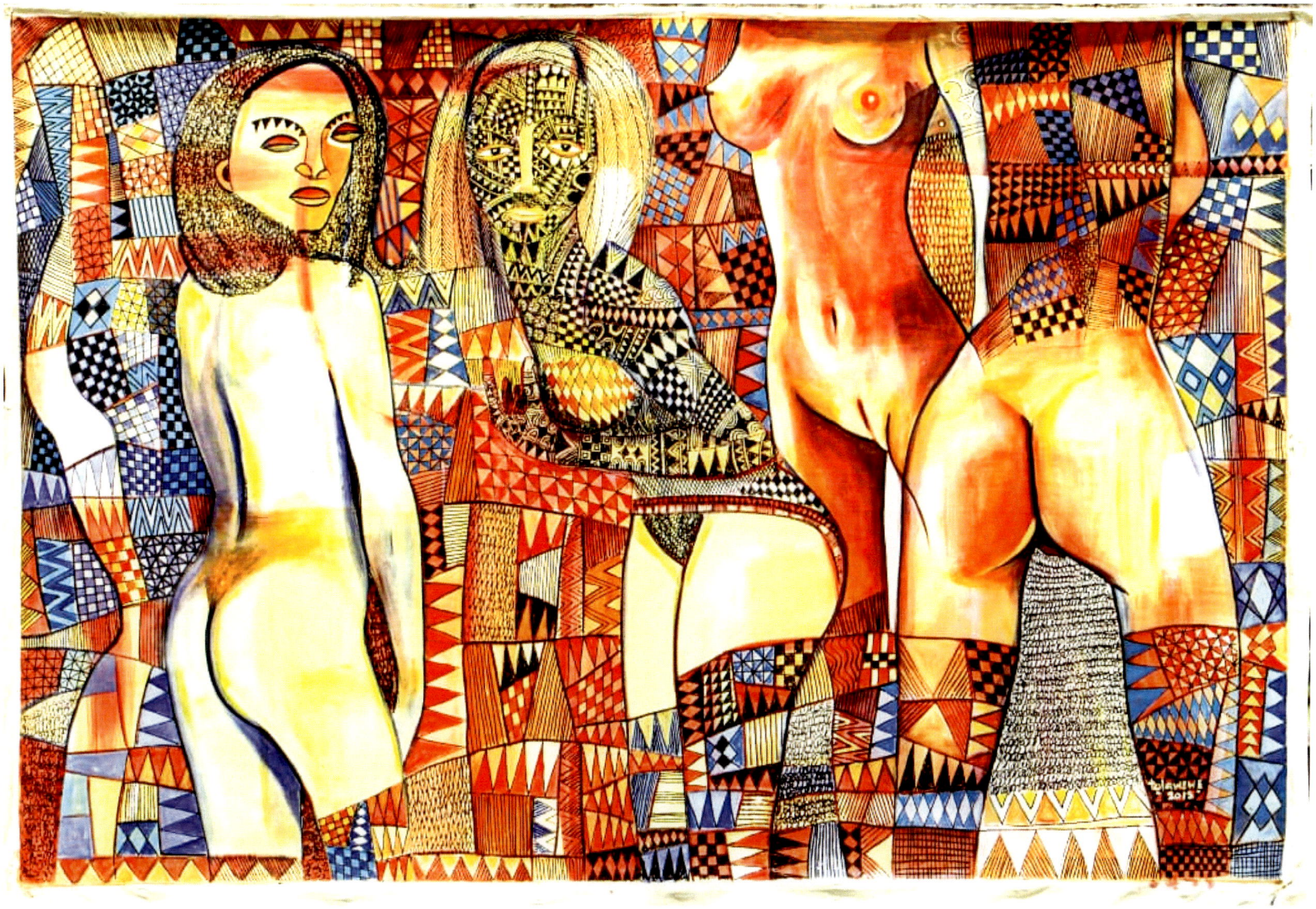

Fig. 11: The Lorde's Gardens of Yemoja, acrylic on canvas, 2015.

work in which the eroticization of the female figure is considered problematic. He understands that the enjoyment of the erotic is in fact an avenue of empowerment from the perspectives of many radical women scholars who assert that there exists "…the false belief that only by the suppression of the erotic within our lives and consciousness can women be truly strong."

More than two decades ago, in 1999, as Wewe drove to Lagos, his car loaded with new work, he mused on the power of love versus the power of war.

"If all they accuse artists like me of doing is loving too much, I am guilty as charged," he thought. "Folks often confuse love and creative desire with misogyny, and I understand why," Wewe says. "There is a thin line. When you exploit women and humiliate them in art, that is a problem. The proverbial 'male gaze' doesn't apply in all situations. The intention of the artist is important. I come in peace and love, and not to kindle an unfortunate gender war. I'm a Yoruba artist and the depiction of male and female nudes, with all their erotic details is a spiritual and divine expression of inter-gender love and desire."

Wewe's aesthetic views are masks from a passionately engaged painter. Within this milieu, his paintings of women conceal an ideological posturing beyond the alluring female bodies. They are world views of gendered commitments, addressing concerns of a world giving birth to its own destruction.

Women are Wewe's most urgent metaphors. Irrespective of age, religion, sexual preferences or social status, women and children suffer when men fight with weapons of war among themselves for power, domination and hegemonies. Love lingers, lost in lust, as human bodies become a commodity of barter and trade, when desperate soldiers of war flood the plains of despair, searching for unfortunate thighs between which to empty their mounting terrors.

Armies of fortune mount campaigns of terror against lands tended and cherished by women; hoping to build their future in peaceful places, women suddenly torn to shreds by shells and bombs flying like predating kites; without care for human life.

Wewe is cynical of the work of creative artists supportive of war; highly paid artists of war implement who design glittering fighter jets. Unlike Wewe, they make ornaments of destruction as shiny bullets fed into the bellies of Kalashnikov machines to gun down villages where the women flee naked and unprotected from the gaze of beholding marauders. Nothing reveals the nudity of life more than women without protection, helpless in the face of the onslaught of invading foreign and local forces.

This, in Wewe's view, is the appalling "male gaze" upon female figures, the glazed over insensitive death-gaze against the vulnerable bodies of women – huddled, quivering, with their little children – their eyes wide with fear, their lives shattered within political borders, with no time to mourn the loss of innocence.

The rampage of patriarchy is fueled on nude female bodies, surrendered to the gaze of war machismo. It is not to be confused with the visual love making of painters: glorifying the timeless divinity of human figures.

He would rather be culpable of love rather than war. That very moment, in 1999, the Taliban was nesting its armies in Afghanistan, and unbeknownst to the civil world, planning to launch the 2001 attack on the Twin Towers of New York. That very moment when the planes were hitting the towers, and people were jumping to their deaths from the top floor, Wewe was working in a gallery in Lagos, personally arranging his paintings on the walls. He froze when the television began to show the attack live. He wanted to stop what he was doing, but he continued, as he deliberated the ironies and necessities of art in a time of trouble. Those attacking New York City were haters of art, people who felt that the artist must not depict any human body, least of all the nude body. If he stopped arranging his paintings on the wall, then he was helping them to fulfill their wishes.

Wewe insists that there is an organic connection between his stylized depiction of the human body to the spirituality of Yoruba religion. Lagos, the large Nigerian city in which he regularly shows his works, is a venue built with the sixteen oracular eyes of Ifá divination of Èkó Ilé, like the structure of the Kabbalah, of Feng Shui's Tao, the gaze of Confucius, and the Torah from Mt Sinai. He affirms that those who founded Lagos and named it Èkó would see nothing wrong with his display of paintings on the wall in defiance of those bombing the amazing city of New York. Between that time and today, he thought, the world has witnessed the rise of new forms of hate, evil and corruption, tainting the enjoyment of our knowledge of a new century.
"I belong to a brigade of love wagers," he says, "and this labor of art is not just for the sake of art. It is a thing of necessity, a contribution to the sanity of humankind. It's like the baker feeding the people with bread. The artists feed the mind of the people with the need for tolerance, for love, for understanding the needs and desires of all in the community. If Lorde likes the female body, though she is a woman, nothing wrong with that. And if others have different preferences, so also be it."

Too many things have happened in recent years, he mused. Two decades ago, as the twentieth turned into the twenty-first century, who could have predicted the rise of the ISIS, the uprisings of the Arab spring, the death of Saddam Hussein, the killing of Muammah Gaddafi and the atrocities of the Boko Haram in Nigeria, Cameroun and Niger? Who could have predicted that Syria in the last twenty years would become the source of the largest numbers of refugees, fleeing a region transformed into a vast warscape without borders? Who could have anticipated the hash tag #Bring Back Our Girls, under which the world launched a rigorous campaign to rescue teenage girls kidnapped and molested by Boko Haram terrorists in Nigeria?

But without that hash tag, how could one understand the work of any African artist, especially one from West Africa, which has suffered so much violent disruptions – from Lagos to Timbuktu – under the march of fundamentalist terrorism? Precisely within this political calendar of global turmoil, the new work of love that Wewe is crafting raises the flag of hope for the dispirited; regeneration of those tormented; rehabilitation of the injured.

Wewe is listening to his painting. "You must take sixteen steps forward and eight

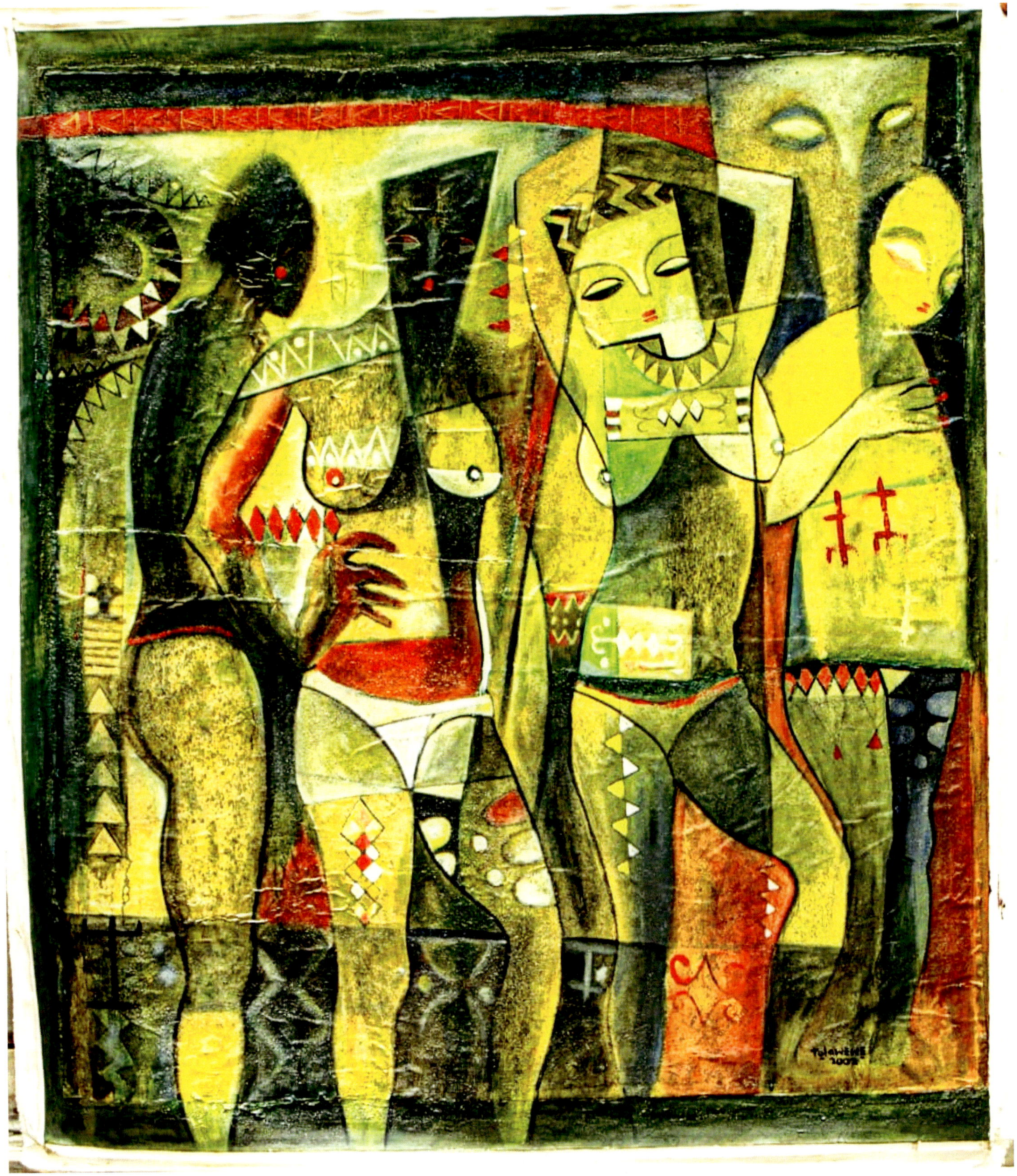

Fig. 12: *Regeneration, Jubilation and Hope*, acrylic on canvas, 2002

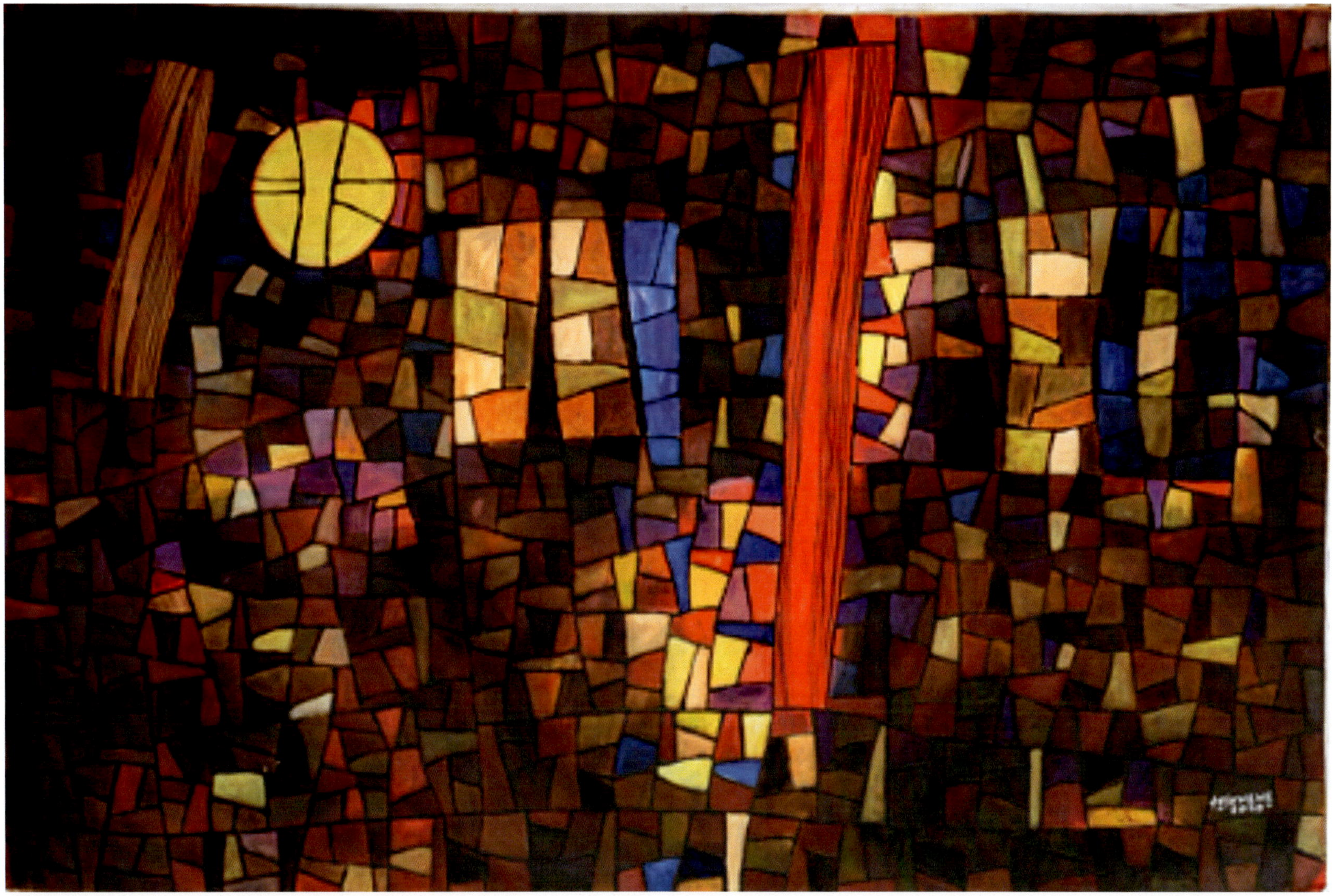

Fig. 13: *Rhapsodies of Colors*, acrylic on canvas, 2020

steps backward towards the morning sun for four days at zero hour," the figures on the canvas (fig. 12) tell Wewe. "You must drive fearless through the alley of trepidation where warriors cower." The paintings always talk to Wewe when he visits them at moments of doubt; they address his dreadful terrors of impending doom. He paints with his ears as full participants and not merely his eyes and fingers. To make a sound painting, he listens to the sound of the painting. And when the painting is done, he listens to what it has to say. Some paintings talk in poetic lines, and others in lyrical prose. A few paintings move beyond mere words and sing in rhapsodic notes of color.

Other paintings stand poised to hold long dialogs, not just with the painter but especially with a wider audience at the art auctions of international marketplaces. Battling the artist and his intuition, some paintings question every brushstroke with resisting rhythms and Wewe must turn the canvas around or climb onto a ladder to address their concerns and grumbles. Some paintings are choreographers and dancers, leaping around with figures of speech and rhythmic meters; others are long-distance swimmers, navigating the oceans of human cultures with invisible vessels of anecdotes and monumental sails, swollen with winds of fortune for those who have come to scale them. But most engaging are the simplest paintings who demand rigorous attention, paintings defiant of easy reading; difficult paintings that sit on the surface of the canvas, compelling the viewer to take a dialogic seat and enjoy a *tête-à-tête.*

Neighborhood Without Boundaries, is a painting which fall within the borders of the simple compositions that interrogate the viewer's mind. It is one of his explorations of the topic of the Ilé Ifè and Modákéké conflict. The work, however applies to any community that is divided within and against itself, into units of conflict that seem irreconcilable. It departs significantly in form from his first painting on that subject about one decade ago. But the content is similar. Ògún's red set the stage for an uneasy terrain of contrasting shapes and compartments. The painting shows the divisions and fragmentation of a community that is essentially the same, but imagines and defines itself through a separatist mentality.

It is also a homage to Ògún, the divine deity of fury and the forge; the blacksmith who shapes agricultural implements and weapons of war; the thirsty drinker of white palm wine and red palm oil; the catalyst of peace and pestilence. Ògún's war is not easy to handle.

Two hundred years ago, Ògún visited the warlike people of Modákéké in the Old Òyó Empire and decimated their community, leading to their dislocation and migration to the ancient city of Ilé Ifè. A neighborhood with invisible boundaries emerged between Ifè and Modákéké and the people prospered in peace, exchanging sons and daughters in marriage, celebrating the same divinities, enjoying the products of their rich vegetation. In exchange for their war songs, Ògún gifted the Modákéké people with prodigious green fingers of agriculture, with which they served their Ifè hosts as dutiful and productive sharecroppers. About one hundred and fifty years afterwards however, Ògún remounted the Modákéké people, inducing them to stake permanent ownership claim to the land on which they have sharecropped for generations. The Ifè owners of the land brooked no such claim and Ògún stained the green Ifè/Modákéké neighborhood in the red of blood with which Wewe imbues this painting.

Dark crisscrossing lines mark the route of migration from Òyó-Ilé – the original home of the people of Modákéké – to Ilé Ifè. Wewe tracks the movement into a pattern that approximates the trail left by mounted horses and motorized tires – linking the past to the present.

To the outside world, the citizens of these two communities seem to live together without rancor, as one harmonic entity. Most of the time, the people live in peace and harmony – until Ògún induces discord. Harmony normally defines their

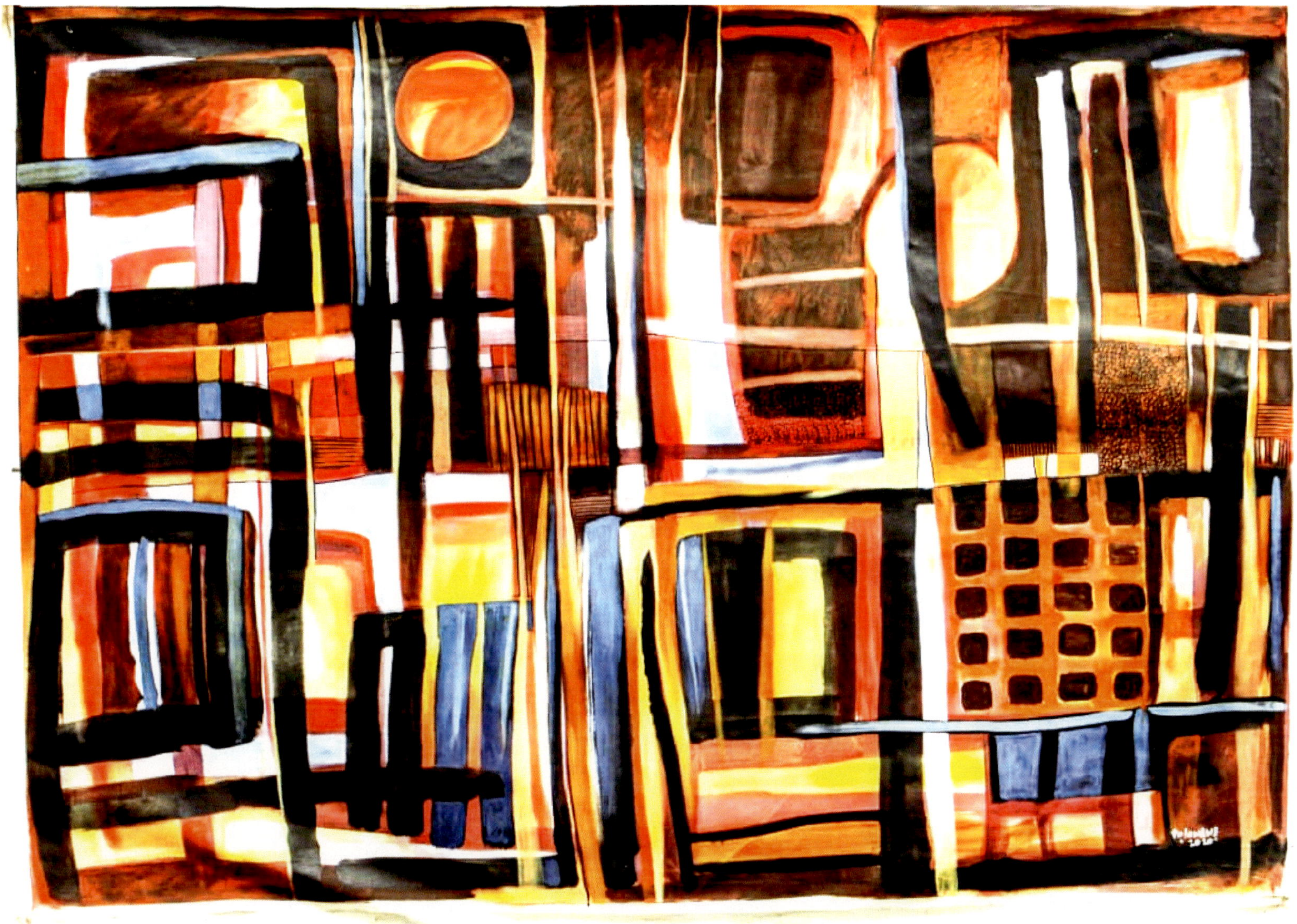

Fig. 14: *Neighborhood Without Boundaries*, acrylic on canvas

relationship from the view of the outsider looking in. But insiders are always conscious of the tenuity of that uneasy relationship, that separates the identity of those living in diaspora from those whose ancestors are Aborigines. Wewe's painting conveys this tenuous tension; as the human figures easily turn to machete blades cutting down one another; as shifting boundaries are constantly drawn and re-drawn; as agricultural fields frequently turn to crimson battlefields.

The last twenty years have been seasons of war and love, Wewe says. Two of the most devastating wars are the campaigns against the Covid virus and the Gender Wars. They seem related in some ways: both are pandemic and keep mutating. Nobody is safe from their unpredictable twists and turns, not even artists, as Wewe says with a knowing laugh. "Love is the only armor of the artist in this war from which there are no foolproof vaccines."

CHAPTER FOUR:

Home is Where the Art Is

Wewe's studio is on the premises of his home in Òndó, a two-story building complex off the main road to Ore, which lies along the highway to Benin City. At the intersection of his street and the road to Òrè is Sabo, the section of the town in which settlers from Northern Nigeria reside. Wewe built that house in the late nineties – the only building in the entire area at that time. When he moved into the house, with his family, they were the only people living in what was at that time just secondary forest on the outskirts of Òndó town. He built the road to the house with his resources, as there was not even a path leading to his place. The area was already laid out in the plan of the city, but it was not yet constructed and had no government amenity.

But in truth, Wewe had company. Right in the middle of the forest, about a hundred yards from his house, was a prophet living all by himself in a shed. Always dressed simply in a long white frock, he wore his white beard long. He spoke with nobody and spent every day and night praying, singing and fasting. From time to time, when he broke his fast, the prophet would venture out from his hideout and walk to the Òndó township to stock up on some food and essential items – soap, matches and so on. Otherwise, the ascetic prophet, who did not touch meat or fish, lived on the fruits, nuts and vegetables that he gathered from the wild.

When Wewe bought the plot to start building his house, he had noticed the prophet. He approached the prophet who signaled with his hands and head that he didn't want to communicate with any mortal. The prophet was exclusively in communication with divine forces, and he moved out there into the forest because it was remote and far from any human contact. Wewe had bought the plot in the remote area also because he wanted a peaceful and quiet place, where he could focus on his art, undisturbed by traffic or constant human company, that could distract him from his creative pursuits. The main difference between him and the prophet was that Wewe was young, in his thirties, while the prophet already looked old. The prophet was tending towards the end of his calling; Wewe was just beginning his practice as a professional artist – passionate, indefatigable, restive. The prophet looked just as passionate even in his old age. Wewe couldn't but admire the fire still blazing out of the old eyes of the aging prophet, wishing and hoping to keep his passion for art even in his old age. Gradually, Wewe began to construct the building and though he did not always run into the prophet directly, he always felt the presence of the recluse, who sang loud and clear from his sacred shed, anytime of the day, or night. Wewe moved into the building before it was completely finished.

If that old prophet could live alone in that bush and retain so much vigor, Wewe saw no excuse for not moving into a house that wasn't fully finished. He wired the house for electricity, and before the area was connected to the national power grid, he used a generator to supply himself electricity. He also drilled a borehole to provide for his household water needs because no government pipe-borne water supply existed.

Once in his new home as a full-time artist, the regular and constant choral activities of the prophet became a meter that Wewe used to measure his creative application and practice. If that prophet worked night and day, Wewe saw no reason to stay away from his painting easel. "My studio is by far more comfortable than the prophet's studio," Wewe said to himself. The "studio" of the prophet was the prophet's shed in the forest and from Wewe's house, Wewe saw the unfailing devotion of the prophet to his divine practice. Night and day, Wewe painted, and his production was prodigious. He would roll up the canvases every fortnight and drive to Lagos from Òndó to supply his clients with work. Wewe's decision to become a full-time artist was daring. There was no precedence among his colleagues for becoming a full-time practitioner because it was typical to take a teaching job after obtaining a degree in art. Wewe did what most people did at that time after taking a degree in art: he began to teach, taking up a lectureship position as a painting teacher at the Adeyemi College of Education in Òndó. At the same time, he began to study the theory of visual culture at the University of Ibadan, where he obtained a master's degree in the history of African Art in 1986. In 1991 he moved to Lagos, where he joined the studio department of the Daily Times – the most prominent daily newspaper in Nigeria at that time – as an illustrator. At the same time, he continued to practice part-time as an artist.

The life of an illustrator and cartoonist was precarious under the military dictatorships in Nigeria, where the press was not free and cartoonists regarded as easy target for censorship, arrests and detention. In addition, Wewe was gradually building a steady body of clientele as a painter.

One of his patrons opened a gallery, Signature Gallery, and invited Wewe to assist him to run the gallery in 1993. He agreed and left his position at the newspaper to run the gallery. This position gave him access to the business aspect of art and an opportunity to meet many art patrons in Lagos. He began to moot the idea of going into full practice but all his friends who practiced as part-time artists advised him against the move, saying that the art market in Nigeria was not ready for full-time practicing artists.

The more he contemplated the risk of full-time art practice versus the creative opportunities and freedom that the move

"There was the practical matter of bringing his work from Òndó to Lagos to market. But there was a direct highway from Ore to Lagos and his house in Òndó was not far from the town of Ore"

might provide him, the more he felt it was the right step to take. He knew it was going to be a rough and bumpy road ahead if he became a full-time artist.

At the time, he had already started building his house. He decided that if he moved into the uncompleted building and started full-time studio practice, he would not have to pay house rent. He had also been saving some money, which he decided would stead him through the first couple of months of having no job that paid a regular salary. If he failed as a full-time practitioner, he calculated, he could always return to a regular paying job. He had nothing to lose and if he didn't make the move, he would never enjoy the opportunity of fulfilling his childhood dream of being a full-time artist.

He decided to take the plunge. In 1995 he left Signature Gallery and moved back to Òndó from Lagos to fully practice as a painter. It was the best decision of his life; it was not easy when he started and he was always scared of failure. He knew that Lagos was where the art market was and it was tempting for him to just stay in Lagos like many other artists did, to seek a location in the art market. But life in Lagos was rough and hectic, a knowledge he had firsthand as a journalist. He did not find the tension of living in Lagos conducive to his creative disposition – the noise, the traffic congestion, the fast, high-paced life that those who moved to Lagos must endure. Living outside Lagos in a city as far away as Òndó would have its challenges, he decided, but he would give it a try.

There was the practical matter of bringing his work from Òndó to Lagos to market. But there was a direct highway from Ore to Lagos and his house in Òndó was not far from the town of Ore. And if he tried Òndó and found commuting from there to Lagos was impossible, he would return to Lagos alone, and keep his family back in Òndó.

After discussing his decision with his family, he made the bold move. They supported his decision. It was timely: the new art from Nigeria was beginning to reach the outside world. Very little however was available.

The artists of the Oshogbo School, associated with the workshops of Ulli Beier, Suzanne Wenger and Georgia Beier, were at that time the most internationally well-known group of artists in Nigeria. The leading artists of the group include Twins Seven Seven, Muraina Oyelami, and Jimoh Buraimoh.[11] This group of artists did not attend the formal art schools within the tertiary educational system in and outside Nigeria.[12] The tertiary-school trained artists include Aina Onabolu, Ben Enwonwu, Demas Nwoko and Uche Okeke.[13] Wewe belongs with this second group. While some of them held art exhibitions now and then, they were not active. There was also a scarcity of opportunities for them to exhibit their works in Nigeria, though there existed a growing crop of potential consumers for art.

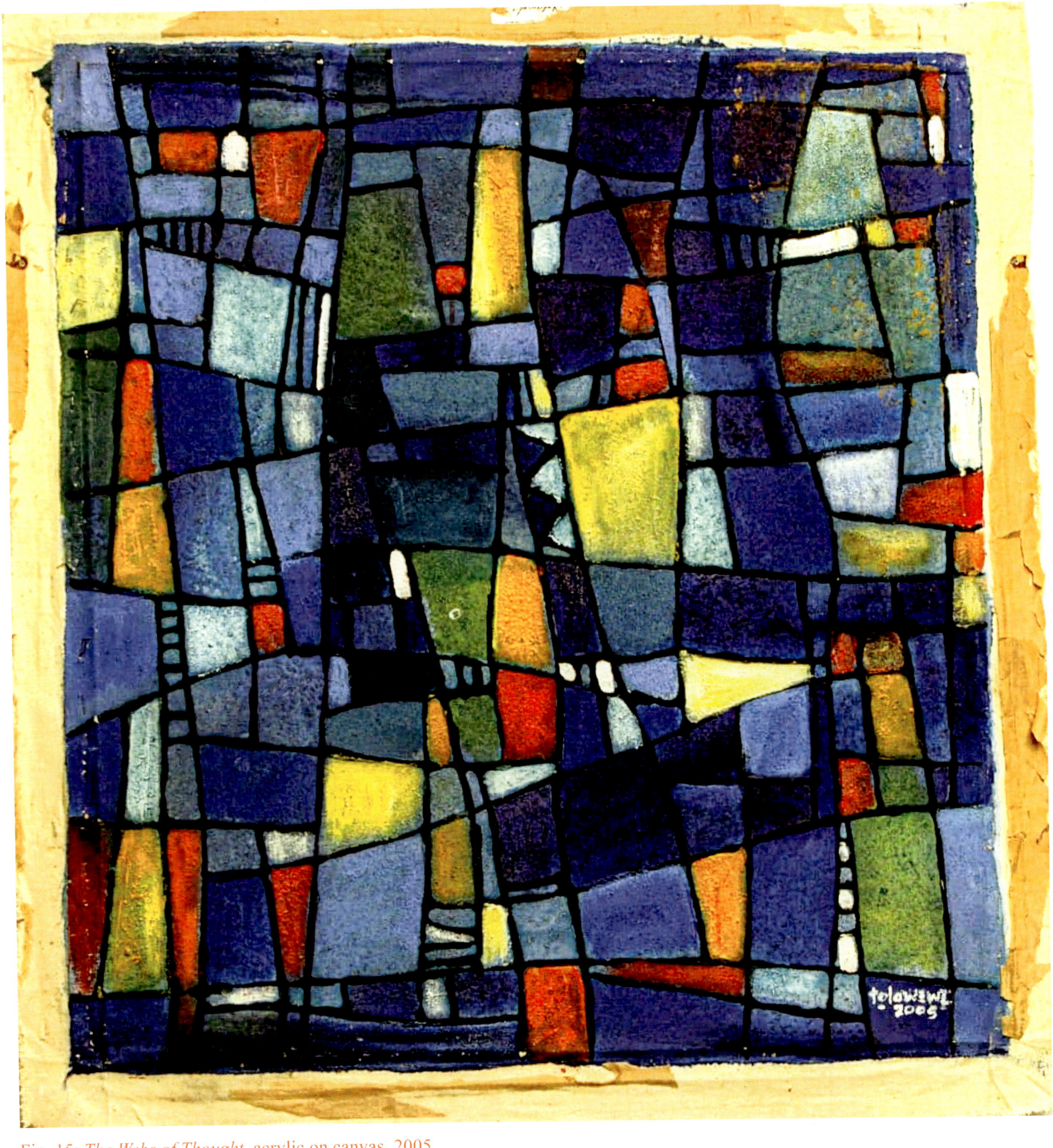

Fig. 15: *The Webs of Thought*, acrylic on canvas, 2005

Nigeria's vast crude oil resources made it especially attractive to lots of expatriates, many of who reside in Lagos (the commercial capital of Nigeria), Abuja (the political capital) as well as Port Harcourt, Warri and Benin City, all cities associated with the petroleum industry. Some Nigerians associated with the banking and other commercial sectors in Nigeria were also interested in collecting the new art coming out of Nigeria. The cultural institutes of various western countries such as the Goethe Institute, Italian Cultural Center, and Alliance Francaise in Lagos and other Nigerian cities also provided some exposure for artists. The members of the Oshogbo school were availing themselves of these opportunities by taking their works directly to any of these individuals and organizations that showed any interest in their works. But the others trained in the tertiary institutions did not embrace these opportunities. It was an opportunity waiting for innovative and enterprising minds to investigate and seize.

This was where the young Nigerian art enthusiast, Chike Nwagbogu, came in. Nwagbogu studied political science at the University of Nigeria, Nsukka, one of the prominent institutions that offered degree programs in the arts during the eighties. He realized that there were many talents producing what he considered "incredible paintings, sculptures and prints."[14] Because he grew up in Lagos and was raised by influential and enterprising parents, he knew many prominent people who expressed an interest in collecting art. He also noticed that it was typical for the producers of art work in Nigeria not to seek a market for their products. He began by collecting small paintings, prints and sculptures from artists in Nsukka and taking them to Lagos, showing them to potential expatriate buyers and making regular sales. He knew exactly where to go and how to present the art. He quickly created a market for himself in Lagos, which he widened by seeking out artists from all over Nigeria and targeting the Lagos buyers.

Wewe ran into Nwagbogu when he decided to go full-time with his art. Nwagbogu encouraged Wewe to focus on producing paintings, assuring him of finding an audience for the paintings. They made an arrangement in which he would buy all the works that Wewe brought to him at a bulk rate, according to the number and size of the paintings.

This arrangement worked for both of them. It enabled Wewe to fully stay in his new home in Òndó and paint all the time. Every weekend, Wewe rolled up all the paintings that he had finished and drove to Lagos to submit them to Nwagbogu, who paid him immediately. At first, Wewe would stay in hotels in Lagos over the weekends before returning to Òndó.

That arrangement changed when Nwagbogu and Tola Akerele co-founded

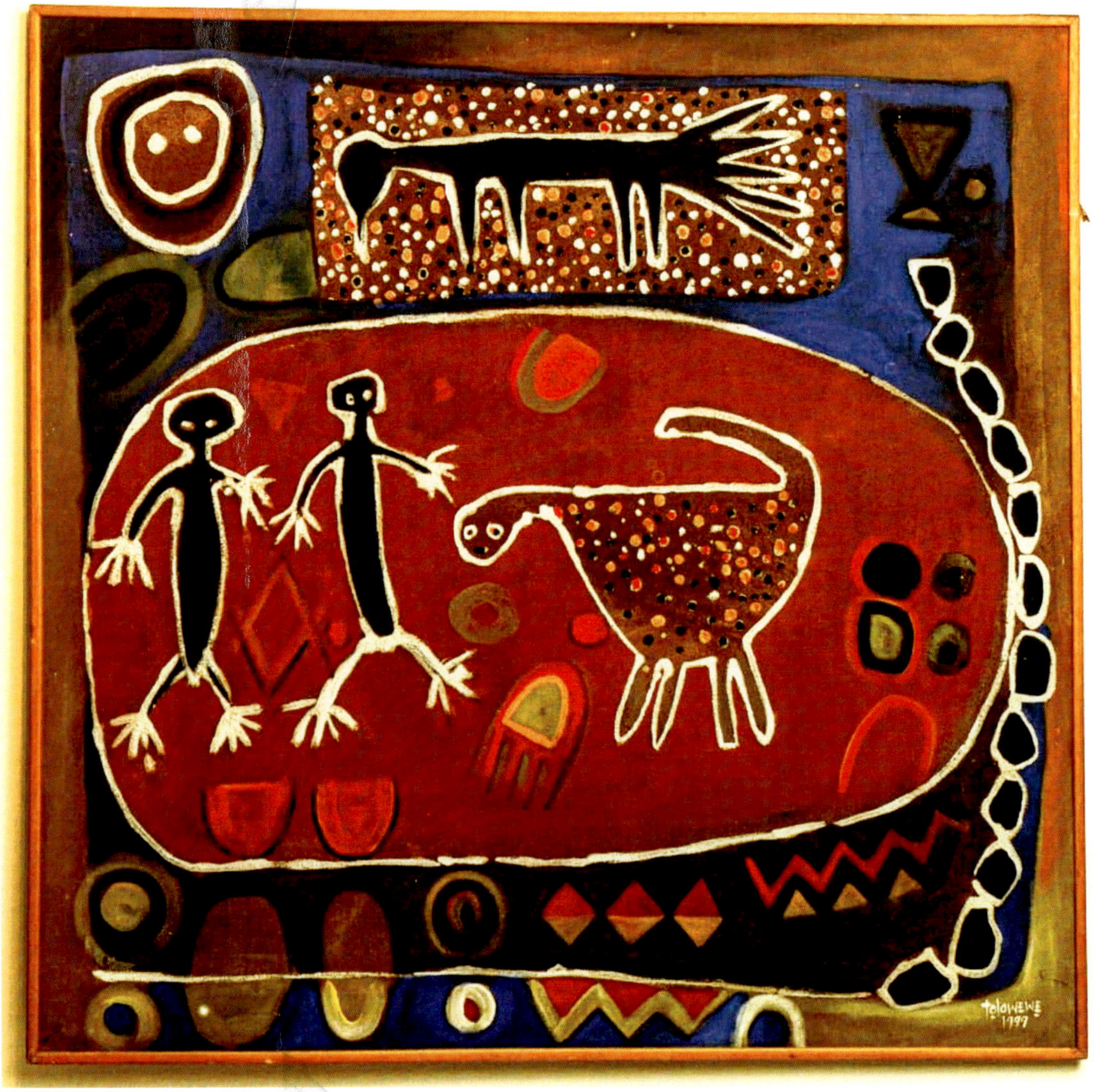

Fig. 16: *Seeds of Life*, acrylic on canvas, 1999

an artsy hotel – Bogobiri, which quickly became the orbit of artists, art lovers and international art researchers in Lagos. Nwagbogu made his hotel available to Wewe who began to stay at Bogobiri on his delivery runs. It was a perfect arrangement for Wewe: he worked hard all week, and spent the weekend at Bogobiri which was great fun; besides Bogobiri's splendid restaurant and excellent bar, it was a beehive of artsy events and gatherings – poetry nights, eclectic music, conversations and discussions about art and the art world in general. Beyond this, Bogobiri became a place where Wewe met other young artists from several parts of Nigeria who Nwagbogu brought to Lagos and offered the same market opportunities that he provided to Wewe.

Nwagbogu and his collaborators had converted the building opposite an exhibition space he opened called Nimbus Art Gallery, where he showed the works of the various artists working with him, to Bogobiri.

It was an important turning point for Wewe. It was also at this time that Nike Okundaye opened her Lagos gallery, Nike's Gallery, in Lekki, one of the more elite areas of Lagos. Nike Okundaye made a similar arrangement with Wewe – he would bring his paintings to her gallery and get paid in bulk for them – enabling him to focus on

"Ọnà is a concentration of artistic energies for aesthetic healing; a search for clarity in the midst of chaos; a devotion to structure in the engulfment of calamity"

the creative part, without worrying about marketing his products.

His paintings flew off the walls like hot cakes. At first, many of the art collectors in Lagos didn't know what to make of his art. It was so totally different from everything they were used to. The art market of Lagos was conversant with the naturalistic style of the Yaba College of Technology which favored the watercolor washes and oil paintings associated with Kolade Oshinowo and his products.

They had also welcomed the innovative creativity of the Nsukka School and the Uli masters – mostly works by Uche Okeke, Obiora Udechukwu and Ghanaian immigrant, El Anatsui.

The Oshogbo Movement they knew – associating them with distortions and exaggerations of forms that were excused as emanations from the lack of "formal" education. But the Lagos collectors were completely unprepared for Wewe's innovative experimentations.
To understand the continued and continuous innovativeness of this art, one must visit the creative impetus that defines Tola Wewe's style.

Towards the end of the 1980s, five graduates of the University of Ifè (now Obafemi Awolowo University, Ilè Ifè) came together to form an art movement called the Ọnà Art Group. These artists are Moyo Okediji, Kunle Filani, Tola Wewe, Bolaji Campbell and Tunde Nasiru. They began to use and infuse the concept of Ọnà – an indigenous form of aesthetic culture – into their artistic practices.

Ọnà is a concentration of artistic energies for aesthetic healing; a search for clarity in the midst of chaos; a devotion to structure in the engulfment of calamity.

A creative energy that started eons ago, ages and ages before the transatlantic slave

trade began in the fifteenth century, Ọnà generates its elements and principles from a fundamental humanistic philosophical system, located within the West African ecological landscape.
The emergence of the transatlantic slavery and the attendant decadence and anti-humanistic focus of the nefarious mercantile activities of the slave culture tasked and strained the development of Ọnà aesthetics.

Slavery, however, was not sufficient to terminate the growth of Ọnà: slavery radically pushed Ọnà deep underground, removing the elements and principles associated with Ọnà from general and public access. Only those who have consciously searched for Ọnà – by delving beyond the surface of pedestrian or easily available aesthetic creativity – can find Ọnà and apply it as a healing tool for the hundreds of seasons of chaos in Yoruba country; especially as the era of enslavement preceded the century of colonization in the Yoruba history of creativity. Others employ mainstream and commercial aesthetics favored by the colonial authorities and the educational institutions of the neocolonial era.
It was within this neocolonial art system that Okediji, Filani, Wewe, Campbell and Nasiru – the foundation members of the Ọnà Art Group – trained at the University of Ife in the seventies and eighties. Though fortunate to have received their art training under scholars who had begun the exploration of the ideals of Ọnà – scholars such as Rowland Abiodun, Babatunde Lawal and Agbo Folarin – the form of artistic training they received was still mostly colonial, manifesting ideas imposed by colonial authorities, who considered indigenous forms of African art primitive, backward and unsuitable for "contemporary" and "progressive" Africans.

The anti-indigenous posture of this education even during the neocolonial era did not encourage the production of graduates that could dedicate their art to counter-colonial initiatives. Rather, the education these young students received further inculcated in them those old colonial practices that were hostile to indigenous forms of art education.

Graduating from this colonial art education, the five young artists of the Ọnà Art Group could not see their relevance within the Nigerian society that they were supposed to service with their creativity. Rather, they saw themselves as alienated individuals, trained to appeal to similarly alienated Nigerians or seek patronage abroad, from the foreign lands of their colonizers, all of which continued to push even deeper, the foundation of their alienation.

It was partly the need to ground themselves in a new way of thinking and partly to reject the tenets of their colonial art education, that motivated these young visionaries to start exploring other approaches to the making and sharing of art.

They graduated at that significant turn of time when the oil boom, which was at its zenith in the early seventies, was beginning to weaken, when the value of the Nigerian currency began to drop and when the expatriate professors that came to work at the art schools in Nigeria began to leave one after another for other opportunities. These expatriates, many of whom had established institutes and centers for African studies, were being replaced by indigenous scholars – Abiodun, Lawal and Irein Wangboje – who presented much more convincing insights into the study of the aesthetics of Southwest Nigeria. It was therefore to the work of these indigenous scholars that the young artists looked for inspiration and leadership.
From the writings of these indigenous scholars – Abiodun, Lawal, Wangboje and others – the five young foundation members of the Ọnà Art Group began to excavate a body of aesthetic principles that they considered relevant to their lives – as emerging creative minds, focused on producing relevant art, that is not alienated from their society.[15]
After organizing several informal thinking sessions at restaurants and bars all over Ilé Ifè and Òndó, they gradually began to build a body of aesthetic elements and principles that they regarded as attempts to heal the crisis they perceived in the art of their time. They codified these ideas into Ọnà – a Yoruba term.

Ọnà is derived from *nà* – encompassing the concept of straightening, stretching, elongating, broadening, widening, unfolding, ordering, adjusting, tidying, arranging, spacing, positioning, cleaning, collating, classifying, aligning all forms of visual, verbal, and other embodied images –all of which are imageries for creative journeys.

The simplicity of the term is also its power. It is a simplicity belying the complexity and sophistication of its possibilities and applications as a system for organizing thoughts, designs, images, sounds, movements, for artistic expression.
Ọnà is a radical devotion to environmental re-orientation and redesigning towards the attainment of joy, truth and understanding – a departure from the pits of pain, deceit and ignorance. How to reorient art to tackle these problems is one of the challenges that the Ọnà artists confronted. It was not enough for them to produce work that is didactic or too sociologically directed in terms of content. The very form of the creative work must be sufficiently eloquent to drive this aspiration and the content should be subtle and refined. The aesthetic aspect of the form should invite the audience into the work in terms of its visual arrangement in a manner that drives the discussion as a major aspect of the meaning.

Clearly, within the Ọnà aesthetics,

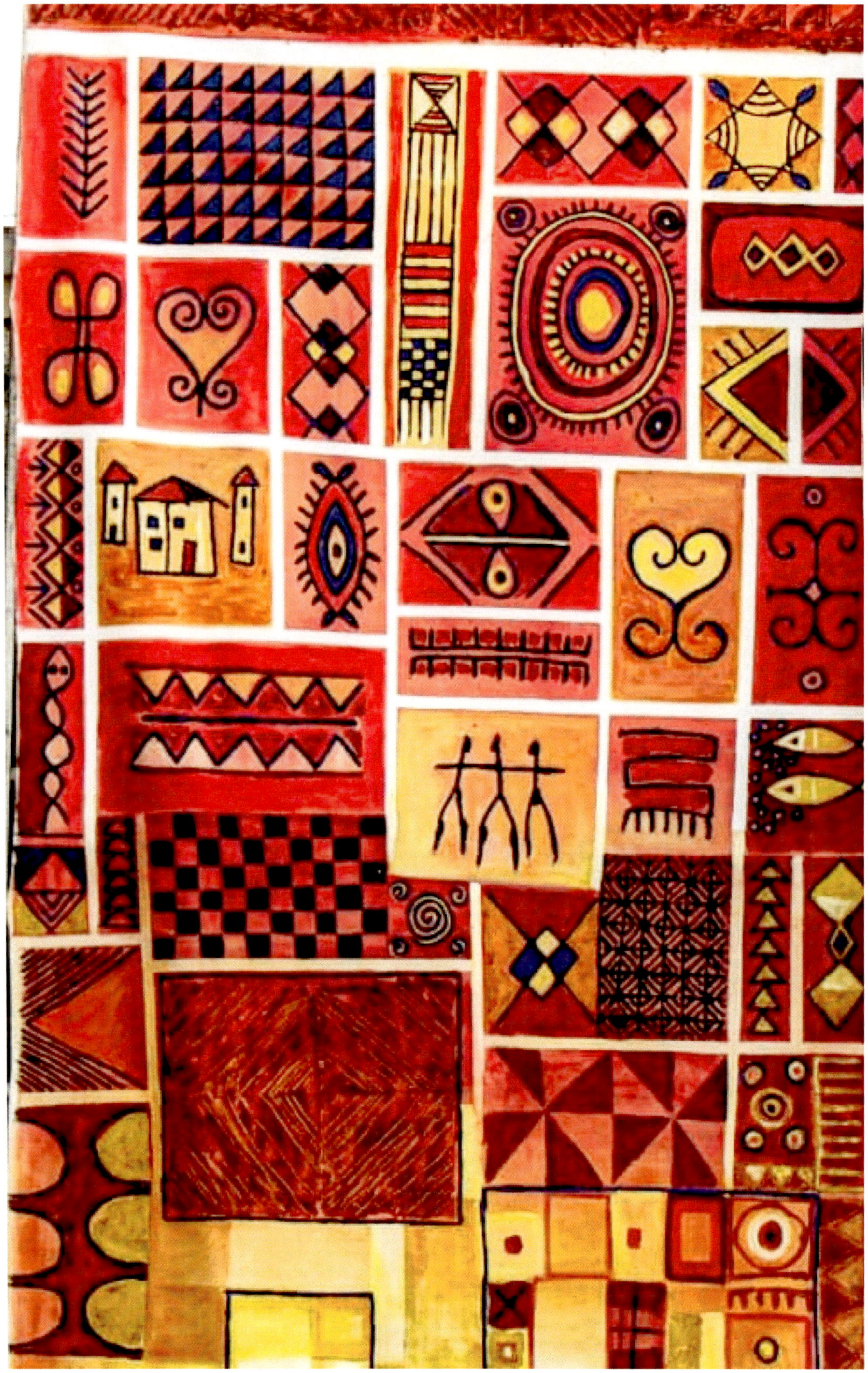

Fig. 17: *Once Upon A Time…*, acrylic on canvas, 2021

the most important aspect of art is its ability to engage and stimulate healthy contemplation, thereby encouraging an *intellecting* community that strives to improve both the individual members as well as the community at large.

But this is certainly not the purpose of all forms of art; certainly not the aspirations of all artists or art collectors. As artists who were trained in a western aesthetic manner of regarding art as sufficiently engaging for its own sake even without any further function, the artists of the Ọnà Art Group – undaunted – set for themselves enormous tasks for which they rigorously searched for solutions.

And this is where the idea of *ètò* comes in as a major component of the articulation of Ọnà. To find a formal approach toward expressing the idea of Ọnà, the Ọnà Five began exploring the notion of *ètò* as a mode of design – beyond the colonial lines of their educational training. If Ọnà is philosophical, *ètò* gives a structural dimension to its interpretation.

Ètò, which is sourced in *tò*, is bifurcated in a Y configuration, one arm defining *tò* – to talk, to narrate, to say, to elaborate, to describe, to report, to recite and to define.

All these words are related to the audio-aural specificity of *tò*. The second arm of *tò*, however, moves in the visual dimension – to organize, plan, arrange, design, outline, prepare, schedule, formulate, frame, develop, devise, concoct, plot, shape, figure, structure.

It is to both aspects of *tò* as Ọnà that the members of the group, including Wewe, began to reach for their structural ideas as they organized their art. The focus is not on making photographic reproductions of reality. *Ètò* does not place priority on

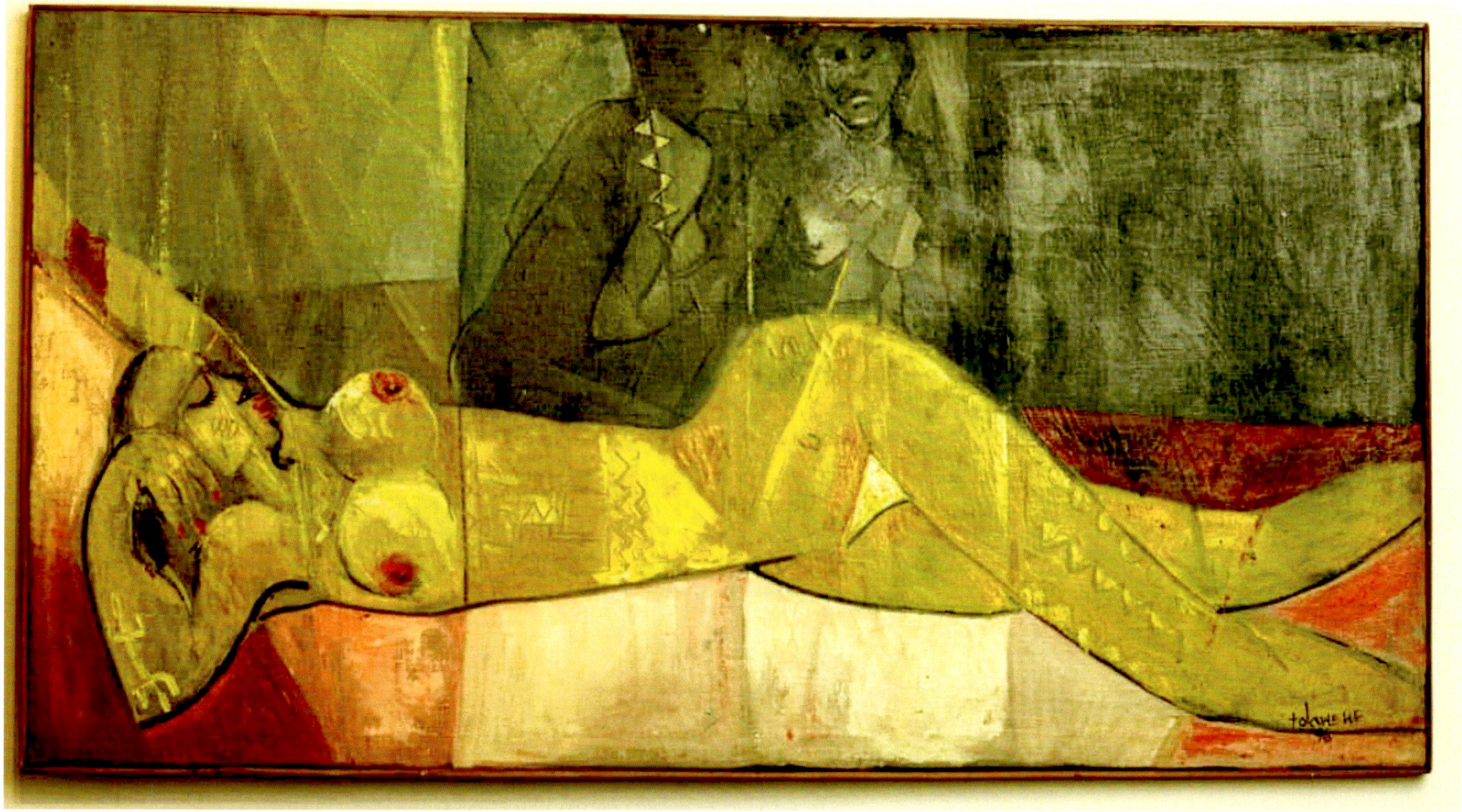

Fig. 18: *Wura: The Jewel of the Lion*, acrylic on canvas, 1996

conveying the physical appearances of things. Ètò engages more the arrangement and rearrangement of things in such a way as to make statements about the need to remake the world, by constructing pictorial analogies to demonstrate our power and commitment to reorganizing life as we know it and living as we find it.

Ètò gives the artist the power to demonstrate a mastery over their destiny – rather than being merely subjects of their circumstances. Reproducing reality as it is found is considered a surrender to the vagaries of life, rather than a readiness to take charge and reconfigure reality. Wewe's work demonstrates this capacity to take charge of the space of composition and reconfigure it. He chooses his colors, shapes, textures and lines according to the mood, values and ideas that he wants to convey in that specific work, and he organizes these components to suit his purposes within the composition. He also creates sufficient space with his *ètò* to give room for elastic interpretations and playful relationships between his work and its viewer, to enable each person find different experiences in the same piece of art.

In the work titled *Seeds of Life*, (fig. 16) Wewe takes an indigenous approach to composition by visiting the forms and iconography of Yoruba women's paintings as found in Ilé Ifè. Abandoning the conventional composition that you find in classic western paintings, Wewe excavates the form of the sacred paintings that adorn the walls of Yoruba shrines and temples. He reconfigures these divine forms, using *ètò*, on a western easel. The result is a hybrid arrangement of forms that derives content and meaning from indigenous sources, yet is arranged within a western idiomatic expression to create a delightful composition of Ọnà; incorporating *ètò* elements and principles.

Wewe rose to become one of the most prolific exponents of the Ọnà aesthetics. His commitment to full time art became an important factor in his contribution to the propagation of Ọnà aesthetics. But when he began to introduce his work to the Lagos art community, he met with some resistance because nobody could understand his Ọnà philosophical approach to composition. The idea of abandoning the tendency by the artist to paint like a camera that many of the patrons had imbibed was not easy to accept for the Lagos art buyers. They didn't understand Wewe's tendency to flatten the picture plane, prioritizing visual poesy as he plays with the surface of the canvas. The references to indigenous and "contemporary" literature were also not quite easy for the patrons to follow, because they were more used to artists who made no such references and simply painted what they saw around them with minimal stylization.

Wewe's *Wura: The Jewel of the Lion* (fig. 18) comes from an interpretation of Wole Soyinka's early play, *The Lion and the Jewel*.[16] Basically, the viewer doesn't need to know the play to enjoy Wewe's work. The rich array of colors, the multiple layering of patterns, the radiating visual percussions, the linear arrangements and the combination of figures on the different strata of the composition is sufficient material to feast a viewer in search of an engaging visual experience. A knowledge of the literary allusions only adds more spice to an already engaging dish.

Initially, the Lagos art patrons were very reluctant to embrace the new aesthetics of Wewe's art; rather they wanted him to provide them with what they were already comfortable with □ themes that had become staple diet in the Lagos art scene □ the Fulani cattleman, the milkmaid, the Èyò masquerades and mother and child themes. Wewe□s art featured none of these conventional references.

Persistence and diligence by Wewe, however, paid off, as a few of the patrons began to listen to the analysis of his work. They began to educate themselves about the purposes and principles of his paintings and started to acquire his work. Some public places, especially exclusive hotels and boutiques, began to collect and display his paintings. Notable collectors such as Prince Yemisi Shyllon and Sam Olagbaju began to avidly push Wewe's work as inspired and distinctive. It worked very well for him. Within a few years, Wewe became the number one artist to collect in Lagos. That was when people began to call him the Lagos Picasso – they had begun to appreciate Wewe's introduction of indigenous African myth, literature, songs and myriads other ideas into his work. Like the European Picasso who changed the form of western art at the beginning of the twentieth century, Wewe became for many art collectors in Lagos, a transformative figure who changed the visual cultural vocabulary of the art metropolis at the end of the twentieth century and the beginning of the twenty-first.

For his exploration of indigenous African sources, Wewe has found Ifá divination literature a rich mine. Not only does he enjoy Ifá literature, he also watches the lines of mystery that Ifá practitioners produce on their *Ọpọ́n Ifá*, in the process of finding solutions to the challenges of their clients. These complex lines that move in short vertical strokes are so interwoven that at a point they produce a horizontal relationship in the mind of the viewer. The priests wipe them off the surface of the tray and make new ones, in rapid succession that create multiple layers of kinetic arrangements, not just on the Ifá tray, but also in the mind of the client experiencing the lines.

It is this pattern of Ifá lines that influences the composition of Wewe and other members of the Ọnà Group – Moyo Okediji, Bolaji Campbell, Tunde Nasiru and Kunle Filani. It is from such lines that Wewe crafted *The Webs of Thought* (fig. 15). The movements of the lines invoke the rituals enacted by the Ifá practitioners in the process of connecting the thoughts of their clients with the decisions of the divinities – at the crossroads of mortal and immortal beings.

In the year 2005 when Wewe painted *The Webs of Thoughts*, Nigeria was experiencing intense levels of violence across the length and breadth of the nation. In the northern and most especially in the middle of the nation, violent activities claimed the lives of hundreds of victims as clashes between Christian and Moslem groups raged across the landscape. Far south in the Delta region of the country, indigenous militias agitating over the mining, ownership and distribution of the oil produced in their area were embroiled in clashes with the federal government, which culminated in attacks against several villages and communities, resulting in the death of hundreds of the inhabitants and the destruction of many communities.

For Tola Wewe, however, Nigeria was a place of economic and creative boom. The conflicts between Ifè and Modákéké were largely over by the year 2002, and he could safely travel from Òndó to Lagos without having to drive through any dangerous territory. He visited Ilé Ifè several times, and in 2003, the writer invited him to a workshop in Ilé Ifè. The workshop, sponsored by the Denver Art Museum, was for a group of traditional priestess-artists, who painted mythic images on the walls of their temples, for the celebration of divine energies. During this workshop, Wewe witnessed the creative processes of these female sacred artists – an experience that added a new dimension to his composition. The purpose of the workshop was to enable the indigenous priestess-artists to paint on canvas rather than the walls on which they conventionally painted.

Wewe was already familiar with the symbols used by these priestess-artists in their compositions and had been incorporating the images into his paintings since the late 1990s. The painting titled *Seeds of Life* (Fig. 16) inscribes some of the symbols. The members of the Ọnà group had become quite familiar with

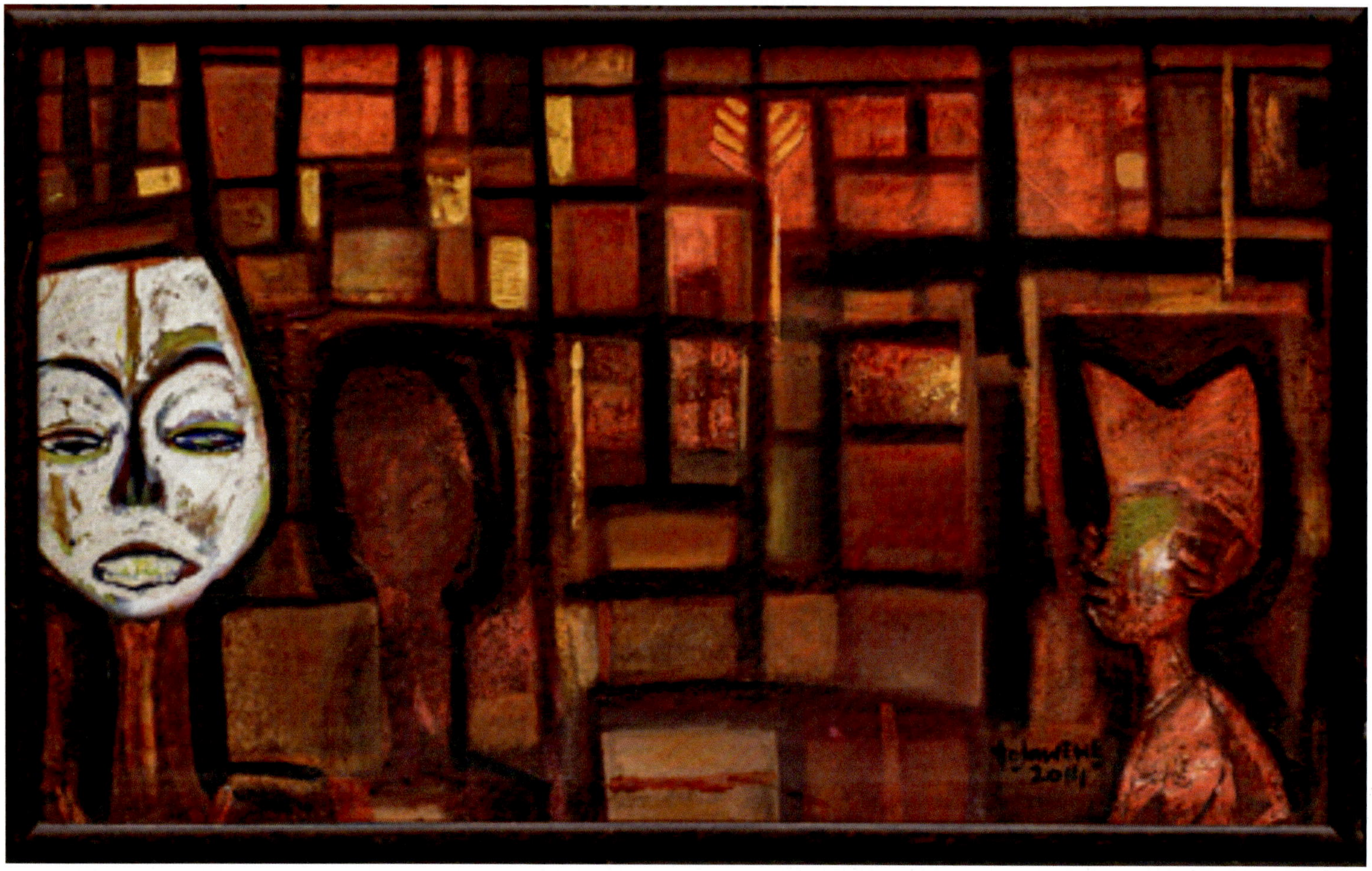

Fig. 19: *Letting the Sunshine Inside*, acrylic on canvas, 2020

the symbols of the priestess-artists after Okediji started working with these women artists from the early 1980s. What was new to Wewe was the experience of directly viewing the women at work as they painted during the workshop – particularly the ritual aspect of their work, in which music, dance and chanting literature were presented as crucial aspects of the women's creative process, despite the fact that they were primarily considered visual artists.

The Denver Art Museum was only interested in the visual aspects of the women's work. As the workshop evolved, however, it became clear that these sacred priestess-artists did not prioritize the visual over all the other sensorial aspects of the creative process, involving all the senses in the creative process – visual, oral, sound, taste, touch.

This observation was to present further opportunities for Wewe to expand his approach to creativity beyond the visual content, which is the product that his viewers and collectors contemplate as they enjoy his paintings. In a manner that is probably unbeknownst to those seeing the work, the process of producing the painting became increasingly important to him, certainly as much as the final product that he exhibits.

"It is the process of performing the painting that leads to the product seen on display," Wewe is fond of saying.

His understanding of the inter-relatedness of the creative process assumed a different dimension when he attended the annual Ifá divination festival at the Òkè Ìtasè, in Ilé Ifè in 2005, following his return from an art residency in Denver Colorado. It was a residency at the PlatteForum – a community-oriented art center that offered Wewe an opportunity to work, particularly with young people, including those struggling with emotional issues, as well as kids from troubled homes placed in foster care facilities.

Wewe described his experience of working with the children from these special backgrounds as an "eye opener." As a large majority of these young people nursed emotional traumas that made them unresponsive to attempts by adults to reach or communicate with them, Wewe described them as "quite hostile" when he at first began to interact with them.

As time wore on, however, he observed that these young people began to open up to him as he shared his drawing and painting techniques with them. They loved the stories that he told them, and soon began to share their own life stories, not only personally with him, but also publicly with their colleagues. Kids who were normally non-communicative, were quick to anger and wore permanent frowns on their faces, began to talk freely, smile, and participate in group work. Wewe gradually encouraged them to use drawing as a means of telling their stories, not merely in a figurative manner, but also to allow their colors, shapes, and patterns to speak when words cannot convey their sentiments. Wewe's painting, *Letting the Sunshine Inside* (Fig. 19) of 2014 is an example of a work in which the colors, shapes and patterns express his feelings, with the inclusion of human figures that are formally subordinate, yet prominent in terms of content. These figures that appear to be experiencing a spell of moody sensations give Wewe the opportunity to use colors as a medium of projecting emotional dispositions. The mask-like figure toward the left of the composition is clearly activating a different emotive sensitivity from the others who seem to succumb, with various resistant energies, to the gloom of the environment.

It quickly dawned on Wewe that the purpose of art is not just to provide pleasure, but sometimes to also support emotional well-being, and even to heal where the opportunities are present, as they were when he was in residence at the PlatteForum in Denver, Colorado. While in Denver, in conjunction with Moyo Ogundipe and Moyo Okediji, they held an exhibition titled *Ablackadabra*, in which they engaged their audience in a discussion of art as healing. During this discussion Wewe, Ogundipe and Okediji entertained questions from their audience about indigenous African aesthetics and healing.

It was in this frame of mind, that Wewe returned to Nigeria in the summer of 2005 with more questions than answers about the place of healing in indigenous Yoruba creativity. These were questions that he took really seriously as his plane landed at the Murtala Muhammed Airport, Lagos.

It was therefore not surprising that as soon as he reached Òndó and dropped his bags, he went straight to Ilé Ifè to study more about the healing practices of the divination systems. He heard that the Ifá center at Òkè Ìtasè in Ilé Ifè is the most

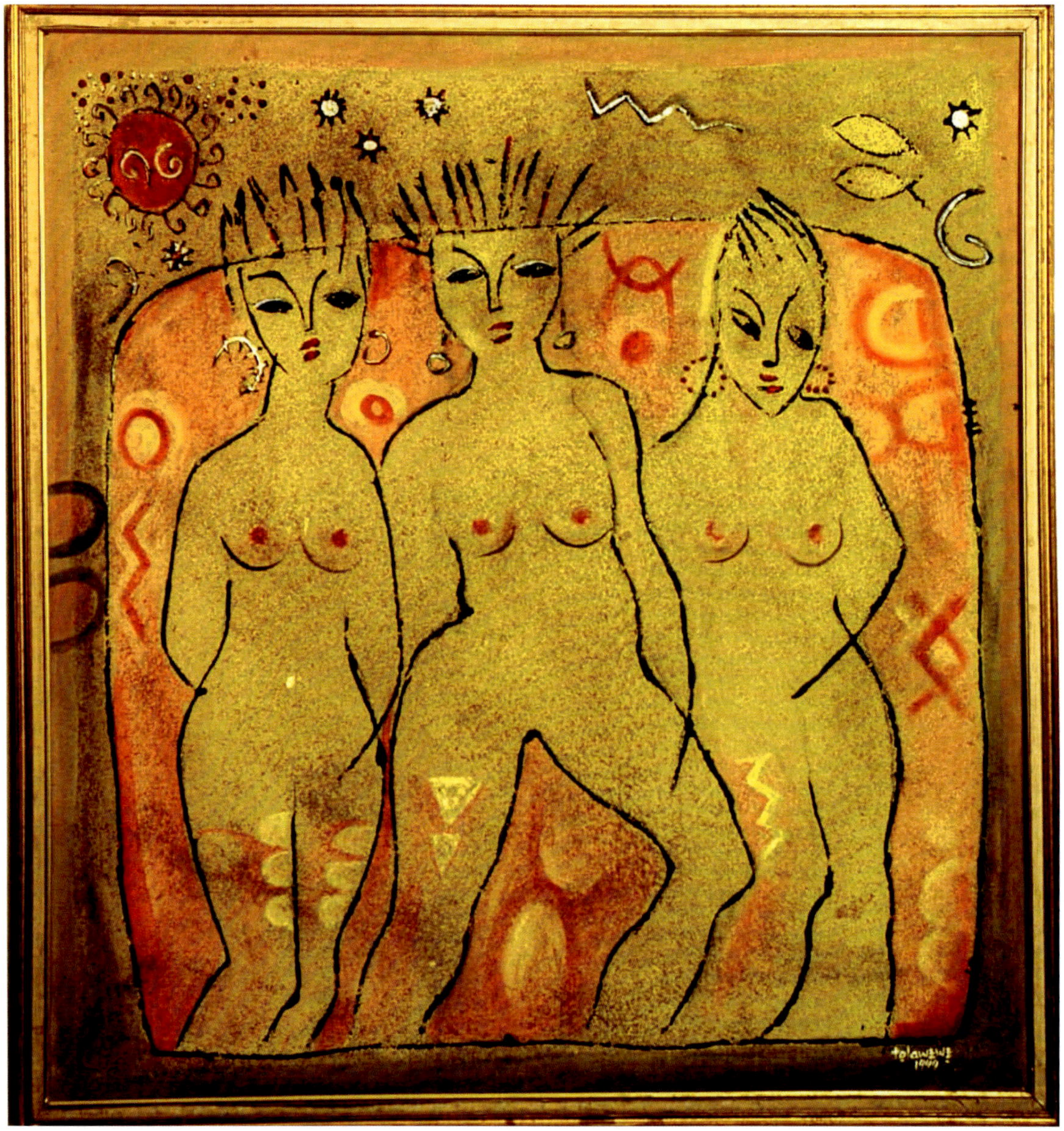

Fig. 20: *Initiation to Maidenhood*, acrylic on canvas, 1999.

important location for the celebration of divination in the entire world, for historical and cultural reasons. He learned also that the world began right there at Ilé Ifè, and that Òrúnmìlà, the spirit of divination, was the primary witness to the process of the creation of the world, therefore, one of the ultimate masters of the act of creativity.

Wewe, therefore, journeyed to Òkè Ìtasè, to discuss with the priests at this sacred spot – located on one of the tallest points in Ilé Ifè, overlooking the entire metropolis. It was quite an important moment for him. He left with an experience similar to what he found at the temple painting of the priestess-artists: that creativity is not merely visual but interwoven with other forms of sensing; including the hearing, the eating, the dancing and the touching. He saw that the diviners have a large body of art around them and employ these art objects as part of their creative activities. He later learned more about these objects in a direct way by watching their specific functions at each stage of the divination process – beyond what he had gathered as a graduate student studying visual culture at the University of Ibadan from 1985 to 1986.

At Òkè Ìtasè, he was counselled to find himself a *Babaláwo* with whom he could work. He started a search and over the years he has worked with several diviners. He discovered that they have varying powers and abilities. Many of them he has retained and he invites them to his studio to divine for him at every important occasion and ceremony including birthing, funerals, end of year transitions and specific periods when he wants to have clarity about certain things in his life. In addition to all of these, he sometimes invites a *Babaláwo* when he wants to create a special painting and needs the words of the diviner to start off the process.

CHAPTER SIX:

The Diviners and the Painter

Somewhere in the far distance, the hypnotic dialogue of the *Bàtá* ensemble color the background as evening falls in Òndó c, an ancient and cosmopolitan hub in south-west Nigeria. Adetola Wewe sits in the spacious studio of his suburban mansion; in front of him, a bottle of schnapps topped with a shot glass, sat in splendid isolation on the round handcrafted wooden table. Loosely knotted and brazenly unruly, his stylish Afro conveys a bohemian disposition, emblematic of his more than three decades long artistic journey – a life passionately dedicated, fully devoted to creative excavations and explorations. Rakishly handsome, his greying beard lends an air of distinguished playfulness as he jokes, chats and laughs with his guests. Seated on a mat on the floor, opposite Wewe, is Aworeni Fatunde—a renowned *Babaláwo* – who has travelled all the way from Ìlá Òràngún for the occasion. Four of Wewe's closest friends lounge on chairs around the room.

Never one to celebrate alone, Wewe has invited them all to join him as he celebrates the completion of his latest painting.

In a ritual that, at the beginning was only once in a while, but has now turned the norm, Fatunde has come to consult and divine for Wewe, to decipher and unravel the message of the divinities, for which Wewe is only merely a medium.

Propped up against the wall, the painting sits about eight feet away from the chatting friends. Babaláwo Fatunde brings out his intricately carved wooden *Opón Ifá*, to begin the divination process. He throws his *òpèlè* on the circular face of his *Opón Ifá* to consult Òrúnmìlà, the Divinity of oracular vision, his gaze intent on the painting. The furrows on his brow, gorged deep by his habitual professional frown, tightens in concentration as he reads the message from the Irúnmọlè.

His gaze shifts to Wewe: "*Bàbá, Ire ni, Ayò ni, Orin ni*....you have painted music itself!"

Delighted, Wewe asks, "*Àgbà Awo, kí ni Ifá wi?* What did Ifá say?"

Babaláwo Fatunde turns back to his *Ọpọ́n Ifá,* on which he throws his *ọ̀pẹ̀lẹ̀* a few more times. Satisfied, he beams at Wewe: "Your painting is not just pregnant with music, it has given birth to percussion. This message calls for a celebration! Your painting is from the lineage of *Ìdígbè*, a special cocktail or *àmúlù odù* that rarely appears, look at it – elegantly organized in its characteristic musical pattern on my *opón Ifá*. It refers to the specific literary verse called *Àpéwò*. The original domain of the painting that you have just completed, therefore, is musicality."

Puzzled, Wewe inquires, "How is this so?

What does it mean?"

Babalawo Fatunde has thoroughly piqued not only Wewe's interest but that of the rest of the group as well. Everybody sits up to listen; intense and attentive, one could literally hear a pin drop in the sudden stillness.

"*Ẹ̀là bọrú, Ẹla boyè, Ẹlà bọyè bọ ṣíṣẹ́,*" Fatunde begins his unraveling of the revealed *Odú* in the liturgical language of the Ifá priesthood. "*Ìdígbè* is a twinned symbol – *Òdí Ogbè* – a hybrid image, an *àyalù* or *àmúlùmọ́là odù*. Only novices would actually break it into its two components: *Òdí* and *Ogbè*. It is a delicately balanced composition of *Òdí* on the right and *Ogbè* on the left. Let's think of it in terms of architecture. Mortar is a mixture of lime, cement and water. We simply call it mortar because masons already know the components of this compound. Builders who don't know the meaning of mortar cannot call themselves adept bricklayers. Those who have practiced Ifá for a long time therefore, formally call this pattern *Ìdígbè*.

They do not singularly pronounce each of the two symbolic components of this hybrid as "*Òdí*" and "*Ogbè*." In full, they would pronounce it as *Ìdígbè, awo Ọlọ́fin*. It is the musical contraction of *Ìdígbè* that defines its vocal identity, just as in your painting. The relationship lies in the translation of sound to image."

To demonstrate the specific configuration of *Ìdígbè*, he marks this code on the *Ìyẹ̀rẹ̀ Òsùn*, the cadmium yellow wood powder, usually spread on the entire surface of the *Opón Ifá* to mark the *Odù*:

I I
I II
I II
I I

This ministerial interpretation of Ìdígbè, in other words, is akin to the way in which artists regard green, orange or purple in terms of colors. As a secondary color, green comes from the mixture of blue and yellow, just as orange is red and yellow, and purple consists of red and blue. Artists do not say "blue-yellow," when they mean to say green. The Ìlá Òràngún priest therefore, insists that it is not just for the sake of poetic beauty that practitioners speak of *Ìdígbè* when they convey the message of *Ìdígbè*; it is the conventional thing to do because music is the key to understanding the transition from saying to seeing.

As is customary, Bàbá Fatunde then proceeds to recite the poetry of *Àpéwò* that has come with the *Ìdígbè* signature, combining poetry, music and body language in a series of ritualistic gestures, reminiscent of performance art. But he is not actually performing: he has become a vessel of divine messaging, conveying encoded motifs of spiritual vibrations to the abode of mortal beings. As the gathering of listeners seemingly hold their collective breaths, he gives vocal cadence to *Àpéwò*, elaborately announcing the name of the new painting with this narrative message from Òrúnmìlà:

Ìdí pá pá pá pá pá,
Ìdí gbè gbèè gbè
Babaláwo Bàtá dáfá fún Bàtá
Níjọ́ tí Bàtá fẹ́ lọ gbayì láàfin

Wọ́n ní kí Bàtá ó kaálẹ̀
Wọ́n ní ẹbọ ni kó ṣe
Ó ní ta ni òún má a rúbọ fún?
Wọ́n ní Èṣù ni kó rúbọ fún.
Ó ní ìgìrìpá òbúkọ

Ó ní eku, kó lẹ́ja, kó lóbì, ó tún ní ọtín
Bàtá gbọ́ rírú ẹbọ, ó rú
Ó gbọ́ èrù àtùkèṣù, ó tù fún un
Ó gbọ́ ìkarara, ẹbọ́ ha fún un
Kò pawo lékèé

Kò pe Èṣù lólè
Kò kọtí ọ̀gbanin sẹ́bọ
Àsẹ̀hìnwá, àsẹhìnbọ̀
Ẹni ìyà sì ni Bàtá tẹ́lẹ̀tẹ́lẹ̀
Tí ayé ti fojú ré nà

Kámọ́ dèènà pẹnu
Bí wọ́n ṣe pe Bàtá
Àti àwọn eléré yìókù
Kí wọn ó pàdé ní iwájú òde ààfin Ọlọ́fin
Láti dá tọba tìjòyè lára yá.

Omele, tí í ṣe ẹbíi Bàtá
Ló kọ́kọ́ bọ́ síta
Láti fi Bàtá ṣe ẹléyà
Emelé lanu ohùn
Ó ní "Ẹbọ kí lo ṣe?

Ẹbọ kí lo ṣe?
Ẹbọ kí lo ṣe?"
Ni Bàtá bá bọ́ síwájú
Bàtá ní "Mo ti ṣẹbọ
Ìdí pá pá pá pá,

Mo ṣẹbọ ìdí gbè gbèè gbè gbè gbè gbè
Ìdí pàá, ìdí pòó
Iwájú jinginni, ẹ̀yìn jinginni
Iwájú jinginni, ẹ̀yìn jinginni
Iwájú jinginni, ẹ̀yìn jinginni
Bùrùkùtù pá ko pá

Ẹ̀yìn jinginni
Bùrùkùtù pá ko pá
Ẹ̀yìn jinginni."
Bàtá tí ayé ti fi ojú ré nà tẹ́lẹ̀
Bí ó ti di pé ó gbayì láwùjọ gbogbo eléré ni ẹ̀yí.

Ó gba iyì, ó gba ẹ̀yẹ
Ni ó bá wá di ọba fún gbogbo eléré.

Translation:

Ìdí pá pá pá pá pá,
Ìdí gbè gbèè gbè
These are the two diviners who consulted Ifá for Bàtá
The day Bàtá went to the palace to seek professional prestige

They instructed Bàtá to be attentive
They asked Bàtá to offer sacrifices
He said, "To whom should I offer

sacrifices?”
They said he should offer sacrifices to Èsù.
He should sacrifice a robust he-goat

He should offer a rat, fish, kolanut and liquor
He harked the voice to give offerings and he gave sacrifices
He heeded the request to appease Èsù and complied
He observed the sound ìkarara, and the sacrifice worked for him
He did not call his diviners liars

He did not call Èsù a thief
He did not turn a deaf ear to the request to give sacrifices
It has been well established
That Bàtá was a pauper
Already dismissed as a nonentity

To cut a long story short
They invited Bàtá
And other musical performers
To converge at the royal court
To entertain the royalty

Omele, who is a kin of Bàtá
Was the one to first perform
Intent on making derisive statements about Bàtá
Omele open his mouth
And uttered, “What stupid sacrifice was it you offered?”

“What stupid sacrifice was it you offered?”
“What stupid sacrifice was it you offered?”
And Bàtá stepped forward
Bàtá said “I offered sacrifice to
Ìdí pá pá pá pá,

I offered sacrifice to ìdí gbè gbèè gbè gbè gbè gbè
I offered sacrifice to Ìdí pàá, ìdí pòó
I offered sacrifice to Iwájú jinginni, ẹ̀yìn jinginni
I offered sacrifice to Iwájú jinginni, ẹ̀yìn jinginni
I offered sacrifice to Iwájú jinginni, ẹ̀yìn jinginni
I offered sacrifice to Bùrùkùtù pá ko pá
I offered sacrifice to Ẹ̀yìn jinginni
I offered sacrifice to Bùrùkùtù pá ko pá
I offered sacrifice to Ẹ̀yìn jinginni.”
Bàtá who nobody considered important
Immediately became a celebrity in the community of performers

He became famous and feted
And was crowned the king of all performers.

Àpéwò – subtitled *Megaracle* – is a musical painting that translates the percussive elements of the *Bàtá* drum into a spectacle of colors. Aesthetically layered, it is a rich cocktail of Mega + Spectacle + Miracle, mixed as music-plus-poetry-plus-image – to constitute an evocative icon that expands the visual lexicon of the global canvas. It constitutes additional evidence that whatever Africans encounter, they colonize; even as they are colonized. They cornered the English language and made it theirs, entirely occupying its premises as if its linguistics was their ancestral masquerade.

Africans have turned the English literary tradition into a weapon of mass expression within the continent – disemboweling its vocabulary, dissecting its sounds, rupturing its tones, doctoring its diphthongs, suturing its consonants, hacking its syllables. The rest is history – Wole Soyinka hijacked its authority, Chinua Achebe broke its teeth, Okot p' Bitek uprooted its homesteads while Ghanaian writer, Ayi Kwei Armah masked its etymologies.[17] The rest of the continent – writers and passersby – ride the vehicle of English language like a native horse. What much they did to the English language, they appeared to have doubled with French, tripled with Portuguese and quadrupled with Spanish – which is so near the Libyan shore that they practically seem to have moored it.

In a dialectically ambivalent relationship with the imperialist history associated with art in Nigeria, Wewe metes out a culturally palpable handling to European art; rejuvenating it with his paintings. He has not only mastered and colonized the western visual lexicon, but has also reframed it into a system of percussion in many of his paintings. He relishes his enslavement of this imported optical grammar and seemingly tethers it behind his backyard like a goat fated for sacrifice to the unruly Òrìṣà Ògún – who guards the road, unapologetically drunk, collecting tolls from everyone, excepting none. Wewe's work – each painting since he began consulting the Ifá philosophical system – is borne along that same convoluted Ògún's passage, which he paints as a canvas owned by all the divine forces of Africa, especially Ọ̀rúnmìlà – *Akéréfinúṣọgbọ́n* (Tiny-one-loaded-with wisdom), *Ẹlẹ́rìíìpín* (Sole-witness-to-the-moment-of-creation), and ¯*Asọ̀rọ̀dayọ̀* (One-who-turns-misfortune-around).

In *Láaróyè's* Intersection, (fig 21) Wewe extracts the essence of the divinity of the crossroad, Èṣù – *Láaróyè*. This divinity heightens the element of complexity and ambiguity into simple forms with the potentiality to explode into fragments or coalesce into unity – depending on the circumstance. Èṣù could mutate from male to female, friend to foe, foreigner to neighbor. Wewe organizes the work along the dark and light colors of Èṣù – with intense depths of blue and red respectively – using the white portions as the focal point. This analytical use of colors also translates into the Yoruba arrangement of colors along the triadic modality: *pupa* (red), *dúdú* (blue) and *funfun* (white).

The orange variation in the painting is from the *pupa* range, a derivative of red. As he explores the mythic colors of Èṣù, he is also opening up the painting to the mysterious penetrations of the transcendental powers of divine spiritual energies.

Wewe attributes his imaginative opulence as an artist to the mysterious plural forces of creative impulsiveness, who grace and groom his hands. These forces have fertilized his studio – not just with innovative ideas – but particularly with inventive parables and visionary acuity that cut across the traditional lines that separate painting and drumming.

"A drummer, for instance, can score percussive arrangements on many of the paintings featured in a single exhibition or in a suite of work," Wewe notes. His painting right hand – which has earned him the nomenclature, *Iwin* – has translated itself into a force of mythological dimension.[18] He maintains he is not responsible for the chromatic poesies that he weaves as paintings and ceramic configurations. All he has to do – he swears – is to sit down and place his hand on the stretched canvas, and he is automatically transformed into a conduit through which the divine forces of positive vibrations manifest themselves, in the forms of unfathomable conglomerations of colorful patterns, shapes, tones and shades; arrayed in light and layers of depths of lyrical configurations.

Wewe's work is a visualization of Yoruba anatomical discourse, using stylistic structures partly derived from indigenous African semantics.

The *Bàtá* tones of *Ìdí pá pá pá pá pá/ Ìdí gbè gbèè gbè* display the broad range of high and low tympanum vibrations available in the genre's vocal cords. "*Ìdí*" begins with the low vowel of the *"ì"* tone, rises to the phoneme of "*dí*," followed by the sustained higher tones of repeated *"pá pá pá pá pá,"* with the last *"pá"* as the uppermost summit of this phrasing. In contrast, "*Ìdí gbè gbèè gbè"* does the very

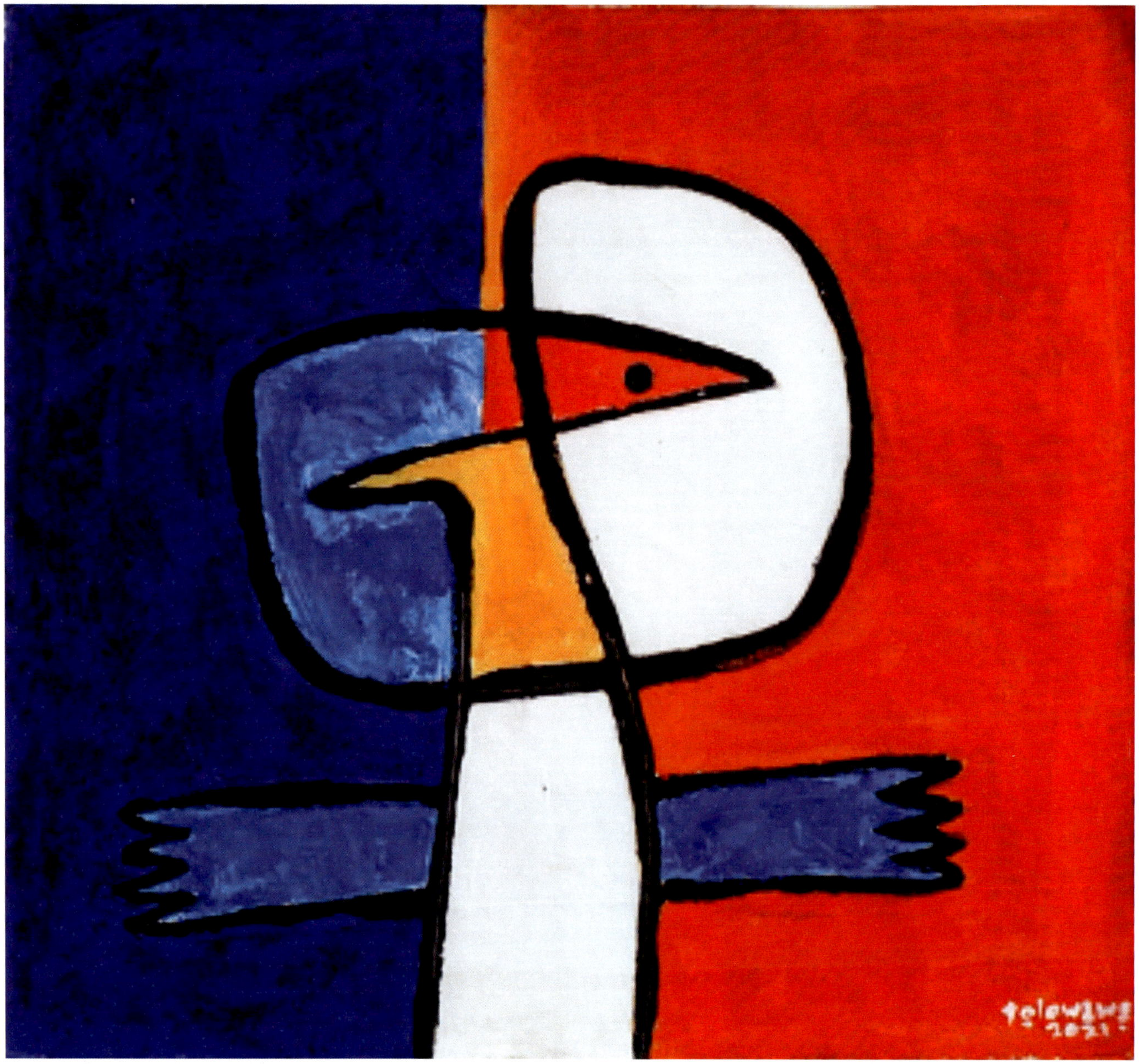

Fig 21: *Láaróyè's Intersection*, acrylic on canvas, 2021

opposite, bringing the keys down with the similarly repeated notes of *"gbè,"* in a sequence in which the last "*gbè*" sound is also the lowest and deepest tone. Regarding colors, the arrangement describes the triadic temperatures – hot, warm and cold—related to the Yoruba trichromacy of *pupa*, *dúdú* and *funfun* respectively. When Wewe arranges colors along this musical notation, the blues, yellows, reds, greens, purples and oranges range along the prisms of tones and shades – sensitively tempered to highlight their utmost vibrancies.

Because the musicality of many of his paintings is from the stammering staccatos of *Bàtá* percussion, Wewe modulates his palette to project the flat lines of the broad side of the instrument, to counterbalance the sharp peaks of the petit side – a tapered cylinder connects both extremes. From the paintings, the viewer feels the obtuse horizontal slapping that the drummer delivers to the broad face of the drum in Wewe's use of thick shapes, slow volumes and toned hues. On the backside, the drummer uses a leather strap to whip acute strokes on the hide of the drum – evoking tight, stinging, pitches. *Bàtá's* sequencing is compositionally dense and biting, compact and slack, compressed and free – enabling Wewe to benefit from

the combinations and blends of colors informing his painterly orchestrations, even in a work as tightly and narrowly colored as *Láaróyè's Intersection*.
Bàtá sonorously stammers and repeats its phrasings "*Ìdí pá pá pá pá pá/Ìdí gbè gbèè gbè*. And beneath the seemingly incoherent replications of patterns that often informs Wewe's more complex surfaces, viewers excavate scattered colors of erogenous banters, as often is the sexualized language in which *Bàtá* speaks. Under *Láaróyè's Intersection*, for instance, Wewe inscribes sexual allusions to the male and female genitalia. A surface or apparent view of the painting might miss this erotic content – as one might miss the eroticism in *Bàtá* lyrics.

Beyond stating the apparent tonal density of the syntactic arrangement in following *Bàtá* construction, one must not translate its vocal meaning to spare the feelings of minors: *Làbò kí n tọ̀ sí - èrò ò pọ̀ bí i tẹ̀ẹ̀kan*.

It was the stage actor, my late friend, Yomi Fawole, who drew our attention to what the *Bàtá* drummer was compacting with his rhythm one day, as we watched Àjàǹgìlá, the legendary Sàngó ritualist enacting a staged moment with humoring gusto and characteristic irreverence. Sàngó – the Yoruba divinity of lightning and thunder – is an erotically charged energy. Sàngó is also the patron of *Bàtá* drummers and dancers.

All I could do was gasp in awed astonishment as Fawole translated the erotic content of the lyrics we were enjoying to us – we had been completely oblivious of this eroticism. A lack of perception of this erotic dimension, as we listened to the *Bàtá* speaking, did not diminish the aesthetic enjoyment of its rhythms.

It is with a comparable reaction that I blink my eyes as I excavate the eroticism of Wewe's *Láaróyè's Intersection*, a dimension that may be totally invisible to an eye not primed to detect it. Similar to some of the sensual words buried inside the *Bàtá* vocal configurations of Àjàñgìlá's performance, Wewe's *Láaróyè's Intersection* conceals iconic patterns – its contents portraying pruriently arousing potentialities.

Just like Àjàñgìlá, Wewe's *Láaróyè's Intersection* captures the color, motifs, rhythms and music of the iconographic repertoire of Sàngó paraphernalia, while retaining the allusion to Èsù. Wewe often layers several allusions to various spiritual sources.

"They are all related," he explains, "they come from the same Yoruba cultural allusions."

He is relating entirely to the music of *Bàtá*, the most important drum in the orchestration of Sàngó rituals, within the choreography of Sàngó, and the image

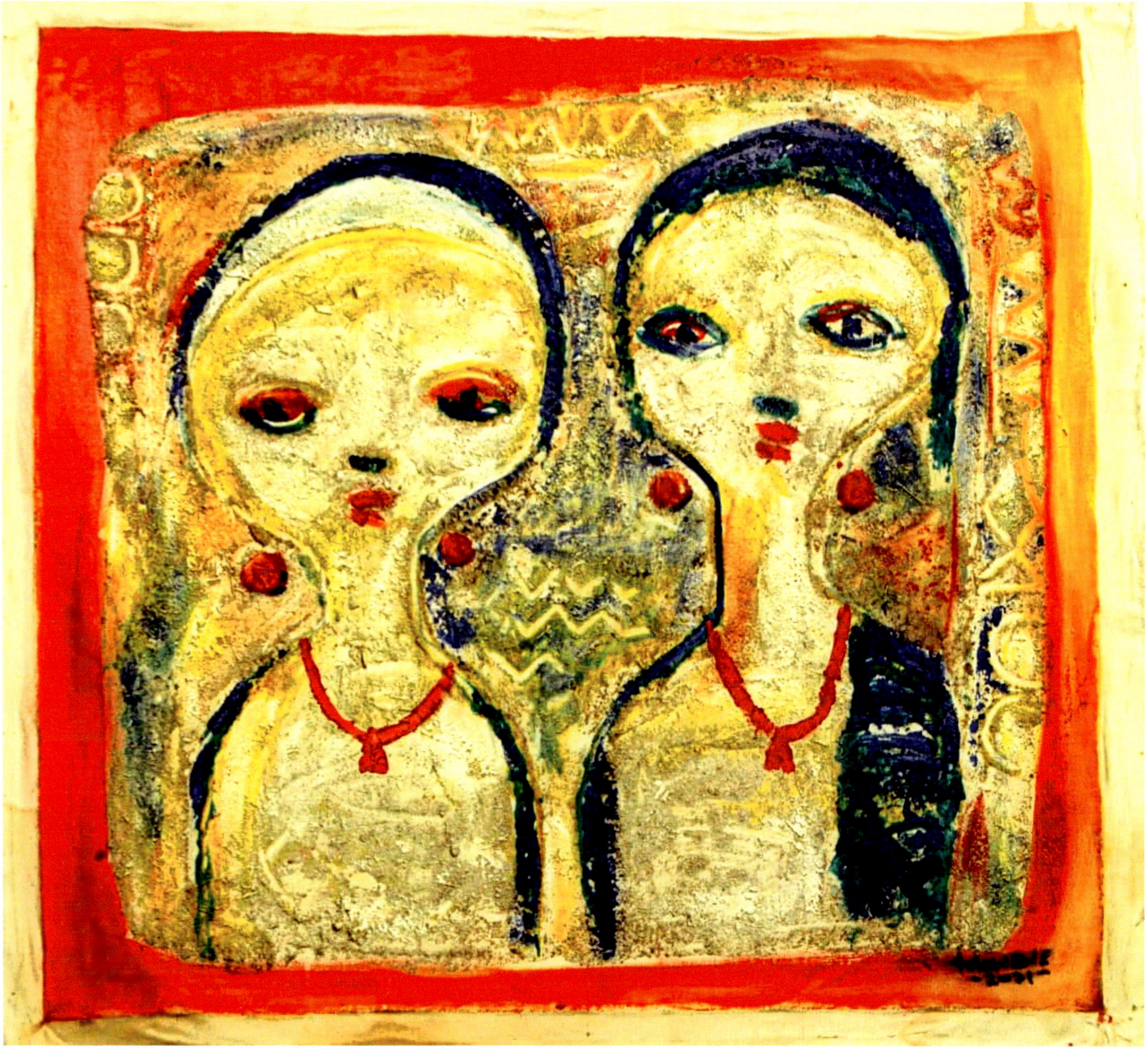

Fig. 22: *Dual: Omo Meji*, acrylic on canvas, 2021.

arranging sequence in Sàngó's temples.

Sàngó, while operating as the divinity of lightning and thunder, is also the deity devoted to the serving of social justice, the one who devotees greet as "*Sángiri, làgiri, ọlàgiri kàkà figba ẹdun bọ̀ ọ́* – The One who breaks, splits the wall with the wrecking kàkà roar and inserts 200 thunderbolts in it."

The phenomenal energy associated with Sàngó liturgy informs Wewe's *Láaróyè's Intersection* as well as *Dual: Omo Meji* (fig. 22), another reference to the *Ìbejí* cult of the twins. Both paintings and many other examples including *Riders of the Thunder Horse* (fig. 23) demonstrate Wewe's rephrasing, reframing, supplementing, complementing, and reversal of colonial western art, as he situates the Yoruba iconographic contents of the paintings in "contemporary" reinterpretations of art historical iconography. Only a cultural initiation into the Yoruba language of *Ojú Inú* – the inner eye – would detect the colonizing-the-colonizer elements

and principles that Wewe embraces to camouflage and stage his works – with the "modern" banner unfurled in global expressive cultures.
As Wewe supplements images with music, some "contemporary" African musicians have visualized music with images. In the painting titled *Bojú-Bojú Masking* (fig. 24), the nearest musical genre in the "contemporary" scene to which viewers may relate Wewe's adventure is the irreverence of Fela's rhythms: it might sound busy and convoluted, even strange and superficial from the perspective of percussion. It was, indeed, once condemned as cacophonous and pornographic before later critics reevaluated his body of music and proclaimed it an acclamation of originality and beauty.

Great works take time to digest.

The composition of *Bojú-Bojú Masking* conceals beauty in the layering of a relatively accessible portrait of a lady with the totally concealed inversion of the same lady in a twin that is initially not so easy to see. Wewe improvises the form of two women partly shrouded in curtains of concealment – an exercise that he describes as "double masking." *Bojú-Bojú Masking* shows that the viewer's imagination is part of the process of unmasking beauty. In this work, Wewe supplements his artistic images with forms associated with mythology, folklore, indigenous tropes and myriads of non-visual resources to colonize ideas coming from the cultures that colonized Africa. The painting therefore seems to imitate Picasso. But as he is fond of saying, "Picasso is the one imitating me; my forms are directly from the African imagery that Picasso colonized in his paintings."

The "colonizing-colonizer" dialectic of Wewe's works is, therefore, intentionally counter-colonial, imbued with values cutting across space, time, mediums and gender.

He has often drawn criticism from those who disregard his strategy of questioning the colonial canon; critics who attempt to impose those colonizing capitals on his creative inquiries.

One of these critics is Philip Feinstein, an African art enthusiast commenting from New York. In a social media conversation with Wewe about his work, Feinstein remarked that "For me, *Bojú-Bojú Masking* is simplistic and confused. It is a bad reflection on African art." He expressed his worry that the work does not sufficiently espouse "contemporary" values because it consists of what he describes as "… brightly colored patterns with lots of little panels and a couple of distorted mask faces." Feinstein's observation, which he quickly deleted after an instant onslaught of contrasting opinions by Wewe's fans, also part of the conversation, is a stereotypical rebuke of the use of mask forms and distortion in African art. It is a trope that

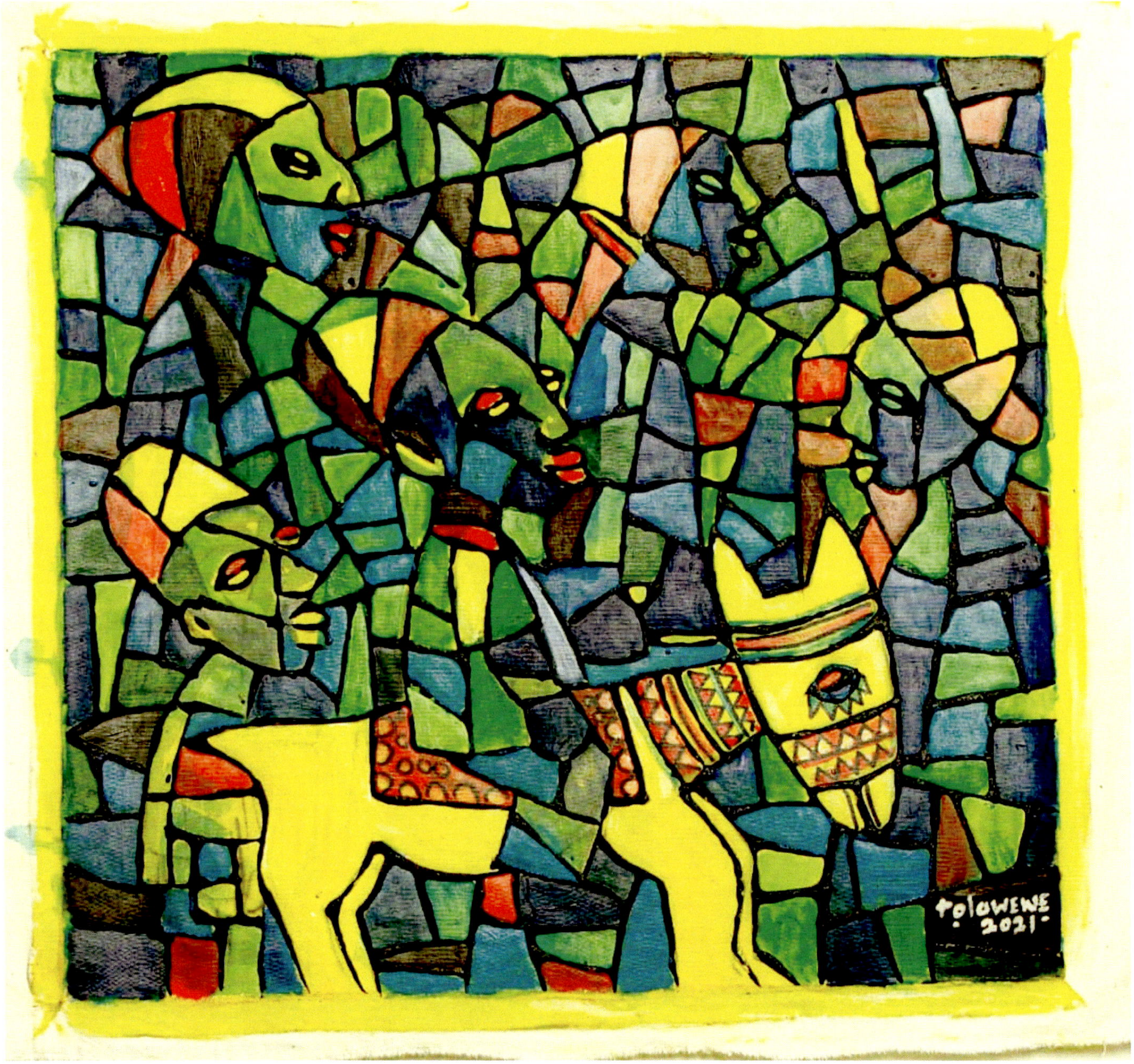

Fig. 23: *Riders of the Thunder Horse*, acrylic on canvas, 2021.

the western colonizing gaze once dismissed as primitive, but has now been accepted as appropriate in "traditional" African art, yet reprehensible in expressions grounded in "contemporary" visual language. Feinstein response, however, does not impress the literary critic, Lolu Akingbola, who, after viewing *Bojú-Bojú Masking*, observes in that same social media thread that, "What the Western eye might sometimes see as erotica simplification is in some other aesthetic traditions a complement of engaged form. Every auditor brings a portion of personal antecedent to a creation. Adetola Wewe is inspired by the aesthetic of the Yoruba World. In an essay in which he cautioned critics to refrain from imposing an occidental gaze on African expressive arts, Wole Soyinka warned that those posit to wear the crown of Pontifex Maximus (of aesthetics) must mind the thorns. And in Wewe's musical palettes, the thorns are sharp and witty. In *Bojú-Bojú Masking*, my eyes see the organic complexity of *Ẹní Ẹwẹlẹ*, the metaphor for 'welcome' and by extension, "inclusion."[19]

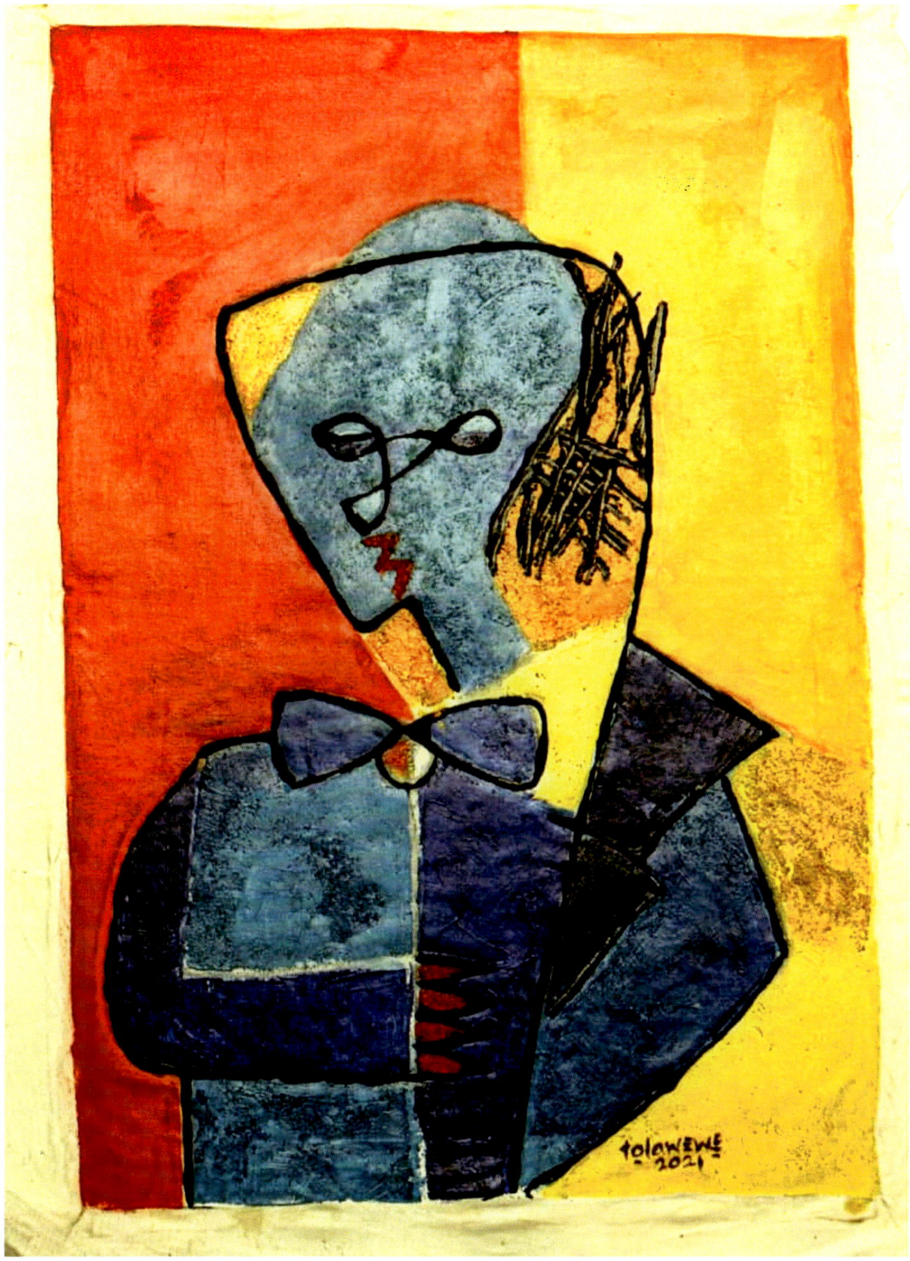

Figure 24: *Boju-Boju Masking*, acrylic on canvas, 2021.

Ẹní Ẹwẹlẹ, to which Akingbola, alludes is the intricately colored handwoven mat crafted in Ijebu-Jesa, an ancient and inclusive Yoruba city. The mat, with its tight crisscrossing of colors and patterns, has the musical intensity of *Bàtá* rhythms. As a mat spread on the floor in the bedroom for people to sleep on, it is a Yoruba symbol of assurance to guests that they are indeed wanted companies in the household.

Yet another comment on the same thread is that of Yusuf Abdulrasaq, an African art scholar: "Listening to the underlying meanings of the vibrations of [the] *Bàtá* membrane in Tola's *Boju-Boju Masking* is like worrying much about the intrigues of the bellows at the blacksmith's shop. The allegory of "làbò" (to open that which is concealed) is unhidden in the coquettish form in *Boju-Boju Masking*. As a son of a drummer, I can decipher the intrigues of

Tola Wewe's drumming the more."

Wewe engages the coded language and music of Yoruba drums in his work, as part of the strategy of rephrasing the dialectic of the colonizing forces that condemned his indigenous traditions of painting – even as they introduced the western idioms of cabinet painting on canvas. Wewe realizes that the indigenous cultures of Yoruba painting as practiced mostly by knowledge-infused Yoruba priestess-artists includes music, dancing and poetry as part of a ritual of invoking spiritual benefits for the community in which the painters work. He, therefore, rephrases canvas painting in "contemporary" or "modern" culture, as a global endeavor that necessarily contains descriptive phrase – outside the syllables of the colonizers. His rephrasing of canvas painting is a subversive creative strategy that transcends the western form of art education he received. Bothered by the restraining limitations of the western art education he received in college – from a pedagogy calling for the stifling of indigenous traditions of painting – Wewe rephrases the visual devices that that colonizing pedagogy enthrones in terms of figure painting, perspectives, monocular perspectives and chromatic restraints.

His disdain for chromatic restrains is evident in almost all of his paintings – especially since the beginning of the twenty-first century – when he began to freely demonstrate his mastery of color, and a penchant for using immensely wide palettes, containing most of the colors of the rainbow. In the work *The Garden of A Thousand Petals* and also in *Ìpolongo*, (fig. 25), a horizontal painting dated 2005, Wewe imagines a Yoruba *Òrun*— paradise —the place in which the ancestors, the unborn, Òrìsà, the Irúnmolè, iwin, ebora and all forms of be-ings reside harmoniously, in eternal beauty and comfort.

Color is the mode of communication in this world; permeated with musical rhythm codes as persistent throbs of ornamental spaces. That world provides abundance for birds, fishes, animals, a countless number of moons, stars and suns, while remaining hospitable to the meta-mortal characters inhabiting the floral llandscape; saturated with chromatic superfluity.

To conceptualize such an abode which originates from his ancestral heritage, Wewe goes beyond the boundaries that separate science and fiction in the painting tradition that the colonial structures imposed on the landscape painting implanted in western forms of art education. That imposed colonial culture – characterized by the teachings of Kenneth Murray in the early years of the 20th century, and imbibed in the paintings of Aina Onabolu – is the subject of reversal in Wewe's paintings.[20] Empowered, he reverses whatever rules might be found in the Murray-Onabolu alliance, and uses that point of inversion as a moment of

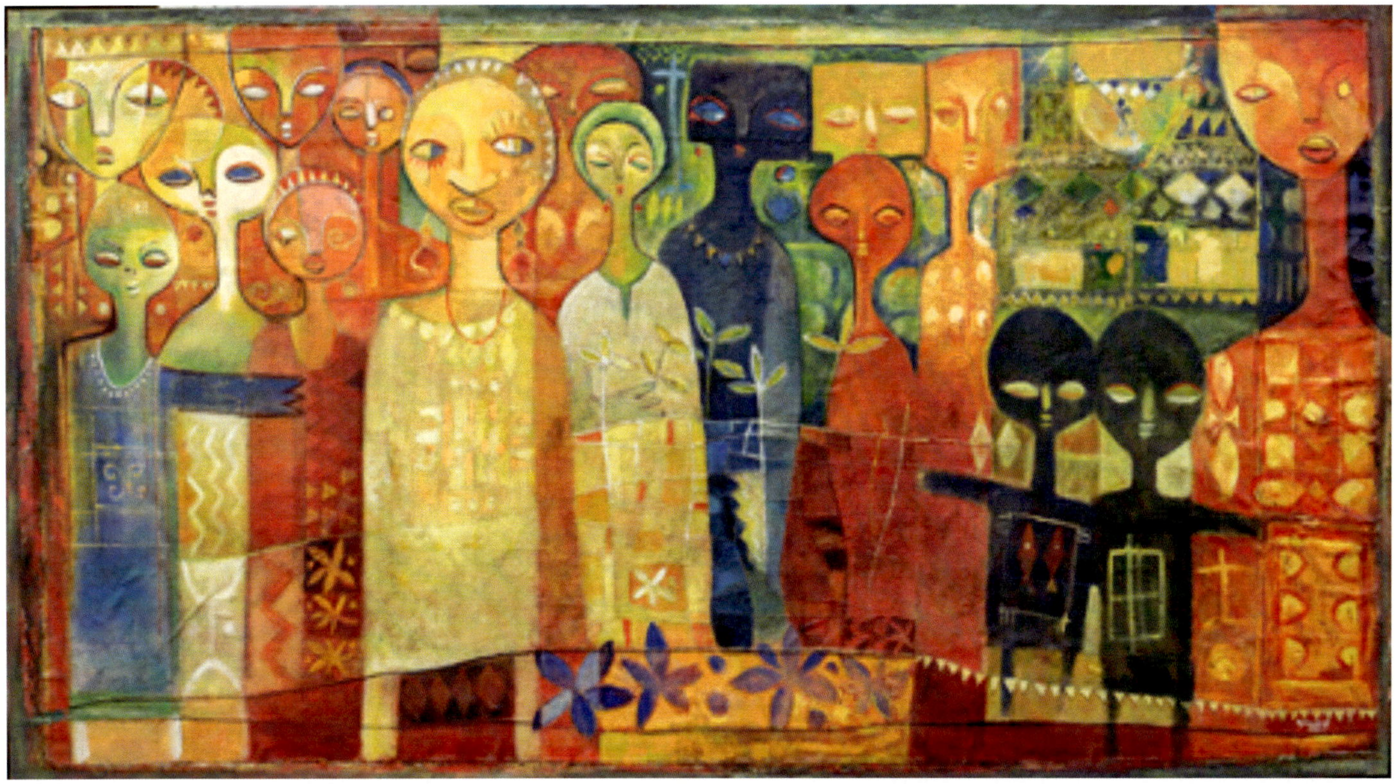

Fig. 25: *Ìpolongo*, acrylic on canvas, 2005.

departure into the improvised spontaneity that permeates the paintings of indigenous Yoruba priestess-artists.

The law of gravity no longer applies because Wewe reverses that code to enable all be-ings to grow wings and fins for flying and swimming; even trees are no longer shackled to a spot, but are transformed into mobile characters that blur the boundary lines of physics and biology – lines that divides nature myopically into living and nonliving entities.

Everything comes alive in *The Garden of A Thousand Petals* – Wewe recalls and reverses the shadow of death that time represents in western colonial worldviews. Time is the first victim of death in this painting, and as time succumbs to death, mortality is revoked and death itself automatically surrenders to time. He asserts that Òrúnmìlà, the divinity of philosophical knowledge, has granted me the power to incorporate new structural adjustments to compensate for the penury of visual and conceptual vocabulary that might exist in my Western-oriented art education."

The Tree of Life, suffused with eternal lamination, is the platform on which death dies in the painting, *The Garden of A Thousand Petals*. That Tree of Life is fecund with fruits, nuts and nectar, from which various forms of be-ings feed in the bright yellow focus of the painting. *The Bird of Life* spreads out its wings at the summit of the tree. That bird is free, just as are all other be-ings in the blossoming and blooming petals of life in this garden of eternal life – where nothing dies.

In *Ìpolongo* (Public Announcement), Wewe depicts the traditional Yoruba town crier standing among the crowd to disseminate the latest news and information to the community. Before the advent of radio technology, the town crier was the one who connected the local administration with the general populace; bringing news from the legislative and executive branches of government to the people. The painting alludes to the indigenous Yoruba consensus decision making process that emanates from the grassroots – the people themselves. The passing of the decision agreed upon, climbs up the ladder, to the offices of the administrative bodies, for ratification and in a continuous circle of input and feedback, the decision is brought back to the public as proclamation.

The members of the public gather around the town crier, typically a male with a sonorous pitch, who casts the information in a colorful manner. Master of the art of public communication and steeped in Yoruba idiomatic diction, he uses proverbs, metaphors and various figures of speech to make the announcement as lyrical as possible. Sometimes the news is not good – as during the passing of important dignitaries or the announcement of an invading mass of locusts, already sighted many miles away. The town crier must find a way to proclaim the most pleasant news to the people, just as he must dig deep within his imagination to announce unpleasant developments without alarming anybody.

"As an artist," Wewe says, "I am the new town crier. I project the voice of the people to the world in colorful and aesthetic ways. My voice is not just personal. I speak for myself, my people and my era. When they look back in the future to the present, they will see that we were human just like then. Time is just an illusion."

Wewe invites his guests to dinner. His wife, assisted by her young consanguine protégés, brings in several large bowls of pounded yam, several bowls of soups, meat, fishes, and vegetables.

"*Àti ẹmu o, àti beer o, àti ọtí o, gbogbo è ló pé si mí lọ́wọ́* – I have palm wine, beer and liquor," he announces.

Before they all descend on the food, Wewe opens a bottle of beer, and with his eyes moving back to the painting, he gingerly drops libation to the divinities.
"To the Irúnmọlè, divine energies who produced this painting, here is my offering. May we gather here soon again to discuss a new painting."

His guests affirm this with a resounding "Àṣẹ…"

"We have feasted the eyes; it is now the stomach's turn. Let the stomach feasting begin."

CHAPTER EIGHT:

The Ceramic Bodies Of Clay

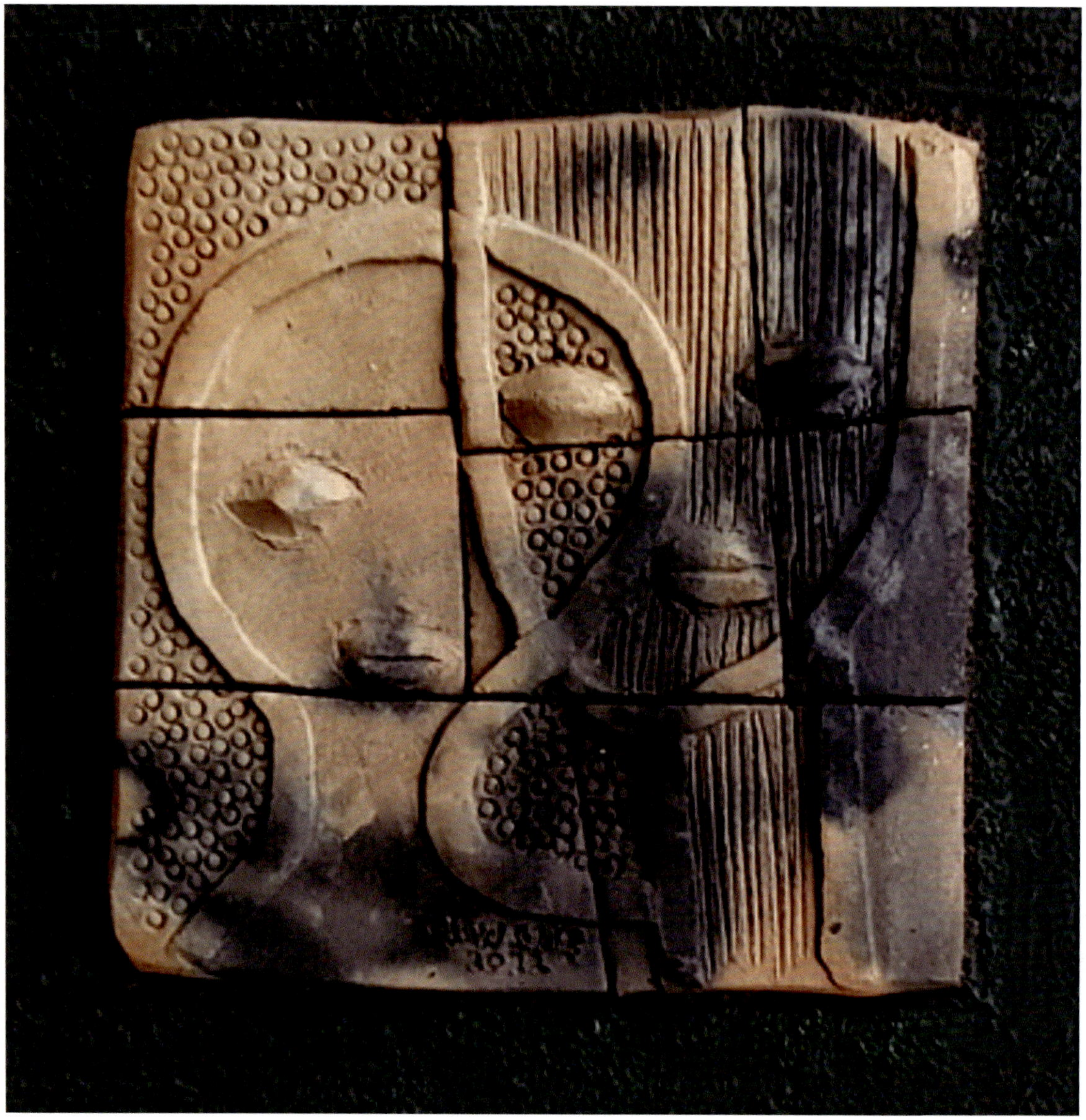

Fig. 26: Tola Wewe, *Young Man and His Wife* II, (*Ìbejì* Series), terracotta and acrylic on panel, 2022.

No longer are the forests green; storms
Assail the palm, the egret and the snail.
Bared, the dark heart of a hidden nursery
Of embers flares aglow, a landmass writhes
From end to end, bathed and steeped
In stern tonalities

- Wole Soyinka, *Ògún Abibiman.*

Slap, thud, slap, thud….It is early in the morning before cockcrow, the sun has not yet stirred, nor have the birds resumed their daily choral duty. You cannot help but notice – Tola Wewe is already beating the clay. Slap, thud, slap, thud, slap….
But, listen; a couple of houses down the street, another beating begins – a man is pummeling his woman; she is screaming and cursing. The leather straps and metal buckles of his belt lacerate the beautiful female body, marking it; cutting it; with violent abandon. (see fig. 26, *Young Man and His Wife* II). Her yells and howls shatter anew, the silent hour of the morning that has already been broken by Tola Wewe's clay pounding. As suddenly as it started, the beating stops and the scream subsides. Only Wewe's steady rhythm of slap, thud, slap, thud continues. Wewe's beating of the supple clay body in his workshop at the back of his house evokes the millions of wife battering taking place that morning, before the birds begin to sing. Wewe beats the clay every day – as the ageless sun struggles to find its youthful feet.

Wewe at work on clay cannot but remind you of the fragmentation and resolution of violence. The loud slaps of his stick on the clay are sharp and persistent; he tears, twists, and pulls the beaten clay to mime the fate of brutalized women – but also to celebrate the beauty of wholesome women. The violent slapping of the clay with his

Fig. 27: Tola Wewe, *The Lovers' Rift*, (*Ìbejì* Series), terracotta on panel, 2022.

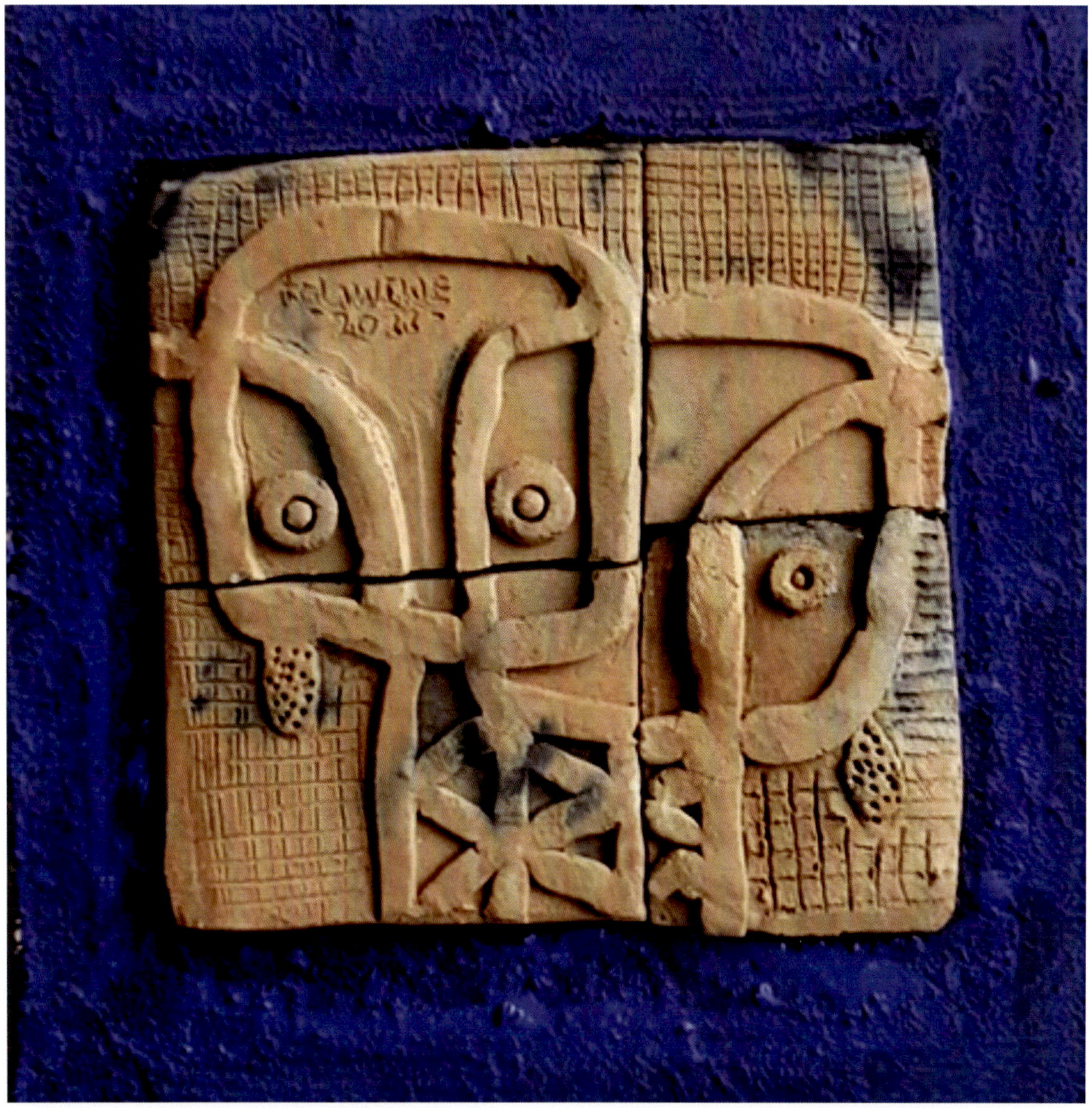

palms and stick, the pinching and pulling with his fingers, the poking and prying of the clay with nails and knives; all are metaphors of transformation and transition. But they are also allegories of violence and the gender confrontations that often escalate romantic conflicts, as couples, like twin figures, develop opposite interests and drift emotionally apart.

On the tiny clay tablets, Wewe spells out the arithmetic of romantic couples – revealing the conflict and complementary structure of binary life. On his clay tablet, one plus one equals three, as an invisible polarizing body enters the simple human union and complicates the relationship of the equation with a wall (see fig. 27*, The Lovers' Rift*). To break this wall of non-communication, Wewe uses twinned figures to investigate and question the dialogues beyond the fragmentation of conjugal interests, when two characters perform within a limited terracotta space. The clay medium is the woman of time. From that female body of clay, the human body was fashioned and to clay the body must return; to be recycled after death.
Within the womb, the fetus gives the first kicks to the wall of uterus in the body of the woman – initiating the fight for life, and starting the dance of death, along the path of primordial violence. With only the heartbeats as the rhythm of transition, the fetus learns to dance in readiness for the larger battle of light and darkness, which commences at birth.

The timeless battle from cradle to casket is the clanging of metallic silence that Wole Soyinka captures in *Ògún Abibiman*. It is the persistence of this battle that Wewe explores in a 2011 exhibition entitled *Footnotes*, as he draws on organic sounds of silence to compose the pictures. The primordial sign of life is the sound of the crying infant; and the primal sign of death is the wailing of the bereaved. When the first cry of life explodes from the infant's belly, it forebodes the final wailing of mourners paying their last tributes. These are the footnotes of life and death and it is from this silent film reel that the colors, lines, patterns, and shapes in Wewe's paintings explode to protect and celebrate the vulnerable body of the priceless female figure.

II

Who remains deceived, who does not know that human hands are incapable of producing the images that Wewe paints! Tola Wewe is a visual, cultural, *Abàmì* magician when it comes to painting on canvas. We call him *Tiwi*, taken from his initials TW, but Nike Okundaye, who knows beans about this business of art, calls him the African Picasso. It is already a well-established fact that he does not make the art with his own hands. We already agreed about this – his incredible ability to paint that large, that quickly, and quite simply that brilliantly, is testament to this fact. He has confessed – at least twice – to the employing of alien *Àjàntálá* studio assistants, appropriating invisible assistants, who visit without being beckoned, from the unfathomable domain of *Àjà Ilẹ̀* (the underworld sky).

As Tiwi paints, they contribute spare mythological hands and eyes from boundless chthonic dimensions. Visitors to his studio witness the wonders of these mythographic *Abàmì* beings, as he moves his hands across vast yards of canvas or when he handles clay with total abandon.

"When everyone is asleep, *Abàmì* visitors start and complete the work for me," he brags.

Nightly, from dusk to just before dawn, Wewe's studio hosts 16 seven legged *Ebora*; 3 thirty-two eyed *Àlùjànnù*; and a sixty-four fingered Iwinlets; among other nomadic spiritual beings. They perform the task of executing his paintings for him. Meanwhile all these *Abàmì* visitors maintain an invisible presence in his studio, even with his fluorescent lights burning so brightly that night looks like day, under the moonless sky. Although he is the one handling the brush, he is not the one doing the sweating. He holds the brush effortlessly, without gripping it too seriously, and the images gravitate without restrains into the body of the canvas; so freely – and sometimes you could have sworn that his eyes were closed, even as his fingers birthed his figures. Free are his fingers of all the rules and regulations of making art.

Tiwi's work is a view of cyberspace, free indeed from the tether of all prisons, oblivious to the ticking of time, released from the logic of space, and defying the grips of gravity. His painting is the epic song of silence that birds twitter when the sun goes up or comes down, when the sky spreads a blank canvas across the firmament – begging for musical colors that no human hand could conduct.

As the painting titled *The First Dawn* shows (fig. 28), it is from this dark canvas that the first dawn broke the waters of incarceration from inside the womb of time; scattered, it spews forth its solar

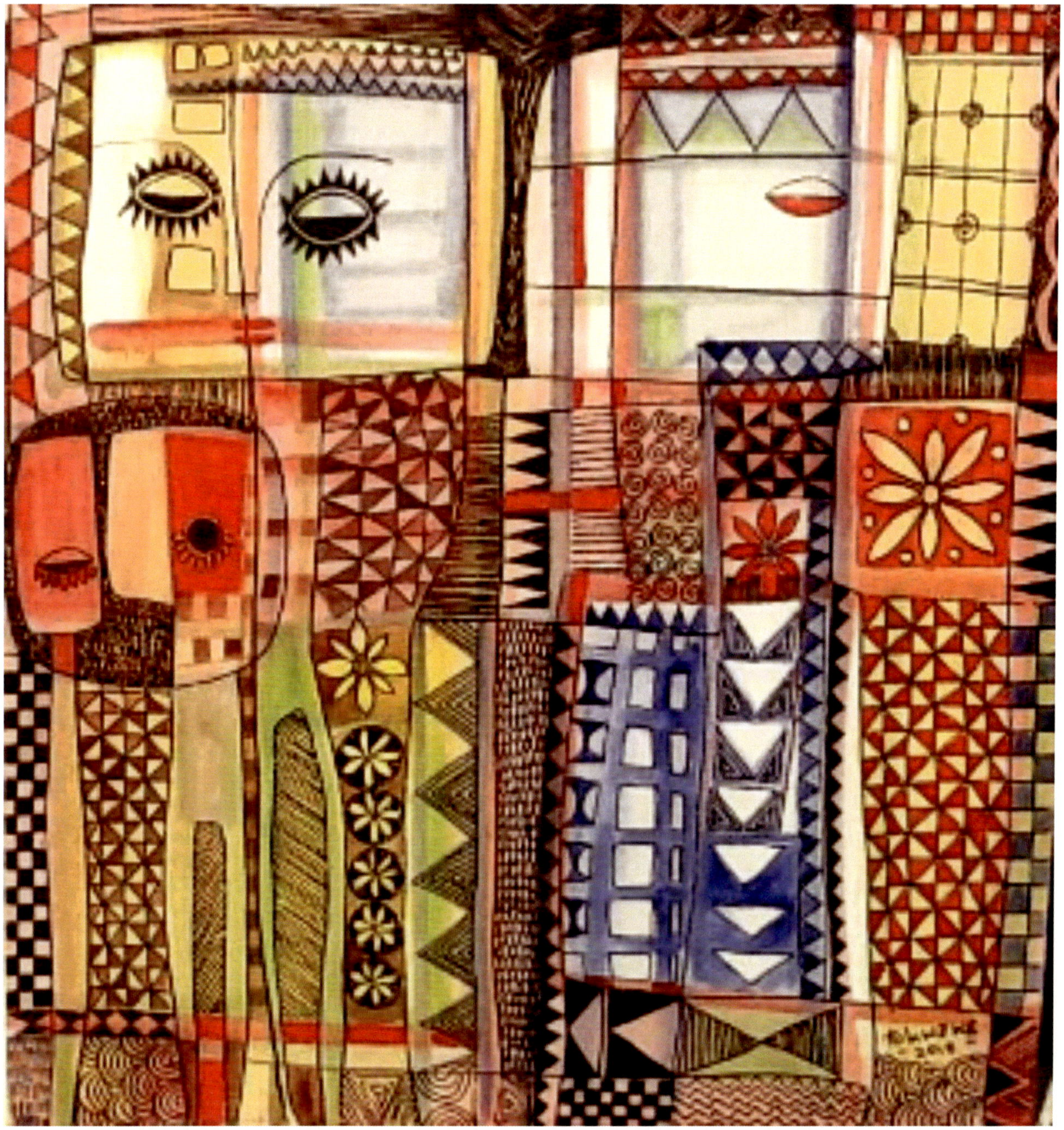

Fig. 28: Tola Wewe: *The First Dawn*, acrylic and oil on canvas, 2011.

secrets, inside smashed gourds detonated by the radiant and combustive energy of Òrìsà vibrations.

It is the aesthetics of healing and hope – reminiscent of the delicate tuning and range of meanings in Dennis Brutus's *Stubborn Hope*. With the intuitive immediacy of visual poesy, Wewe conjures the magic of color over the loom of primal rainbows, hailing the sun to rise anew from the prismatic shards of shattered gods. He crafts silence to frame the canvas with songs, stories, parables, signs and symbols, beams of light and lodes of rainbows, unlocking mysterious passages with labyrinthine corridors of transformation – after the caged bird stopped singing of slavery and colonial hegemonies. When Tiwi rubs red on his canvas, therefore, it is green with life; he balances the complimentary colors of silence on canvases stretched to the point of dancing. When he loads the orange color on his brush, he spells with rhythmic calligraphy, the violet color of silence on luminescent blue hues, and chromatic purple duets. "Grown old," writes poet Kojo Laing, "are these strong elements of tragedy."

Silence is the highest strain of tragic music – when the rising tides of pitch and the soaring inner notes hit their crescendo. A muse who has pulled poems from prison bars – even after the master jailors swore all locks had clanged close – nobody but Fela Anikulapo knows the meaning of deafening silence nearly as much as Wole Soyinka. In the epic poem, *Ògún Abibiman*, Soyinka measures silence with the meters of proverbs, when the divinity of metals, Ògún ÒnÍrè, rejected dialogue, in preference for silence. Silence dethrones dialogue—the Nigerian Nobel laureate declared. But Tiwi's silence enthrones dialogue with color. His instincts understand that Soyinka's silence is replete with footnotes – because in life, as in Death and the King's Horseman, there is no word, nor room, for "dead silence" as a functional vacuum of existence under servitude. The time line is all too familiar now, as its footnotes directly reference sporadic spates of resistance struggles by the 99 per centers across America and Europe, escalating recently across Wall Street, on 9-11-2001. The D-Day was "March 3rd, 1976," Soyinka writes in the preface to *Ògún Abibiman.* "Samora Machel, Leader of the people of Mozambique, announced to the world a symbolic decision which primed the black fuse on Southern Africa: the Mozambique nation had placed itself in a state of war against white-ruled Rhodesia....The rest is history."

From the flames of this triumphal moment in African history, Wewe lights the torch with which he mixes his pigments within the primal fluids of pregnant instincts, primordial principals, folk passages, and ancient warriors.

To paint is to fight for life. A formidable Ògún Onírè field marshal, Wewe roared with the braggadocio of an ancient warrior, "I hear the cries of my people," in my conversation with him in the late 80s. "The cries of oppression, the cries of the suffering masses. They are cries of protest, cries of hunger....I hear the shootings of the 'men-with-guns'. These shootings are reactionary. I may be hungry, I may be denied medical care, despite all these woes, I love my country."

For Wewe, the question was carved down to a legible, sublime, and irreducibly gendered shape: what has symbolized the ruins of war more than the female body? What wears the treasures of peace better than the female gaze? But war is war – when mere words are contested worlds of life and death – especially when a woman as figure of speech is leading the way; the visualization of Samora Machel's "Aluta continua" woman – masked under the wrappers of the female maternal icon; a baby strapped to her bare back, crisscrossing rows of gun-belts cradling her khaki-clad breast and hips as sexualized outer bikinis, brandishing a silhouetted AK-47, armed with ample breast milk for her baby.

Wewe demonstrates with his brush that the female figure embodies the battles of life: that from the milk of maternal breasts, masculine dignity collects and erects the flag of courage. That from the thighs of mothers and daughters emerge the manhood of fathers and sons. That when African women go into labor, they crouch on bended kneels – and cry "*Imẹ́mẹ́, Imẹ́mẹ́!*" – before painting the silence of childbirth with the screams of broken waters. It is a battle cry that women raise as they move into the mythic terrain of mortality, to birthing children from the womb of life.

"*Imeme, Imeme!*" This is the same scream that warriors hear when they march with courage to confront oppression and injustice with nothing more than naked maternal gallantry.
"*Imeme, Imeme!*" – what did you imagine birthing labor was going to look like, to sound like, to taste like, to feel like? Because it was so sweet, did you not imprison yourself with your own hands; with your own keys? Did you and your lover not lock the door and throw away the key? What now is the meaning of all this "*Imeme, Imeme!*" twittering about with the sweetness of a poetic passage in front of Wewe's visual treats and tricks?

III

"*Imeme, Imeme!*" is the moaning sound of the brush on a palette with paint, as Wewe joins the battle to save his mother, his country, from the politics of waste, greed, and death. Unknown criminals who asked for ransom kidnapped Wewe's mother in November 2010. She was held in captivity for more than two weeks, as negotiations went back and forth.

The political resistance movements had bred outlaws who preyed on the citizenry with the military skills they had acquired from their liberation training. These outlaws had infested the Niger Delta from where they launched raids inland to kidnap, rob, and assassinate for money. One of these militant groups kidnapped Wewe's mother. He organized an elaborate search for his mother and finally succeeded in obtaining her release, after paying a heavy ransom. In a ritual involving a complex choreography of phone calls and a tiring blind chase through several cities in Ondo, Edo, and Delta states, the outlaws released her to a team of security consultants that Wewe had hired to conduct the campaign to find his mother.

But one of the ways through which Wewe negotiated her release was through homeopathic magic: in which an idea could be translated into the visual dimension, in order to embody and capture or reach that idea, process, object, or concept in actual life. The conjurer could write an event with graphic signs and whatever he or she writes would happen in real life. The transition of idea to graphic image is therefore a point of vulnerability or strength that Wewe manipulates as a crossroad or intersection

for releasing his mother. By composing iconic paintings celebrating her release, he activates the process of actually releasing his mother in the real world.
Wewe, therefore, produced a prototypical icon (see fig. 29, *Return of Our Mother*), the highlight of which is the figure of his mother as an equestrian general, returning from a triumphal battle, doing a victory lap in her home city. It is invariably a white horse that she rides; the large area of white attracts the viewer's eyes and unifies the composition, while Wewe draws attention to the central homeopathic function of the painting. The placement of her figure on the horse is an iconic convention for representing Òsun, Oya, and Yemoja, the Yoruba Goddesses of femininity, reproduction and beauty.

This iconic act also marks the symbolic investment of his personal mother with the care of the whole community. In playing the communal maternity role, she becomes the mother of the whole community. She acquires the power of an Òrìṣà, and becomes invincible when she discharges her duties as the mother of all, as Wewe depicts her in his series of paintings titled, *Return of Our Mother*.

The style that Wewe visits in this painting is totally different from the style of his work in the late 80s, when Nigeria's concern (or lack there-of) under military regimes was different from its present concerns. A different world produces a different experience and provides a different style for expressing that experience. In the late 80s, his work was formally literal, as a brutally mimetic representation of reality. In the style used in *Return*, he has mastered the aesthetic of Onaism, which provides him with a direct access to ancestral connections and resources, that are not the focus in the Western aspect of his hybrid education.

In Nigeria, those were the days of the Maitasine saga, the precursor to the ongoing Boko Haram campaign of terror. Mohammed Marwa, aka Maitasine, was killed in Kano by members of the Nigerian security forces in 1980, during one of the bloody insurrections for which his group was notorious and dreaded. His brutal killing, documented with graphic pictures, published on the front pages of daily newspapers and displayed on television, did not bring an end to the campaign of blood mounted by the members of his group, who practiced an unorthodox form of Islam that shunned the use of technology, which they were persuaded is the work of Satan.

Everything emanating from Western culture is satanic? Or what exactly did this group want beyond the causing of chaos? Before the Nigerian military forces silenced the sect in 1985, Maitasine followers had killed several thousand people in Northern Nigeria. The sectarian attacks initially focused on Christian victims, but soon expanded to include Moslems who

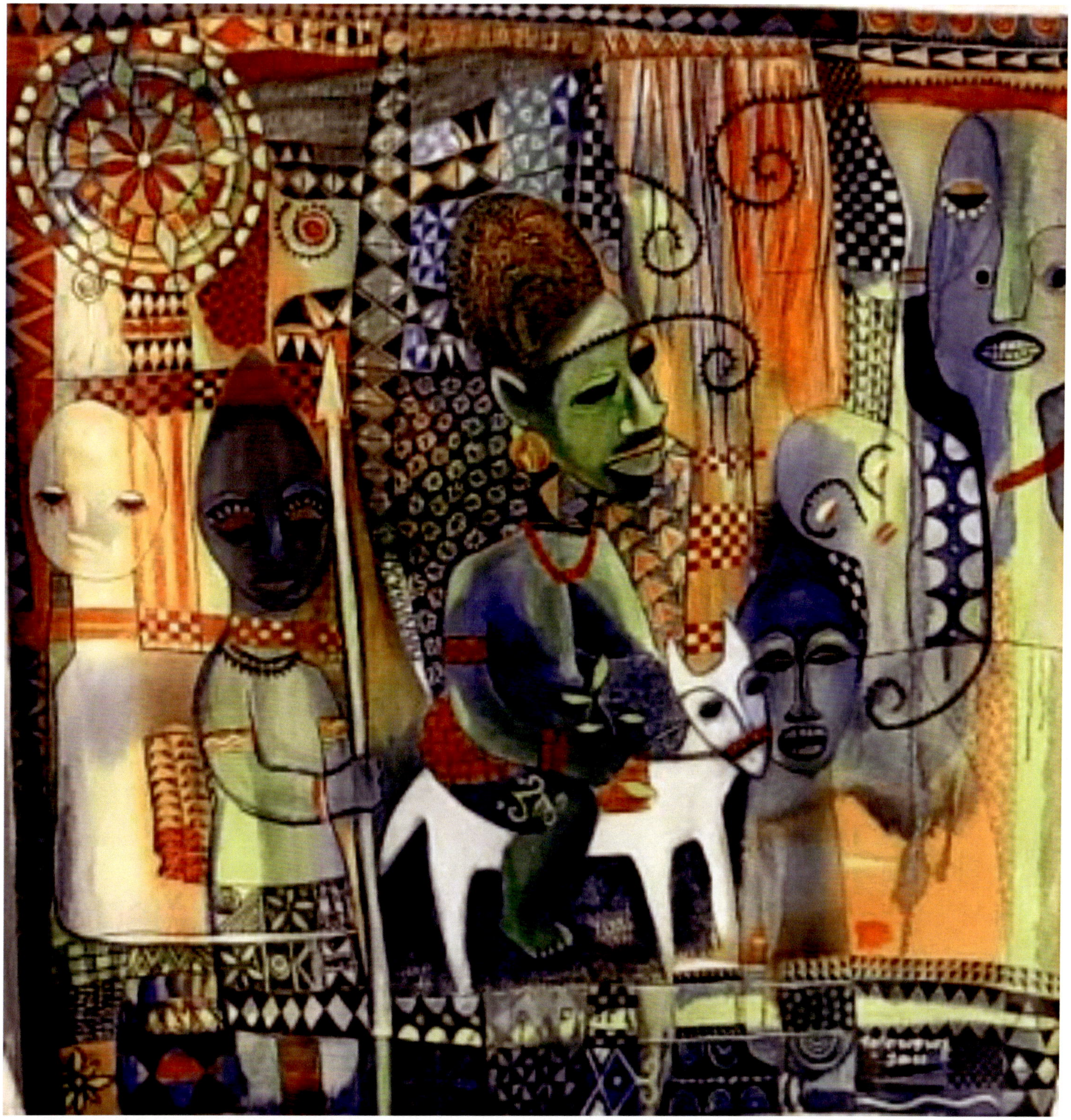

Fig. 29: Tola Wewe, *Return of Our Mother*, acrylic and oil on canvas, 2011

practiced the orthodox forms of Islam, instituting all the five tenets.

Wewe did a painting that he titled *Maitasine* in the late 1980s. It is a graphic work depicting the close-up of a faceless character in the gruesome act of butchering a fellow man. In the background is the image of a mosque and a church. Wewe emphasizes the bulging muscular arms of the assassin, as the killer thrusts the sharp dagger into the heart of his victim. Flowing freely from the mortal wound, blood runs off the surface of canvas – and seems to continue endlessly beyond the frame of the picture. With the painting, Wewe elaborates on the nefarious activities of this group as it began to stage a return in the late 1980s. It was not simply to draw attention to the excesses of the group and the self-inflicted tragedy of religious warfare; his intention was also to warn Nigerians about the sporadic violence that has defined the nation since her independence from colonial rule.

With this painting and many others that he executed in this same period, Wewe established himself as a nationalist artist who positions his work as an opportunity to serve his people; he creates work that makes ethical, mythic and lofty visual statements.

In the 1980s, Wewe's politically engaged paintings were ideological in the literal sense. His vision refused to condone the destruction of the country that he chose to fervently love, even as this destruction festered, only to be followed by promising spates of good hope.

Before the current Boko Haram's campaign of terror, Wewe had witnessed the hideous campaigns of destruction during the Ifè-Modákéké battles, along a route that he frequently plied as he traveled from his studio base in Òndó en route Ìbàdàn, before joining the expressway to Lagos. He took this route because he needed to make a stop at the University of Ìbàdàn, where he was completing the course work for his master's degree in visual studies, under the supervision of Dr. Cornelius Adepegba, the renowned art historian. For his first degree, he had studied painting with Rowland Abiodun, the distinguished art historian at Amherst, and we had countless discussions in those impressionable days, when his ears were still located on his shins. What is common to his teachers is that they were all art historians with strong studio backgrounds. They helped him in shaping his vision, even as his hunger, passion and intrinsic energy fed his desires, moods and sensibilities.

The early 1990s came with a different brand of violence – related to election politics – with the formation of resistance movements including the Oodua People's Congress, Oodua Liberation Movement and the Revolutionary Council of Nigeria, in Southwest Nigeria. Just as these activities ended with the re-establishment of democratic rule in Nigeria in 1999, a different form of political and violent activism erupted in the Delta region, perpetuated by different groups including the NDPVF (Niger Delta People's Volunteer Force), MOSOP (Movement for the Survival of Ogoni People) and MEND (Movement for the Emancipation of Niger Delta).

Now that more ambitious and violent strains of radical groups and activities threaten the very foundations of Nigeria with terrorist acts, and the entire world hangs suspended in curious anticipation of being in the center of a gigantic and seismic cultural cataclysm, one would expect Wewe's body of work to be a hideous catalogue of bloody scenes, destruction, mayhem, and chaos. Isn't this what we see on television and the Internet on a daily basis? Isn't that what the newspapers print as headlines?

But Wewe, now older and wiser, has changed his pictorial tactic without turning his back on his love – Nigeria. Using a tactic similar to the poetic strategies adopted by artistic revolutionaries including Leopold Senghor of Senegal and Dennis Brutus of South Africa, Wewe has adopted the romantic metaphor as the thematic thread running through the body of his work. In addition, he moved from a mimetic representation of depicting things as seen in actual life, to a more fluid style that enables him to improvise, analyze, and dissect reality, without enslaving himself to any direct depiction of things as they appear.

His new style is a series of visual episodes along the passage of memory, through which he takes the viewer in this exhibition. This explains the title of the 2011 exhibition, *Footnotes*, as a reference to his more recent styles: the styles that enable him to travel to deeper levels of visual engagements, into the hearts of his subjects. In this relatively recent menu featuring a wide variety of tastes, the viewer is able to savor the differences, coherence, and focus of Wewe's iconic stability – he images his country in the form of a female figure, which he paints with incessant passion and compulsive dedication. As his clearly meditated and rigorously articulated political choice, Wewe becomes a love painter, refusing the option of maturing into a gore painter, even as Nigeria covers itself in more ignoble blood baths, and the world looks stranger than a Nollywood tale.

Wewe's weaving of romantic wefts with political warps borrows from the arsenal of negritude ideas, though Wewe does not subscribe to the racial essentialism of neo-negritude avant-garde art. Rather, he learns from the revolutionary thrust of African writers in the era of the anti-apartheid and anti-colonial struggles. Soyinka noticed this literary strategy as early as 1950s. In the introduction to *Poems of Black Africa,* his 1975 anthology of poetry from which

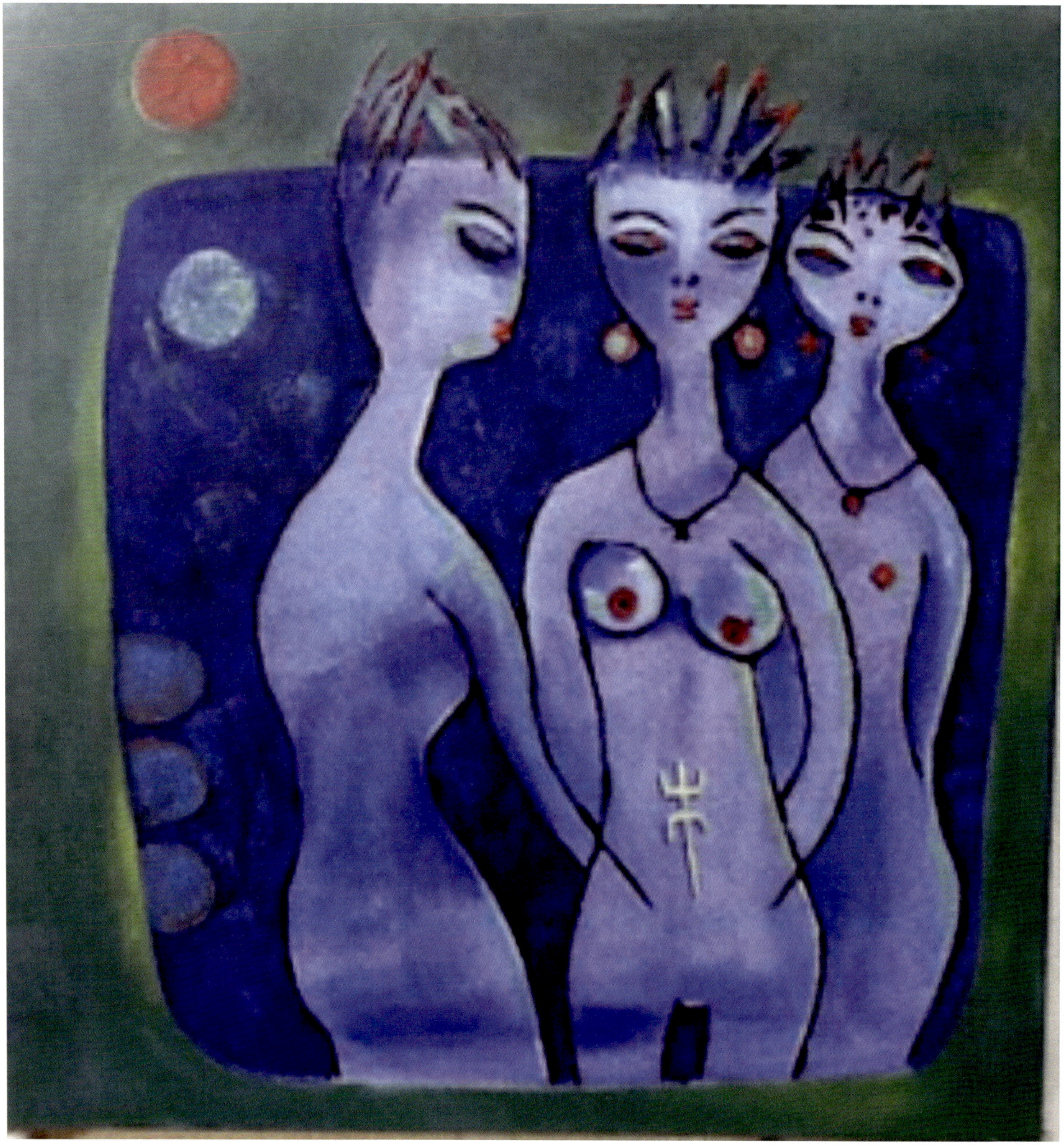

Fig. 30: Tola Wewe, *Waiting In the Nightwind*, acrylic and oil on Canvas, 2011

I extract the following lengthy passage, Soyinka wrote,

"What gives, for instance, the love poems of Dennis Brutus their raw, passionate desperation is the fact that they are just as much poems about love as they are poems of indictment…against the brutish environment from which such emotions are painfully wrenched, that they speak of internal refuge and outer defiance, hope and resolve, within one breath. Even when the poem emerges as essentially tender, its poignancy remains a yet more lacerating accusation. Senghor's leaping meters of human passion are equally cries of nostalgia for a distant homeland and for that missing essence of himself, which he later celebrated more overtly in the doctrine of 'negritude.' The objects of his love sooner or later become completely identified with homeland; his invocations take on the spiritual urgency of an initiate awaiting fulfillment from ancestral presences."

Around his hybrid theme that combines feminine mystique, "ancestral presence" and nationalist fervor, Wewe is most indebted to Senghor. Some of the paintings in this exhibition borrow their titles from Senghor's "Night of Sine." In the first lines of the poem, a romantic protagonist reveals his naked adoration of a lover:

Woman, rest on my brow your balsam hands, your hands gentler than fur
The tall palm trees swinging in the nightwind Hardly rustle. Not even cradlesongs,
The rhythmic silence rocks us.
Listen to its song, listen to the beating of our dark blood, listen
To the beating of the dark pulse of Africa in the mist of lost villages. [21]

Wewe reads this exaggeration with a convivial visual response, through the vision of the triadic thirty-two eyed *Àlùjànnú*, with wide-lens pupils arranged all over their bodies, without any of them quite visible. In fig. 30, titled *Waiting In the Nightwind*, the sun and the moon mingle in the twilight zone of an idyllic landscape, serenading the African muses of the Three Graces. The day, with its parting songs of green vegetation, yields olive hue to the cool blue of a freshly minted night. The parting sun blazes with romantic passion, blushing red in its verdant fecundity of complementary hues.

But it is the melting moonlight that defines the mood of the standing figures. Wewe borrows amorous tints from the radiant sun to crown the women's breasts, which he compares with the softness of the moon floating on a sea of cyan shades. The swaying female bodies present themselves with the gentleness of palm trees listening to the songs of the night wind. Initiates of a water goddess, the women wait in suspense behind the secret garden of an unknowable night – their tremulous bodies tabooed with forbidden fruits. In preparation for their abstruse rituals, the first Grace on the left decorates the belly of the central figure with a totemic gecko, as the third Grace waits her turn with solemn anticipation.

Titled *The Silence of Rhythm*, Fig. 31 is culled from a slightly longer line of Senghor's poem which in full reads, "The rhythmic silence rocks us," in the first verse in the poem, "Night of Sine." What better than a painting to convey the complexity of silence, which enables the artist to embed sound as pigments, without giving the chromatic notes any audible volume? The denial of volume however does not eliminate the vibration of rhythm that travels in leaps and bounds along the multiple axes of colorful grounds. To convey this invisible sensation in optic dimensions, Wewe introduces geometric movements along the bodies in his painting: three seated women with a standing fourth.

Now you see the figures, and then you don't; shapes shift, surfaces curl, patterns twirl, movements frolic, chaos reigns; in an openly choreographed arrangement. At first unseen and unheard, the women in this work do not occupy space or time – they

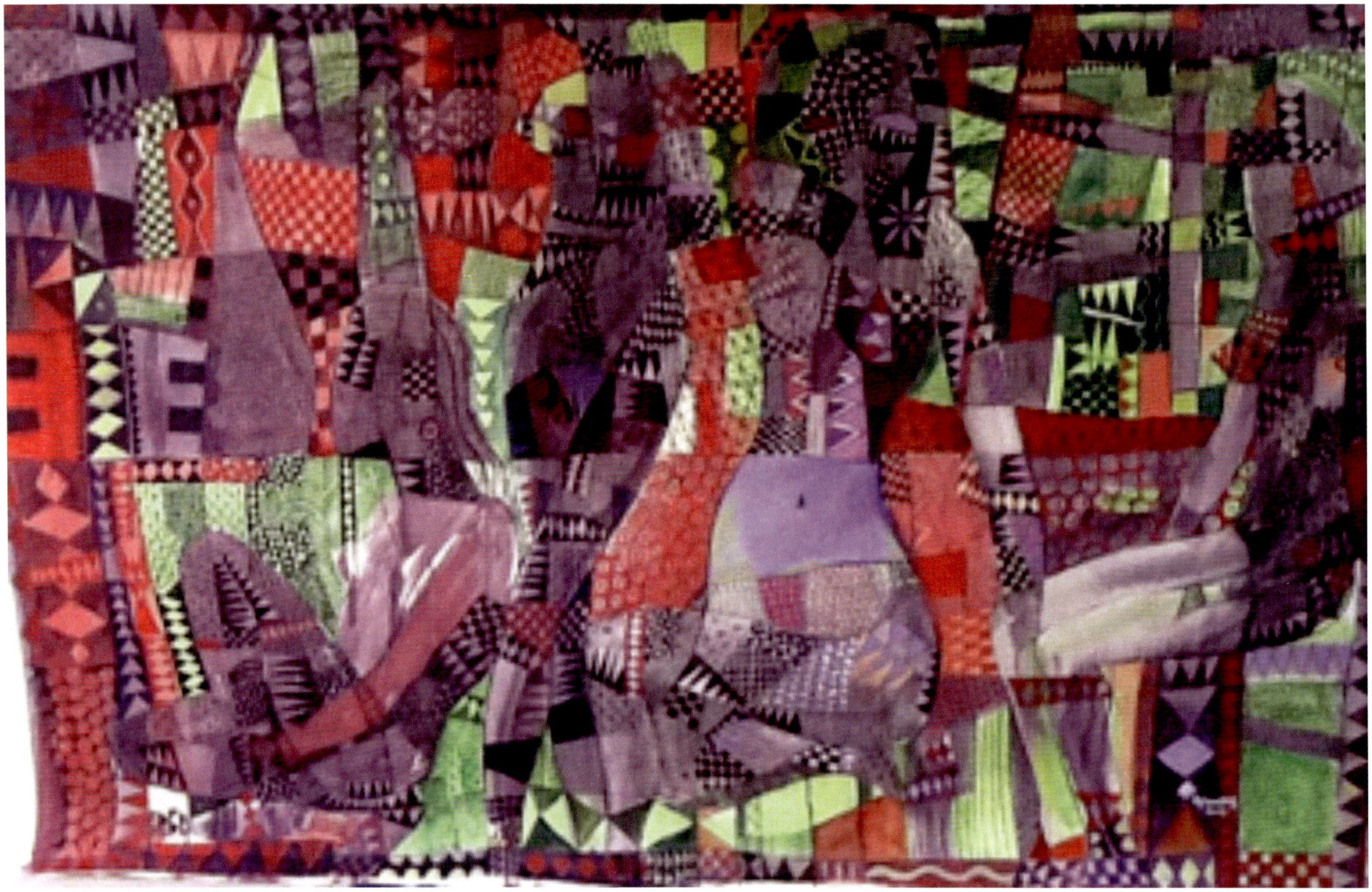

Fig. 31: Tola Wewe, *The Silence of Rhythms*, acrylic and oil on canvas, 2011.

are located in Soyinka's four hundred and first-dimensional "fourth stage."

The women are buried into the painting by the aforementioned sixty-four fingered Iwinlet, with the 16 seven legged *Ebora* and 3 thirty-two eyed *Àlùjànnú* as studio assistants. Is it any wonder then that only a seminal excavation can exhume the central figures from their dense background in Soyinka's marketplace of "Myth, Literature, and the African world?"

In the 1950s, Senghor, in his negritude writings popularized this path of romanticism. Who says Soyinka, a critic of Senghor's negritude, does not understand that men are lured into strange crossroads of life and death – in the landscape of the Òrìṣà, when, finally, silence is invoked? In his review of *My Name is Red* by Orhan Pamuk, the 1998 Nobel laureate, Irfan Zafar wrote, "Painting is the silence of thought and the music of sight."[22]

The thoughtful silence and the musical view are not contradictions in this outlandish work that suspends reason and logic behind a mythic dissolution of light – enjoyed as waves of color.

In terms of number and distribution of the women, the painting relocates the viewer to the dawn of colonial era, when in 1830, imperial France penetrated North Africa. In *The Women of Algiers* by Eugene Delacroix, three seated Arab women suspend time in an opiate stupor, as their African maid, standing, attends to them. While artists as diverse as Pablo Picasso and the Algerian painter Houria Niati have sorely processed the raw content, Wewe's interpretation of this theme is stylistically fresh, musical, and convoluted.

The Mist of Lost Villages is the title of fig. 32, a landscape that presents Wewe's mnemonic tactics in the form of recollections and remembrances. But memories are documentary images that we draw with the expressive skills of recollection. The villages lost to Wewe's infancy are now recalled to the service of the canvas. But the village is not real. Washed with the white coat of distance, the village appears behind the fog of time; and displays its details like a stall in the market place. It is a village that functions as an equation for all villages – the architecture, walls, plants, sun, moon, fishes, and fabrics are present without a single human representative. But if the village is abandoned, who is culpable for this desertion, but the man who leaves his traditions and spirits – in search of alien treasures? Or the one who neglects the ancestral land, the motherland, in search of distant places?

Is this a metaphoric loss of mother? Wewe suggests in the painting that the fate of man is to be weaned from the mother; to seek solace in the breasts of foraged lovers, who must be fished from the sea, which he locates at the bottom of the landscape. To look back with ambivalent nostalgia for a lost past – for a mother who died while the hunter ventured into the wilderness – is to grope for words when the mother tongue falls silent.[23] The village is the childhood from which travelers disperse into the city; only to journey back in their minds and retrieve whatever images the psyche returns from the foggy mirror of time.

IV

Footnotes appear at the end of the page. Wewe's painting marks a significant footnote to "contemporary" African art as it transits from its birth in the early 20th century, to the end of a page in the early 21st century. Wewe watched this passage of a page – an entire era in African art – in the clanging dramas that characterize the transition from one artistic era to another. Within the footnotes of time, readers and viewers may recover the circumstances and events that moved "contemporary" African art from its birth to the end of a page in recent years.

What is the end of this page in African art? To enjoy a larger view, let's examine the footnotes in Arthur C. Danto's book, *After The End of Art*: "Modernism in art marks a point before which painters set about representing the world the way it presented itself, painting people and landscapes and historical events just as they would present themselves to the eye. With modernism, the conditions of representation become central, so that art in a way becomes its own subject.... The question then would be: who was the first modernist painter—who deflected the art of painting from its representational agenda to a new agenda in

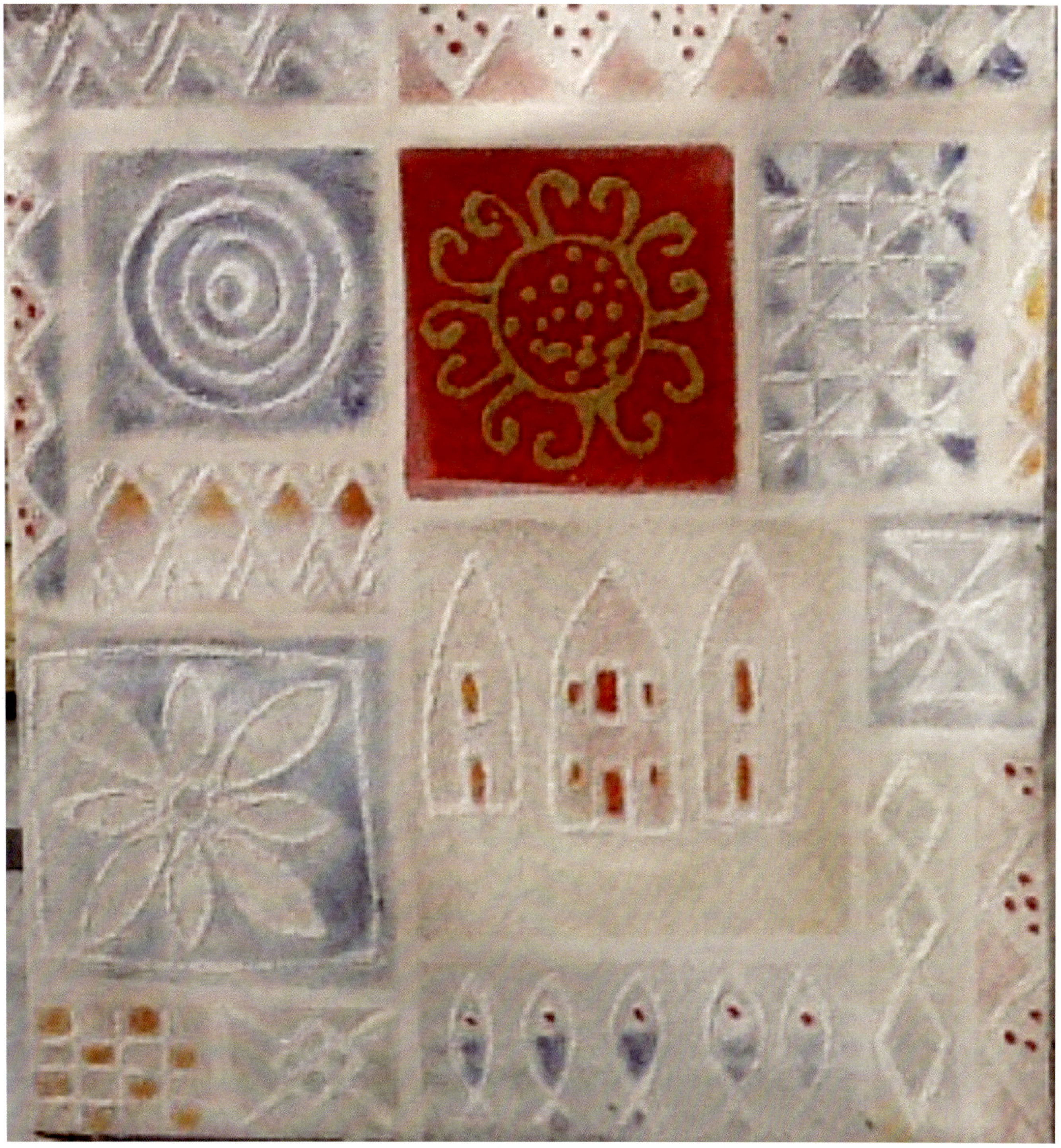

Fig. 32: Tola Wewe, *The Mist of Lost Villages*, acrylic on canvas, 2011.

which the means of representation became the object of representation?"

In indigenous Yoruba art, the painters did not "set about representing the world the way it presented itself." It was the contact with the west at the beginning of the 20th century that initiated attempts to represent the "world as it presented itself." Yoruba artists who learned western painting techniques, such as Aina Onabolu, and a little later, Akinola Lasekan, created works in which they represented the world exactly as they viewed it, with no attempt to abstract or stylize the figures in any way. Building upon the heritage of this early realism in Nigerian art, artists including Enwonwu, Uche Okeke, Yusuff Grillo, and Onabrakpeya began to develop strategies to move away from the representational modes of Onabolu and Lasekan.

To Wewe, the question is this: what deflected African artists from representing reality as it appears to the eye? And in a personal way, what is responsible for this transitional passage in the microcosm of Wewe's own art?

His exploration of the Yoruba concepts of Ọnà presents Wewe with the opportunity to explore artistic questions as periodic footnotes to art history, as commentaries about the freedom of the "contemporary" Yoruba artist, of the African artist, of the metamodern artist, to see the world in other ways, beyond the way it presents itself to the ordinary eye.

Footnotes are bridges that writers construct to define and reconfigure key ideas in a passage. Footnotes link a notion to other notions, a figure to other figures, and a passage to other passages. The answers are not fully realized yet, as Wewe's exploration continues as footnotes to his earlier styles.

Slap, thud, slap, thud goes the rhythm of the visual music of resistance that Wewe conducts to break the gender silence. Behind this silence lurks a gruesome catalogue of global, domestic and cultural violence, especially perpetrated on the bodies of African women. In the morning, when passersby hear the "slap, thud, slap, thud" sound coming from Tiwi's studio, they know that soon the first birds will start singing – as the sun breaks in silence from the embrace of dawn.

With metamodernism as a footnote of premodern, modern, postmodern and postcolonial art, Wewe defines the end of art in terms of the purpose of art. What is the end of his art? As he turns a crucial page that he marks as a footnote, the end of his art is to bring attention to the fate of women in Africa: through the adoration of the African woman's body. It is the metaphoric and metamodern celebration of the female body as the figuration of Our Mother, our nation, our being. This is Wewe's footnote at the bottom of a page in African art and culture. African battles have shifted from struggles against colonial domination. With these metamodern pieces, Wewe acknowledges this shift by breaking the silence and drawing attention to other forms of cultural violence. Consistently and firmly, before the crowing of the dominant cocks, he beats and pummels the soft clay body, with the persistent rhythm – slap, thud, slap, thud, slap....

It is plain to see that Wewe's ceramic plates are all cracked, cut and pasted, displaying the lesions and scars of a troubled era.

A Yoruba proverb teaches us that one must show the eye the clotted pus that one removes with a finger from the same eye, otherwise the eye would deny that it excreted the mess. With his celebrated 1912 painting, *Nude Descending the Staircase*, Marcel Duchamp did not precipitate the early twentieth century holocaust that chased his fleeing nude down the stairs in blurry motion.[24] Yet the French painter added grace and rhythm to the panic of that nude. Wewe's terracotta pieces exhibit the fragmentation of a wounded culture; yet the broken pieces cling to the hope of survival and possibilities of rebirth and growth, as the growing shoot cracks the ground and seeks the sun, while killing the very seed from which it springs.

Alas, what more could Wewe do but paint to the music of gory vision while seeking the grace of glory – as the female bodies flee from the incessant stutters of machine guns radically seized by the phallus – in Syria, Nigeria, Afghanistan, Iraq, Palestine, even in Jerusalem?

The music of our time is recorded in Wewe's assiduously taken pictorial minutes of our hour. The world is still young, a mere bittersweet sixteen. If you listen carefully to Wewe's patterns, you can hear the invisible onomatopoeia of our immature era of war-and-peace-talks; she is twittering: Rat-tat-tat-tat-rat
Tat-rat-tat-tat-tat
Rat-tat-tat-tat-rat
Tat-rat-tat-tat-tat....

CHAPTER NINE:

Abstractions Between the Silence and Noise of Painting

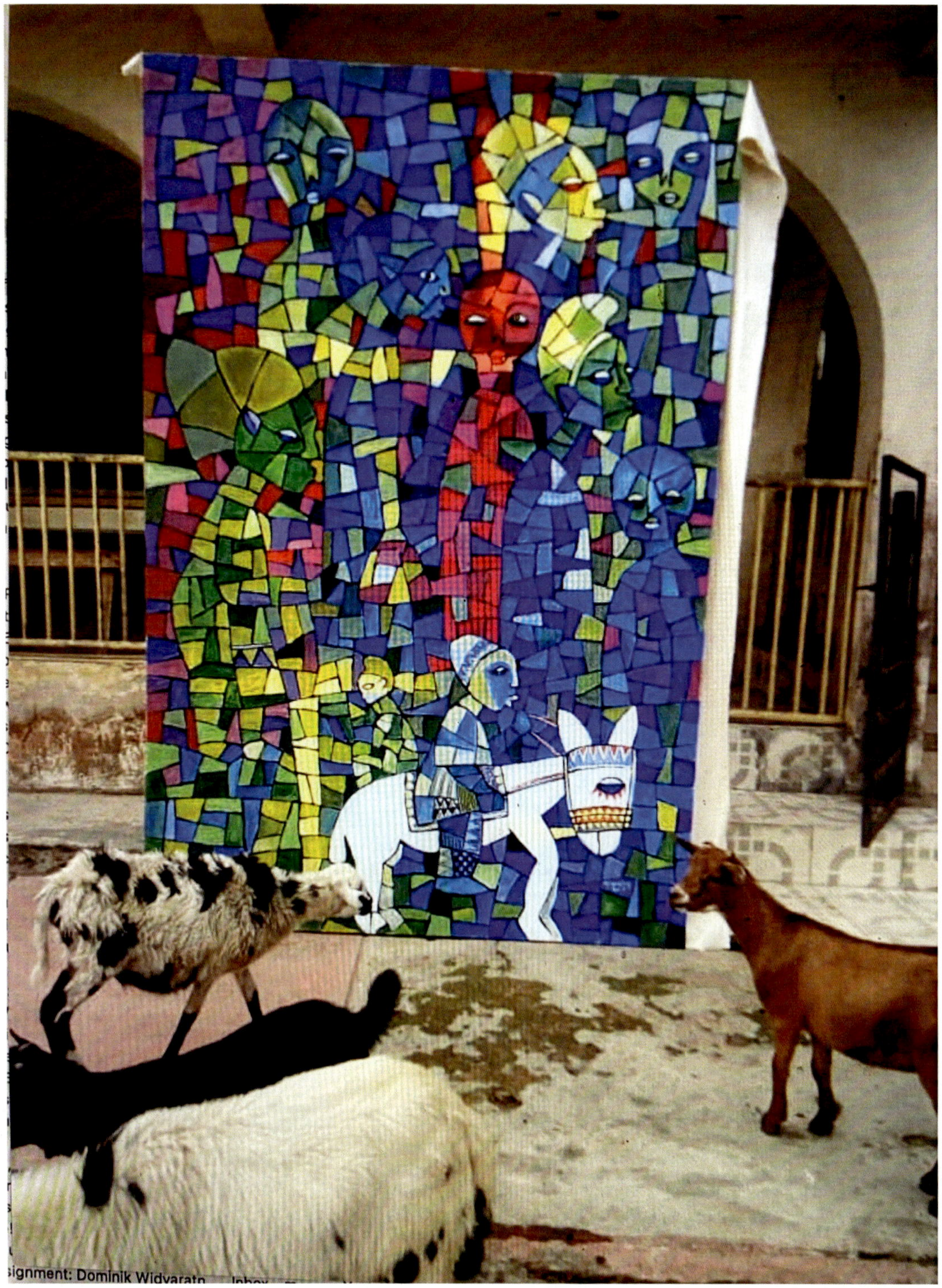

Figure 33: The animals and the painting.

Just before the Covid-19 lockdown in Nigeria, Adetola Wewe began to observe a pattern of behavior among his domestic animals; he found it rather strange.

His residence and studio is also a farm. Goats, sheep, chicken, ducks, rabbits all patter about at their pleasure while his ferocious guard dogs keep them all in and everything else out. Wewe began to notice that the animals would gather in silence in front of his paintings – appearing to study them. The animals would stare transfixed for hours at a time; with some settling down on their haunches, just to keep staring at the compositions.

He decided to document it. One weekend, Wewe completed a large painting for a client, and placed it outside his studio to get a long view of it as well as to record his animals' reaction to the painting. He had deliberately painted a white horse at the bottom of the painting. Almost spontaneously, his sheep and goats came out from the shed and began to focus on the highlight of the composition – the horse and its rider.

"This is quite fascinating," he thought. They remained fixated on this painting and gathered around it until evening, when they had to be forcefully herded into their sheds for the night. Many people have called his work "abstract" art. But here were animals mesmerized by it. (Fig. 33).

He was still reflecting on the ideas of realism and abstraction in relation to the strange event of his animals' attraction to his paintings when the order to shut down and lockdown came. Covid-19 had become a pandemic and had finally entered Nigeria.

As a graduate student, he had written an essay in which he had argued that animals have cultures like people and they act and react in ways that align with their purposes and abilities. His professor had vehemently disagreed him, maintaining that animals have no culture and simply followed their natural instincts. Wewe had argued back that humans, like animals, follow their natural instincts too, but his professor shooed him out of his office, laughing uproariously in final dismissal.
During the Covid lockdown, Wewe wondered where his then professor currently was, how he is doing and what he would say to his photo documenting the animals gathering to study his painting.

As Tola Wewe emerged from the lockdown of the Covid-19 pandemic, his collectors and admirers wanted to know what he had been up to. What happened to him during the pandemic? Was anyone in his family or neighborhood sick? What medications, if any, did he take as preventive measures? Did he socially distance? Did he even hold private shows in his home for some collectors?
"They were me asking me all these questions, especially the press, with my phone ringing off the hook. Things were stone quiet during the lockdown of 2020. Frightening. At the beginning, it was dreamlike, like a shock. There was nobody to talk with, but thanks to the Irúnmọlẹ̀ that at least we had our cellphones. But once you got off the phone, your immediate environment felt unreal; it was really quiet. Even I was also quiet during the lockdown. But I was still surprised at the large number of people interested in what happened to me during the pandemic. They wanted to know what happened to my art. Was I painting at all or was I even painting more? Did the isolation change my style? Lots of questions like that. They asked what the meaning of my work was and if the pandemic has changed my symbolism? Did I still paint abstract art? I wanted to retort back: did I ever paint abstract art?!"

The questions and hypothetical answers about abstract art and Wewe's work transports us back in time and space; almost twenty years in fact. Christmas festoons decorated the streets as the snow drizzled steadily that December evening in the early 2000s, and the heater in my truck was turned to its maximum capacity. The late Nigerian artist, Rufus Orisayomi, was with me in Denver, Colorado and we were on our way to see the opening of Tola Wewe's exhibition on Santa Fe Street. Wewe was already waiting for us at the art gallery where his work was showing; we were running late. But I could not drive any faster because of the snow; we ran the risk of the truck skidding out of control, despite its four-wheel gear. To take our minds off the weather, I turned on the radio, which was playing a tune by the Brazilian artist and former Minister of Culture, Gilberto Gil. It was an instrumental arrangement that blended African, European and aboriginal Indian music into a haunting composition.

I was convinced that Rufus would readily enjoy the African percussion that formed a strong background to Gil's music. In 1977, Rufus had met Gilberto Gil in Lagos when the Brazilian musician visited, as part of the Black contingent from Brazil to perform at FESTAC, the international cultural jamboree. It was therefore shocking to me when Rufus grumbled, "What is the point of music when it has no song. All sound and no meaning. I hate instrumentals!"

I decided to let his comment slide, thinking it was more about his madness at the falling snow than Gil's music.

But he continued: "It is like tea without sugar. No! It's more like *gàrí* and *ẹ̀gúsí* without meat."[25]

His comment caught me totally by surprise. Rufus was an excellent percussionist. He was an integral member of the *Orí Olókun* Theater group that emerged in the late sixties at Ilé Ifè, under the direction of Ola Rotimi, Sam Akpabot, and Peggy Harper (all late). Rufus had studied with all these distinguished artists, and was a star artist who performed regularly during their shows.

Rufus's statement was particularly surprising because all the teachers with whom he studied prioritized instrumental music and used it extensively in their performances. But I was all the more amazed because Rufus was one of the few Nigerian painters working in the idiom that is popularly described as "abstract art," art that did not attempt to represent "life as it presented itself," to use the idea of Danto, the art critic.[26] I therefore knew exactly how to address his remark. "Rufus," I responded, "you just said instrumental music makes no sense because it contains no lyrics, but don't you think that sounds ridiculous? It's just like saying abstract painting makes no sense because it has no figures."

I had gotten his attention. "How many times have people told you that they cannot understand your work because it is 'abstract'?"

"Countless times," he responded. "Right, I see what you mean. I guess instrumental music makes sense when you think of it as abstract painting without human, animal, or any figures."

That was easy, I thought. "And vice versa," I continued. "Abstract art makes sense when you think of it as a visual form of instrumental music." Rufus nodded in agreement and paid closer attention to Gil's music. This analogy between "abstract" painting and instrumental music was a statement that I repeated often that evening, as I explained Tola Wewe's work to the specially invited visitors. These were members of the Douglas Society at the Denver Art Museum where I was the curator for African and Oceanic Arts.

I had purchased a few works by Nigerian artists for the permanent collection of the Denver Art Museum, including mixed media painting by Rom Isichei, drawings by Wole Lagunju, videos by Rufus Orisayomi and a couple of pieces by Lamidi Fakeye. When Wewe visited Denver in 2004, he made some drawings that I also acquired for the museum. Besides this, I had organized a highly successful exhibition for Moyo Ogundipe at the Denver Art Museum. The exhibition received considerable coverage by all the news media and was regarded as one of the most successful exhibitions of "contemporary" art in Colorado.

The audience that trooped to the Santa Fe gallery for the opening of Wewe's work therefore had seen "contemporary" African art before, although it was (and still is) a rarity in the United States.

Seeing "contemporary" African art in the Denver Art Museum was one thing; understanding its aesthetics and meaning, however, was a totally different matter. To the typical museum visitor in America, African art does not include anything on canvas. African art to them is still frozen in the past and refers to "functional" objects in wood, which they refer to as "tribal" art, produced anonymously in villages, and used in rituals and performances that evoke strange ceremonies of witchdoctors, blood, barbarity; maybe even human sacrifice and cannibalism.

In most major museums in the United States, "contemporary" African art is not shown. The boards of directors of museums discourage the purchase or display of any object not in conformity with the primitivism fiction and envisioning of Africa as a dark continent, that has not successfully crossed from the past into the twentieth century, not to talk of the twenty-

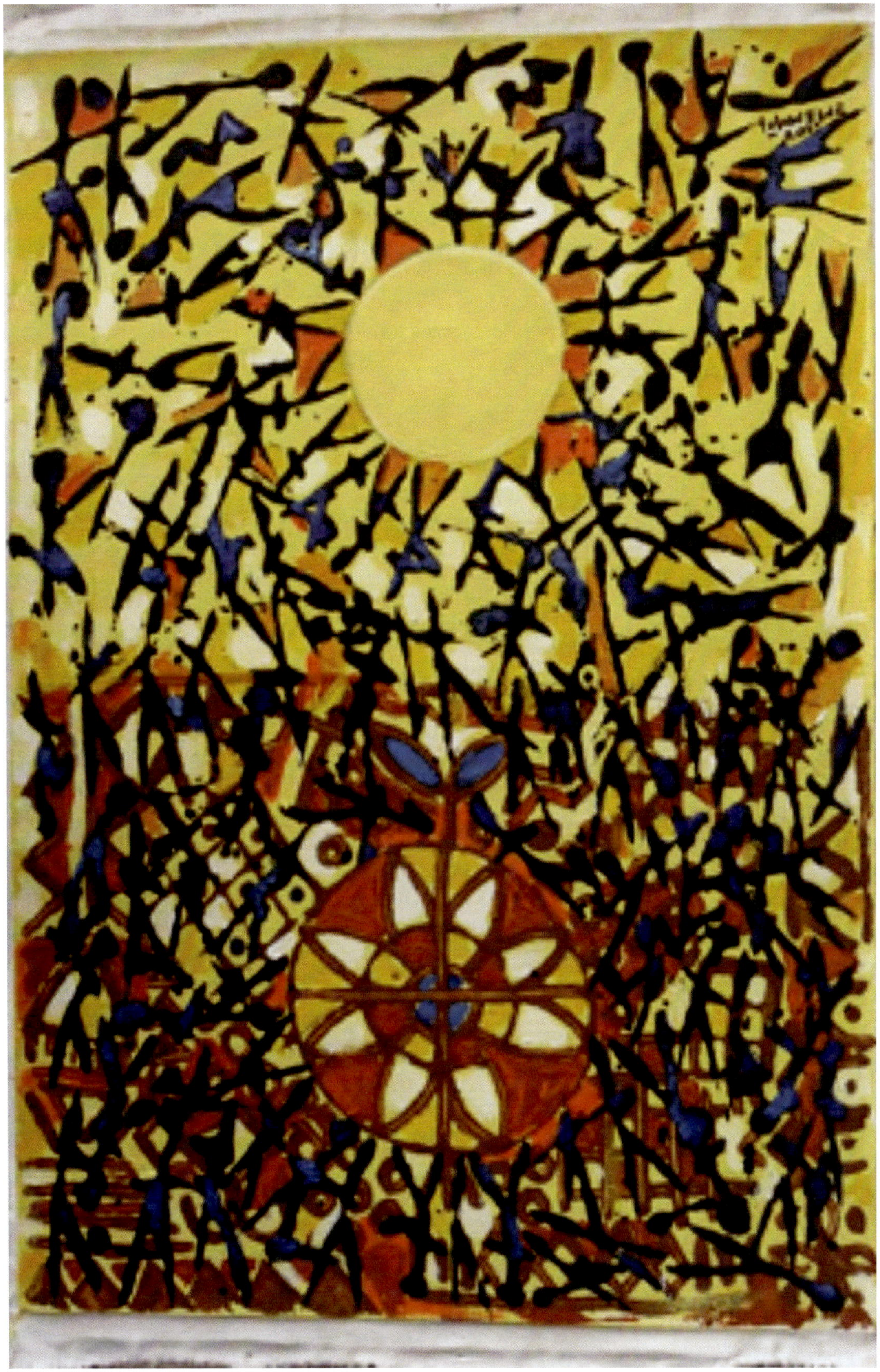

Fig. 34: *Breaking soil*, acrylic on canvas, 2021

first.

One of my purposes when I became the curator of African and Oceanic arts at the Denver Art Museum in 1999 was to challenge the notion that African art belongs only to the past. It was not an easy task, given the formidable forces and institutions that have thrived for hundreds of years, and have built their reputations on the construction of a primitive idea of Africa; and its arts. When I began to address the issue of "contemporary" African art at the Denver Art Museum, not a single "contemporary" African art object existed in any art gallery or in any known private collection in the entire state of Colorado! My bosses at the museum, therefore, did not know what I was talking about when I informed them that I wanted to collect "contemporary" African art.

It was a battle that I fought throughout my ten-year tenure at the Denver Art Museum. Most of the time it was a tiring task that threatened to wreck my resolve and destroy my morale. The persistently recurrent statement that colleagues threw at me was, "There's no such thing as 'contemporary' African art. It is either 'contemporary' art or it is African art. You can't have both together."

My first big break came with the Moyo Ogundipe exhibition in 2002. But even with this show, I had to make a compromise: I was only allowed to show Ogundipe's work, if I displayed it side by side with the old pieces that have become the stereotypes for Africa. I decided to craft an exhibition with the title, "African Renaissance: Old Forms, New Images in African Art."

The conceptualization of the exhibition enabled me to present a narrative in which the "traditional" art objects fluidly merged with the "contemporary" forms; Ogundipe's paintings contains images of some of these old objects anyway. Ogundipe, by that time, had become a member of the Ọnà Artists.
The exhibition instantly transformed Ogundipe into a celebrity. Simultaneously showing in the museum when his work was on display was a blockbuster exhibition of Impressionism paintings. Museum visitors and patrons in the United States love Impressionist art more than that of almost any other period. At the Denver Art Museum, after visitors completed the viewing of the Impressionism masterpieces, some of them who had time to kill strayed into the temporary display gallery showing Ogundipe's work. They were so awed by the irrepressible expressive power, the attention to detail and the mastery of color in Ogundipe's work that they went out and spread the word.

Before long, Ogundipe's show was drawing as many viewers as the blockbuster exhibition of the European Impressionist paintings. The exhibition received television, radio, and newspaper coverage, and visitors came from far and near after learning about the beauty of the works from the news media.

The runaway success of Ogundipe's show convinced the Denver Art Museum to begin to purchase "contemporary" art pieces from Africa. The climax of these purchases was the acquisition of a monumental work by El Anatsui, which the museum commissioned in 2007. It was my last major contribution to the acquisition efforts at the Denver Art Museum.

In addition, the collection of African art objects was brought out from the basement storage of the museum, where it had been stacked when I was hired as a curator. When the Denver Art Museum was expanded in 2006 by Daniel Libeskind, he incorporated a specially designed gallery for African art objects in the ultramodern museum building he designed.

But in 2003 when Wewe opened his show

in the Santa Fe art district, there was no gallery for "contemporary" African art at the Denver Art Museum. All the "contemporary" art pieces that I acquired for the museum were in storage. I often led groups of museum enthusiasts to the storage space to show them what I had acquired. Many of these museum patrons came to Wewe's opening and it was my duty to take them around the exhibition and explain Wewe's work to them. Some of them were perplexed by some of the "abstract" images in Wewe's work.

To these people, who needed to see figures before they could find meaning in an art object, I presented the analogy of music.

"Imagine you were listening to jazz or classical music without lyrics," I told them. "Or that you were simply listening to a bird singing. You allow yourself to enjoy the rhythm, colors, lines, and movements of the instrumental music. When you translate these same elements of composition into a visual language, Wewe's abstract forms will become meaningful to you."

With Wewe's work, I began a dialogue with the audience about abstraction in "contemporary" African art. It was an enjoyable Yuletide evening where we wove the wefts of instrumental sounds, into the warps of abstract painting, to explain the mystery hidden inside Tola Wewe's painterly compositions.

Wewe recalls one of his earliest memories of growing up in Shabome, a community in the dense network of creeks that empty into the Atlantic Ocean, along the West African coastline, around the vast seascape between the Bight of Biafra and the natural seaports of Badagry and Lagos. Wewe's father was a successful forester who traded in lumber. Wewe's father and his men felled huge trees in these creeks, tied them together into rafts and sailed them to the seaports for their onward journeys to Europe and America, and nowadays, Asia. A small motorboat in the command of a great crew, could move a mountain of trees, the size of a soccer field, from the hinterland, through the creeks, to the lagoon, and onto the ocean, along water paths totally invisible to the non-initiate, ignorant of secrets and knowledge of the trade, passed down the family for hundreds of years – before, during and after the transatlantic slave trade.

When followed for a couple of miles in a paddled canoe, a seemingly tiny and insignificant stream in Shabome, Wewe's hometown, opens out into the vast network of creeks emptying out through the lagoons into the ocean. A vast part of the wonder of the landscape is the variety of constantly changing plants, animals and soils, transforming the appearance of the ageless water. The water seems to be the same; but everything within and around the water changes every time it collides with the water.

Water is the fuel of life: whatever water touches starts a new life and finds some agent of collaboration and transformation. In that organic setting of spring, decay, death and rebirth, nothing appears to be happening in nature as reality rolls on in cyclic progressions of day and night, with short mornings, middays and evenings. Timelessness is the temporal dimension. On the landscape in Yoruba country, day and night, one sees the same picturesque sight of tall palm trees, standing like posed models against the skylines, with their peculiar leaves forming asterisks of decorative stars; they stand in silhouetted designs reflected on the glistening surface of the water. The pattern is an endless stretch of time in suspended patches of light and dark palettes – as found in Wewe's paintings. In the light-scape, nothing is insignificant; the more normative is the more provocative in the scenery of the creek and the painting.

"In these musical spaces of light and dark forces," Wewe says, "what is visible to the ordinary eye is little. You must wash your eyes with the waters of the location. Otherwise, you will see nothing. Each location here is different as its waters are different. Each water is a mirror of the sky and when you wash your eyes with the water, you will see things differently."[27]

It is in that journey into a landscape where the lagoon meets the huge lumber of the West African shores, where the water spirits form a colorful pattern toward understanding the mysteries lurking behind the surface structure of the map, that Wewe finds the palette for weaving his colorful fabrics on canvas. The blues of the water, the pastels of the soil, the brown barks, the greens of the forests and the reds of Ògún □ the divinity of time and waste, in whose wars humankind has situated their foibles as cultural engagements and expressions.

What, therefore, presents itself to the eye when Wewe is looking at the world? It is not the same modern eye that Danto describes, but a metamodern eye that informs Wewe's perception of the world.[28] Reality, as it presents itself to Tola Wewe, is therefore, a space of infinite expansions and limitless flights along the crossroads and bridges of the sacred and the secular – where the idea of one existing outside the other is inconceivable. It is from that terrain of an open frontier of cultures – where south meets north, and east and west melt into hybrids and other cultural indeterminacies – that Wewe pulls out his work, using conceptual compositions with no wall between polar imaginations of the visible/invisible, living/dead, fiction/facts.

It is a metamodern adventure. The fortunes and images of life follow the fluidity of the creek waters as it changes color, density and texture under the billows of the wind and the sun, as the paddles slowly and steadily move the canoe forward on the golden water, streaked with the silver glitters of light.

The indigenes of Shabomi blend cultures from several southern West African communities – Yoruba being the strongest influence – with words, phrases and inflections inherited from Edo, Itshekiri, Ijaw, Urhobo and other cultures. Their family structures indigenously support tight-knit kinship where everybody in the community is related and treat each other as stemming from the same ancestral root. Within that homogenous pattern, nevertheless, is a mass of different fabrics and yarns, each with its own distinctive color, texture and design. Each individual within each family is a different design, an *Ènìyàn* □ specially granted the power by the Divinity to pick and choose their individualities. The syllable *-yàn-* from *ènìyàn* grants each individual the power to choose throughout life; together with the readiness to take responsibility for the choices made. You are the choices you make; just as the choices you make redefine you.

"Everybody minds the business of everybody else by minding their own business and allowing others to mind theirs," Wewe says with a smile.

It was in that atmosphere where the sea and the soil dance to the music of the wind, that Tola Wewe grew up to the wonders of the world.

"My father had five wives and many children," Wewe recalls. "He was a practical man: work hard, know your trade, bargain hard. He could not even understand what I meant when I told him I wanted to study art at the university," Wewe said as he painted. "Law, engineering, medicine, pharmacy, even teaching Papa understood perfectly. But art? Quite simply not."

He had always known he would be an artist. Quite early he realized that making art brought an attention and an instant gratification that he enjoyed tremendously. He enjoys sharing his work with the world; his painting is the barometer with which he regularly measures the vigor of his body and spirit; and the health of his environment.

As he narrated, the Covid-19 pandemic lockdown has intensified his practice of the art of herbal medicine. He comes from a culture in which 100 proof liquor, with a 50% alcoholic content, is the preferred agent for extracting the active ingredients from herbs. He boils and soaks his various herbs – nuts, roots, leaves, seeds, barks – in alcohol to provide Anti-Covid medication. He takes these teas and tinctures daily as spiritual support in his fight against the Covid and he takes the vaccines as additional charms and amulets.

Though Wewe was born in 1959, just a year before Nigeria's independence from direct colonial occupation, he says he has always been in the world, and would forever remain there.

Early in his career as an artist, he saw art as a means of delivering direct criticism of the political social order. Over now are those days when art for him was a tool for criticism: he has been at the center of government as the Commissioner for Arts and Culture of Ondo State in Nigeria and has seen how and why the government is prevented from working – to benefit the ruling elite and strangulate the lives of the rest of the people. He understands that the issue is not merely political. The sociological contradictions come from deeper spiritual conflicts that are yet to be interrogated. It is to these sociological sublayers of reality that he aims his paintings, as a song of triumph against the angel of death and pain that Covid unleashed on the world.

A strong element of his healing material is spiritual, because he thinks the body cannot heal when the spirit is sick.

"This is why I work during the night, when all the spirits wake up and humans go to asleep."

The paintings when done at night, he says, become spaces of rituals for the spirits, who promptly pick up his tools and complete the paintings for him before the break of dawn. He becomes a witness to his own painting, he says, as he enjoys watching the creative process from a body that is performing the work that the spirits are producing.

"Every art that comes out of an artist's studio today must face the challenge of healing the body and the spirit that this Covid pandemic has pummeled and injured. When the spirit is strong, the body can handle the virus or any other ailment."

The Covid-19 ailment has affected his country, Nigeria, most profoundly, and perhaps more devastatingly than most countries. Nigeria has not till this moment been faced with so many difficult political, economic, security, infrastructural and developmental challenges; all at the same time. In all of its over sixty years of independence, Nigeria has always managed to survive. But these days, he thinks the nation that the British built in West Africa might be mortally wounded.

Wewe never bought the independence story anyway. "Nigeria is totally dependent in all ways. It is dependent on food, industrial products, electronics, trade, health care and in all other ways on the outside world." Because Nigeria was birthed to be culturally tied to the apron strings of Western Europe, Wewe recognizes her vulnerability, a vulnerability which only heightens her beauty for him. This intersection of vulnerability and beauty is an aesthetic position that comes from Wewe's conceptualization of the black female figure – continuously, repeatedly violated, yet undiminished.

Wewe's construction of this feminist icon of vulnerability is not from the influence of the Negritude era that the poet Leopold Senghor celebrated from the middle of the last century, and which Ben Enwonwu defines with a numerous array of paintings from the late 1950s until his death in 2009. Wewe's feminist construction comes from an age that grew up post-Negritude and did not have to spend long periods on alien soil to earn their first degrees. The generation of Enwonwu and Senghor had to travel to Europe to get their university education. For poets like Senghor and Soyinka, or painters like Enwonwu or Etso Ugbodaga-Ngu, it was almost inevitable to travel abroad – away from Africa – to get a university education.

For Wewe and his generation, Nigeria already had universities offering degree programs. The political situation has also changed from that of colonial occupation to a pseudo free state. Nigeria is now ruled by fellow Nigerians, unlike the case of the artists of the Negritude era, coming from territories in Africa colonized by their Portuguese, French and English conquerors. Though the European countries ran distinctive colonial polities to suit their interests, they were united by the color of their skin against the indigenes, who were also integrated – beyond the individual European-drawn national borders – by the colors of their skin.

Even in Africa, the skin was the color of offence and defense as colonial lines drew the cartography of Negritude subjectivities. Wewe finds the music of the inventor of AfroBeat music fascinating for its historical allusions. The aesthetics that came out of that tensile relationship engaged the west as a colonizer, as documented in the narrative epic of Fela Anikulapo Kuti lyrics:

We dey sit for our land jeje (We sat in our land quietly).
We dey mind our business jeje (We were minding our business quietly)
Some people come from faraway land (Certain people came from a distant land)....[29]

Fela sang the classic story of all indigenous peoples suffering from the aftermath of Western colonization. This entire indictment of the plight of Africa as emanating from the colonial impoverishment of Africa, comes as a conclusion in Fela's declaration: "That is why Black man dey suffer today"

This colonial impeachment rightly or wrongly underlines Negritude aesthetics, not only as a unified experience, but also as provided in specific countries.

Wewe did not have to deal with the aesthetics of European colonization in any direct manner. Indirectly, yes, because he wouldn't let you forget that the fanfare of independence ceremonies

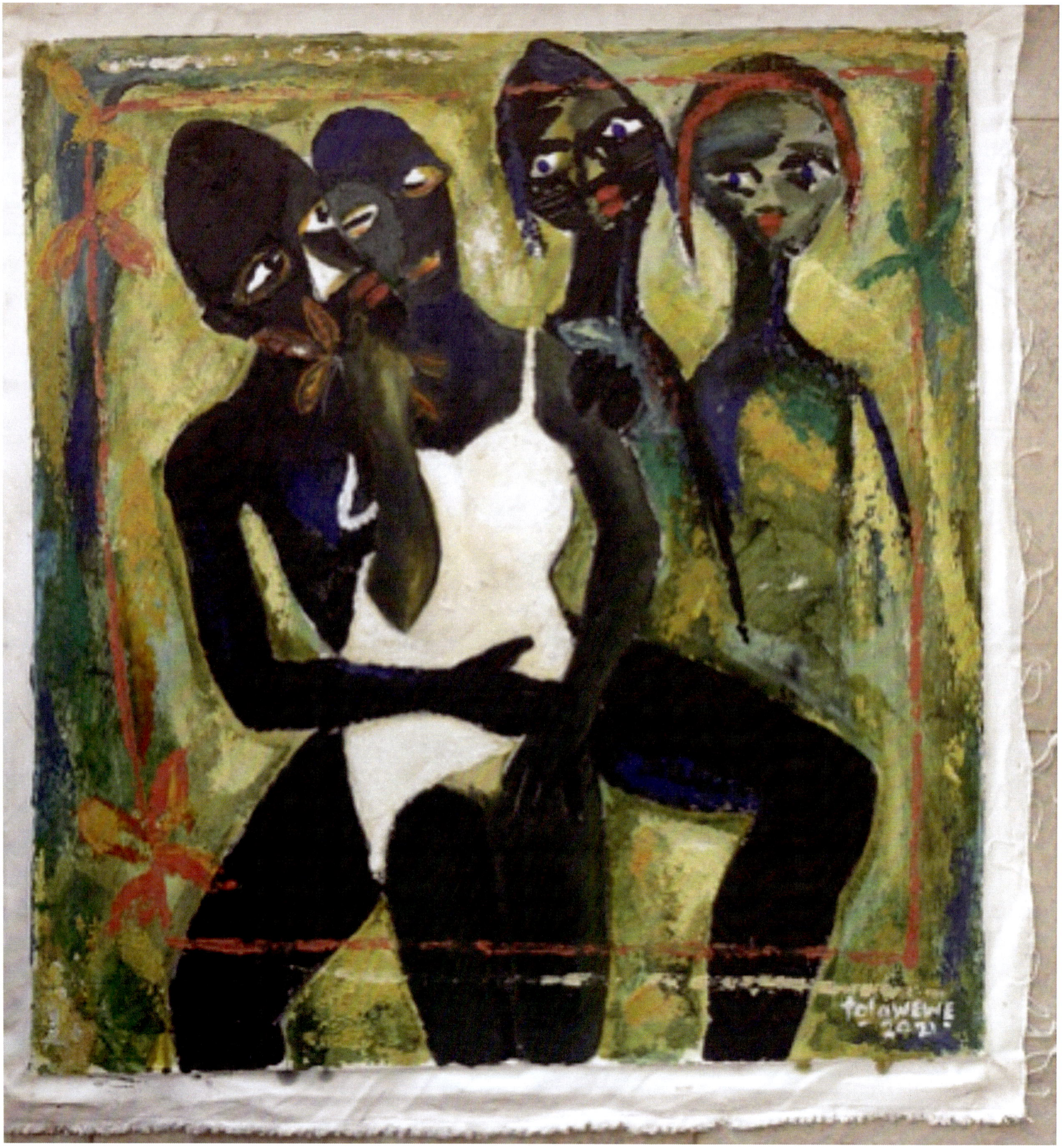

Fig. 35: *Seven Songs*, Acrylic on canvas

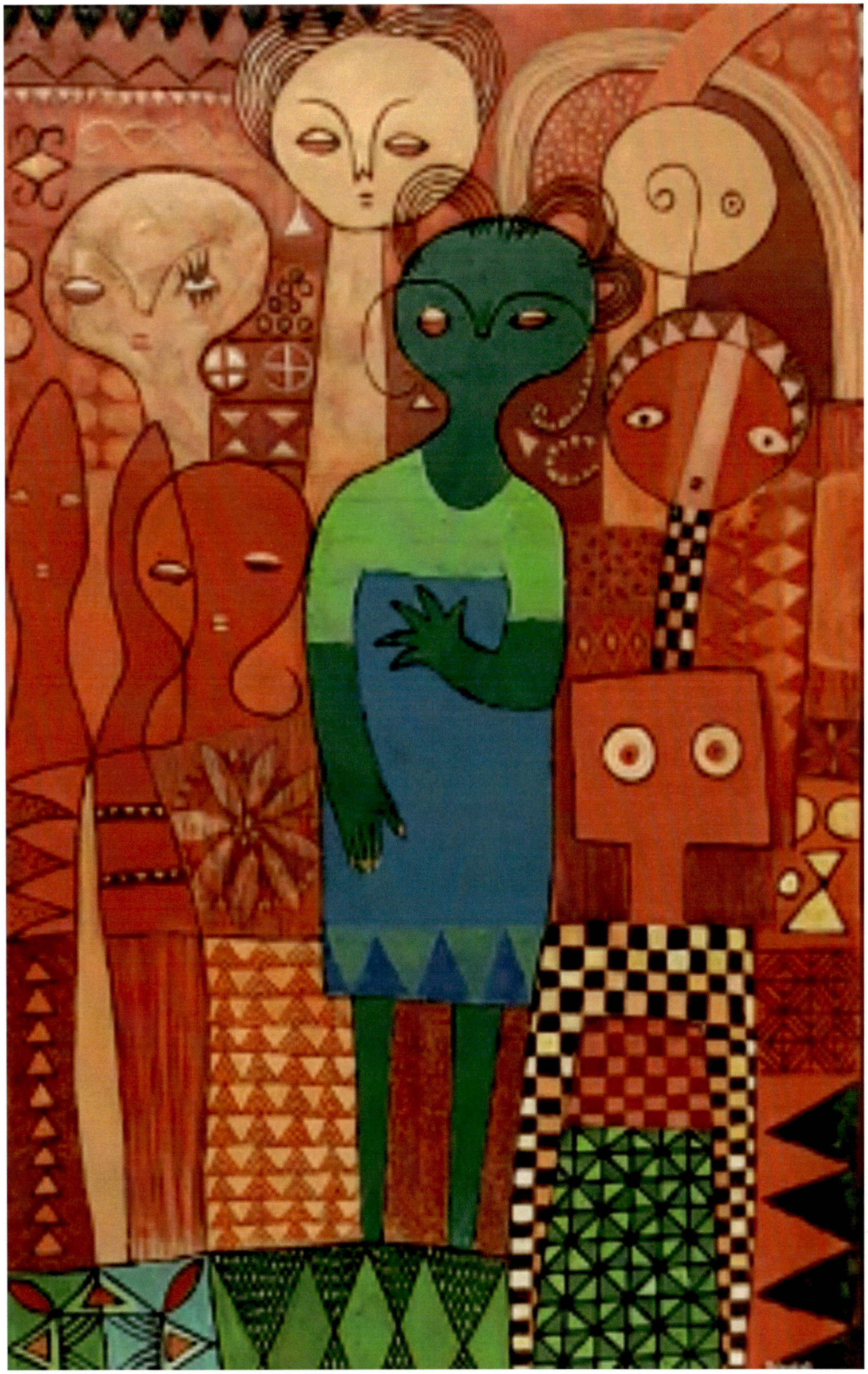

Fig. 36: *Ìyálóde (The Women Step Forward)*, acrylic on canvas, 2020

for African countries are just rituals and the repeated performance of fake news without verifiable substance. It was within the notion of an independent country constructing the necessary infrastructure of independence that he grew up in the 1960s. He benefitted from the construction of universities in different parts of Nigeria as an important agenda of the emergent nation. He attended and graduated with honors from the University of Ifè (now Obafemi Awolowo University), before proceeding to the University of Ìbàdàn, where he received his Master's degree in African Art History. He thereafter gave two years to traveling around the creeks of his homeland, looking for and avidly photographing the paraphernalia, rituals and performances of the water spirits which flourished in the wetlands. He held discussions with the devotees of the water spirits about their images. He studied the language and music of the water spirits, some performed as enactments in elaborately decked boat floats.

"I absorbed the colors, patterns and rhythms of the water spirits into my consciousness," Wewe says, "and they populate my canvas whenever I paint. They relieve me, take over the paintings and do the pictures for me."

In his 2021 painting, *Seven Songs*, he inscribes the female figure as musical patterns animated by choreography and chromatic lyrics, in which a male figure, in the company of female characters, is playing with gender stereotypes.

"Not all music is blues," he says. "Some are disco. Others are jazz. Some are in fact difficult to characterize, despite what you seem to hear. *Seven Figures* would lure you into easy thinking."

The music inside this painting is from the stammering staccatos of the *Bàtá* talking drum. It is part of a series of paintings in which he highlights the influence of *Bàtá* drumming on some of his compositions. *Bàtá* is dense. It seems to stammer and it repeats its phrasings. And beneath its incoherence, you find scattered colors of □pornographic□ banter. But the Bàtá music talks only to those who already understand its language; thus, it has an unruffled structure of simple sounds with seemingly no meaning. It sounds abstract to those who cannot pick out the text and lyrics from the instrumental. This is the same visual approach that Wewe adopts in the painting, *Seven Songs*, with his iconic explorations of rhythmically broken space and time sequences. (Fig. 35).

Wewe's attitude towards the spirituality of African sculpture and other cultural references is not a Negritude nostalgia for a lost homeland that the generation of Wole Soyinka, Senghor and Enwonwu faced and expressed in their works in alien European lands. Wewe experienced no such separation from the land that the inevitable education in the alien locations of the colonial capitals necessitated for the earlier generation. Wewe is from, of and in the land. His gaze falls on the land directly, and on a people suffering and lacking in the midst of plenty, not under the rule of colonial officers, but under the rot perpetrated by Nigerian politicians in conjunction with military and civilian government officials. The large masses of the people build their own social structures as survivors of systemic pressure from local and global exploitations. Already built into the body of the gender relations, the imbalance between the male and female interaction is stressed by an unequal power structure promoting patriarchy. (See Fig. 36, *Ìyálóde*)

He saw closely and in clarity the system of corruption and ineptitude that leads to the victimization of the weakest – the women, especially the unmarried young lady, the elderly women and very young girls. He experienced firsthand the commodification and merchandizing of the female body, as his old mother and little niece were kidnapped and held for ransom for over two weeks of chaotic negotiations with bandits and terrorists. He marked the recovery of his mother and niece from the outlaws in the form of a series of paintings showing a woman riding home in triumph on horseback. His vision of women as the target of terror, violence and deprivation has found expression in his paintings, with women as the dominant themes of his compositions.

The women in Wewe's work are not the mythical ideological Black female figures with serpentine twists found in Ben Enwonwu's Negritude women. The women in Wewe's work are people he has actually met in real life or in his dreams, people living the daily history of his motherland and the struggles of his biological mother, or those fermented in the torments and pleasure of his vision. The female figure in Wewe's work is a statement about his hometown Shabome as much as it is about Nigeria. If she is sensuous, so is his nation. If shown as forlorn or fortunate, these are the realities of the struggling country, with the women bearing the brunt of the grunt.

If not to Negritude, to what philosophical orientation then does Wewe lean for his creative lifts? Fela's music provides another window into Wewe's work: *Ayàkàtà!* The moment of Wewe's emergence from Covid-19 lockdown is likened to the moment Fela was released from prison by another military dictator, after he was jailed by a different military dictator, who regarded Fela as a loud-mouthed artist who needed to be kept quiet for the good of everybody.
In "*Beast of No Nation*," the song Fela released after being incarcerated for nearly two years, Fela complained that people were bothering him with questions about his incarceration – "Dem dey worry me," Fela repeated over and over, turning it into the chorus of a long passage in this monumental song. It was also in this song that he released the essence of his music as "*Áyàkàtà*!." It is in this sense of *Ayàkàtà*! that one must understand the music of Fela as an ideological statement of victory against oppression. If you hit them hard enough with music, they will fall down and flip over – *Ayàkàtà* – in disarray, chaos, dismay and defeat.

It is with this *Ayàkàtà*! aesthetics of hitting and defeating the negative energies, viruses and spirits in the Covid-19 and other toxic aspects of life that Wewe has positioned his new works. The realization of his purpose became clear to him after the Covid-19 lockdown. He has been hitting pretty hard against the aesthetic standards of the canon throughout his career. The results have been rewarding and challenging at the same time. In *Silence I*, 2021, (Fig. 37) he looks back.

Wewe, in this work, recalls the deafening silence of the period of the Covid-19

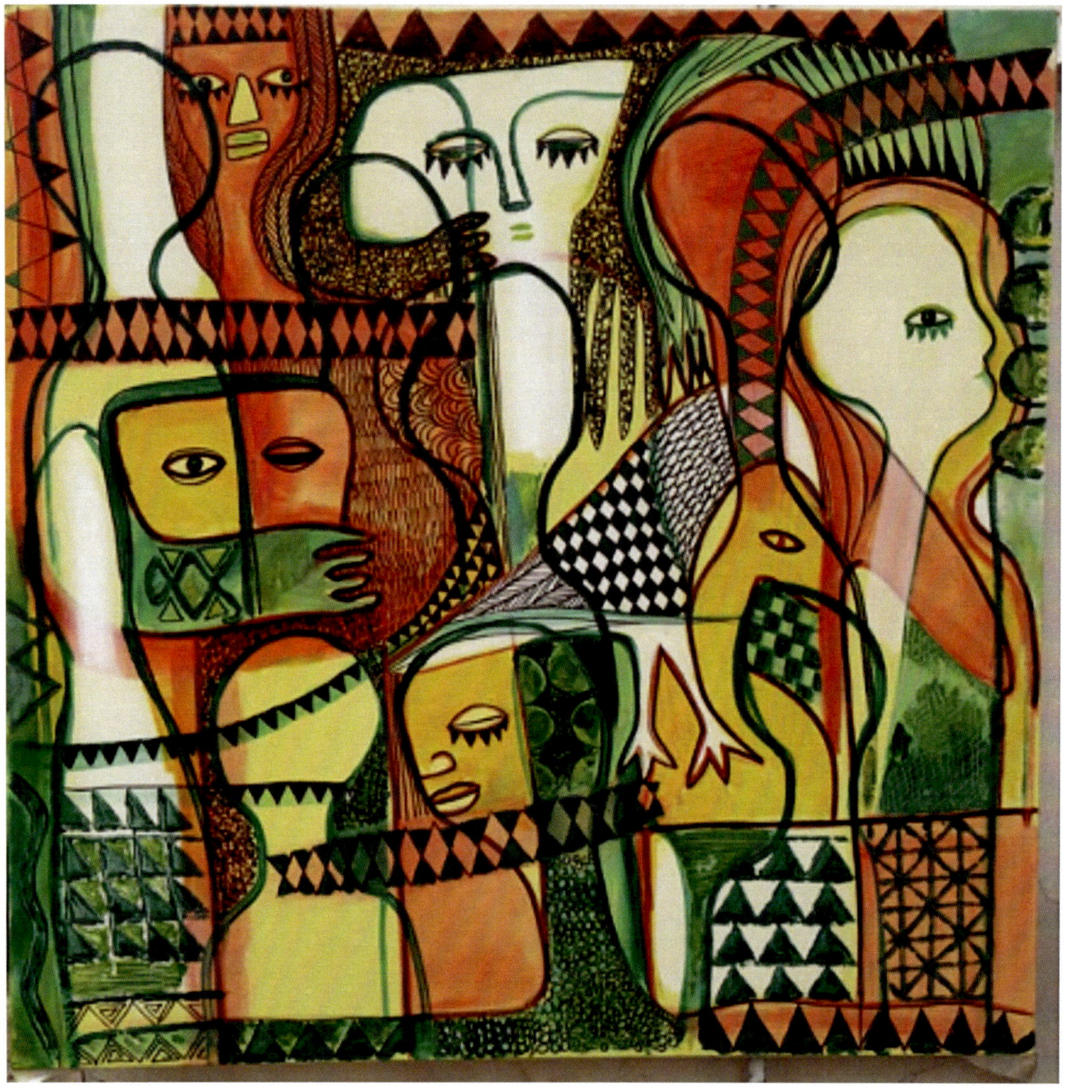

Figure 37: *Silence I*, acrylic on canvas, 2021

lockdown in Nigeria. Nothing seemed to move or speak. As he listened daily to the audio of his city, the voices of the birds subtly overcame the voices of people; more and more, the sounds of insects, rodents and reptiles became audible. The power of *Silence* lies in its visualization of life as a study in contradiction: it is a deafening silence. The contradiction in the painting stems from its use of contrasting complementary colors of greens and reds, embedded in the neutral tones of white highlights and deep dark resonances.

In legal terms, it is a document that enjoins the viewer with the right to remain silent – as a tactic of interrogating the probing eyes. The mouth may remain silent, but never the mind, never the spirit, even when a subject is asleep. The dialogue that a sleeping mind conducts with invisible forces is silent yet sufficiently articulate to sustain a dream, which transports the body out of the immediate environment to climes beyond the reach of the physical plane – out of the vulnerability of pandemic afflictions like the Covid.

To the viewer confronting the questions within the composition, the answers may proceed along the strategies of "Silence is the best answer for a fool." The fellow who is silent is a potential sage: only the breaking of that silence exposes the fool or the sage in that silent fellow.

On the other hand, the Yoruba have a proverb: "*Àìlè lanu sọ̀rọ̀ ni ìbẹ̀rẹ̀ orí burúkú*." (The inability to speak with one's mouth is the beginning of misfortune) The paradigm therefore persists: to speak or not to speak. That is the question that emanates from a Shakespearean dictum: "To speak is to be; not to speak is the negation of being and the beginning of not being."

Silence is the punctuation mark between words that makes speaking audible.

Silence is also the background color of all music. It is in a silent space that a clear musical note can be played or recorded without distortion.

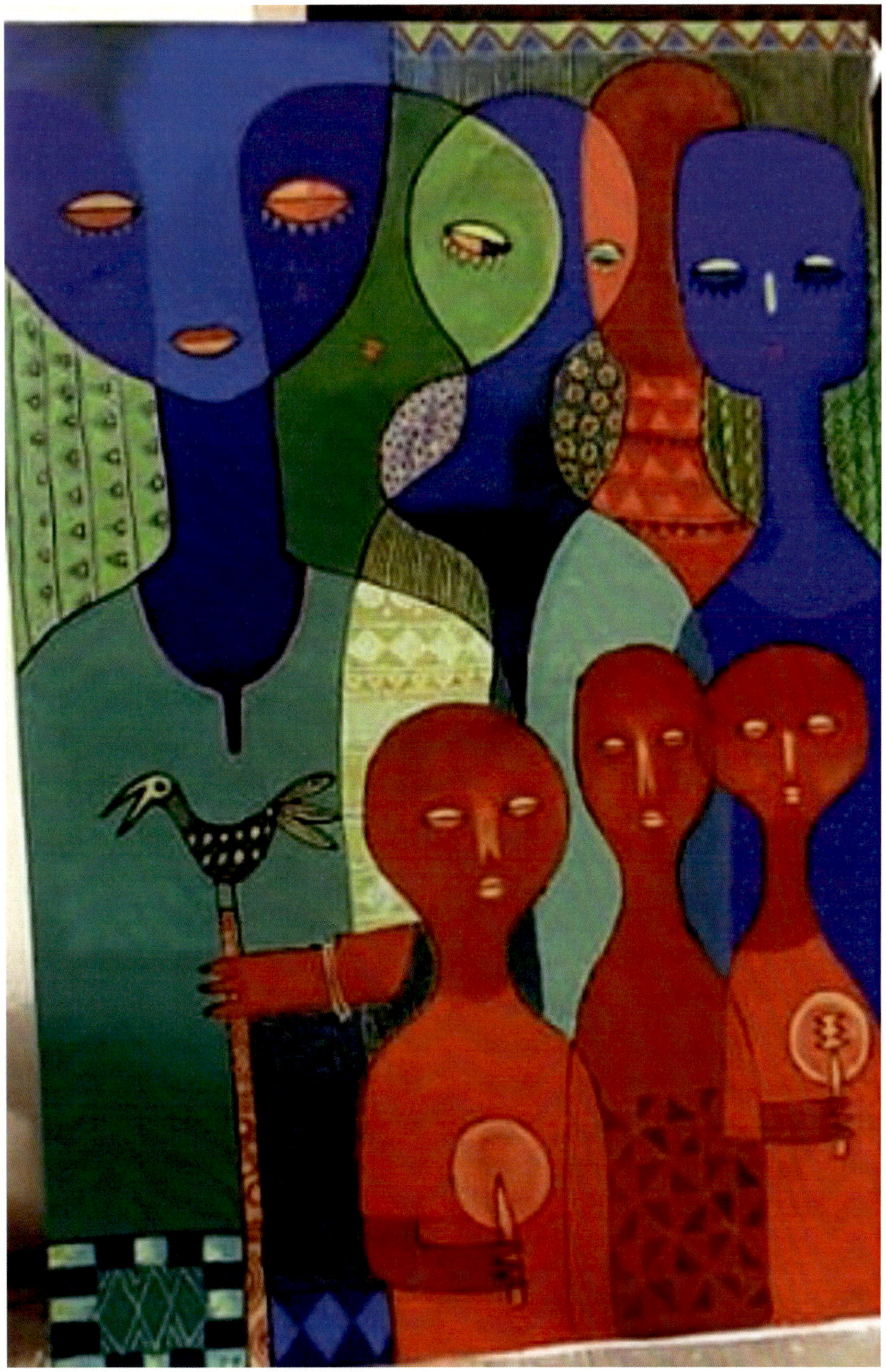

Fig. 38: *Silence II*, acrylic on canvas, 2021

Wewe has built two paintings, *Silence I* and *II*, using a birdlike character as the agent of silence in a deafening market where wheelers and dealers are buying and selling without uttering a sound. (Figure 38). The silence of a market, however, is a dangerous omen: when a market is silent, it is about to explode.

"When an entire people are silent, one must be very careful" he says. "The silence in our land today is the deafening silence of a market where people are buying and selling things, but not speaking to one another."

In 2021, he held an exhibition at the Nimbus Gallery, Virginia, containing paintings that he produced during the Covid 19 shutdown in Nigeria. In the exhibition, Wewe's attention is directed toward the healing of the body and the mind. The paintings he selected for the show, with the curatorial assistance of Chike Nwagbogu, are visual journeys into the forests where he has plucked various blends of leaves, barks, seeds and roots and transformed their ingredients into optical signs on canvas, whilst retaining the therapeutic values of the natural components. Is it "abstract" painting, after all? Is it a song without lyrics? Or more a situation of instrumentals whose very articulation spells out the lyrics in different meanings to different ears, through the eyes and nose-poking curiosity? Wewe smiled, his eyes ablaze with excitement and passion. He didn't answer the question. He seemed provoked beyond words.

When he does that, he wants to paint another work to explain what he means, and wants to be left alone in the studio to work with his water spirits.

CHAPTER TEN:

Departure and Return

"Please could you find out how much it will cost me to extend my stay in Austin," Wewe said. "I'm not ready to leave yet."
"You have gotten a lot done," I replied. "Fifteen large paintings in thirty-two days. And couple of small ones."
"Exactly what I mean," he responded. "We didn't go out to enjoy any of the night clubs you mentioned. We just worked all day and all night. I need to take some time to relax. Maybe just one more week. We can travel and see the state. Or something. Maybe even just stay in Austin and visit the nightclubs; party a little."

"Okay," I said. "Let me get online and see what the ticket change will cost. One week extension, you said?"
He nodded.
"American Airline, right?"
He nodded again. "I sent you the itinerary by email, now. Just check."
I checked and found his tickets. I searched and came up with an evening flight.
"It will cost you two hundred and seventy-five dollars to change your ticket. Should I book it?"

"Yes,' he answered. "Use your credit card. I'll give you cash."

I booked the flight, printed his new itinerary and handed it to him.
Thanking me, he went to the fridge to get himself a bottle of beer. He looked down at the bottle and then changed his mind. "We hardly touched this liquor," he said.
He was referring to a cocktail that he had prepared with some nuts he called "Wonder kola." He had cut the nuts into small pieces and soaked them in some strong liquor we got from the grocery. It was a strong mixture; after taking shot of it, I had decided I would not be having too much of it.
He grabbed a cup, poured himself a generous portion and drank it up straight. Then he poured another which I also gulped straight down as he handed it over to me.

He grabbed some chicken from the fridge, microwaved it and carried the entire cocktail bottle to the sofa along with the bowl of chicken. He settled down and began to drink.

"My week-long holiday begins now."

He had barely finished the first glass of his liquor when he drifted off to sleep, snoring loudly. After a while, he started talking incoherently in his sleep.

XXXX
When the kidnappers arrived Shabomi, the night was an endless pool of black ink. Beating light patters on the dark surface of the waterbed, the rain drizzled continuously as the seven kidnappers tied

"They sought the empowerment of the poor peoples of the Niger Delta, in the impoverished and neglected parts of Nigeria, from which the country taps its oil wealth"

their motorboat to a natural dock on the creek, after a totally uneventful landing. "All clear," Sergeant, the leader, whispered the pre-agreed signal that it was safe to leave vessel. As far as Sergeant could tell, there was no one in sight. But the night was not quiet. The sounds of marine insects and other amphibian creatures added invisible layers of colors and textures to the darkness of the night. Just before dusk, fishermen from the village had sailed far into the Atlantic to set their fishing nets. They were not expected back until dawn, when they would return with their catches in time for the morning fish market.

Because their eyes were used to the darkness, the kidnappers could make out the various dug-out canoes docked at the small Shabomi port. One of the canoes was motorized. Like a cricket negotiating its way through the thickets, the men of the underworld moved briskly as they picked up their AK-47 from their vessel. Each kidnapper carried an automatic rifle, an axe, in addition to a highly polished and deadly sharp machete hanging from a scabbard tied to the waist. Sergeant crossed himself. Bringing his palms together, he whispered a quick prayer. His fellow kidnappers did the same. With Sergeant leading from the back, they began their swagger through the village, on their way to Madam Wewe's villa.

They knew exactly where to go and how to get there. These were professionals who also doubled as agents of political freedom fighters. They sought the empowerment of the poor peoples of the Niger Delta, in the impoverished and neglected parts of Nigeria, from which the country taps its oil wealth. Sergeant had cut his teeth kidnapping expatriate oil workers employed by the multinational oil companies. Violence was the only game he understood. This operation had several purposes; an opportunity to raise money for their cause being just one of them. He knew that some of his colleagues were in the business mainly for the financial benefits. But he also knew that a good number were dedicated freedom fighters. To his surprise, he has also since learned that some of his colleagues killed for the sheer love of violence

But he never killed for pleasure. He killed when it was absolutely necessary. He took pride in himself as one who understands the art of brutality and who has mastered the subtlety of this art. Sergeant was afraid of no mortal. He kept his eyes on his goal and he has never failed. He believed that God was on the side of the poor and saw himself as the embodiment of the poor and downtrodden. He worked hard, and believed in God. He paid meticulous attention to detail, and believed that God protected him even though he worked in the underworld.

Together with two of his boys, he had visited the village several times before this night of the operation to map out the terrain. Madam Wewe's house was right in the middle of Shabomi. A mansion that stood out from the rest of the town, the building had an imposing presence among the small bungalows that stretch over a landscape of about one kilometer, before merging almost seamlessly with the sea. A few buildings constructed on stilts stool elegantly on the water line.

Sergeant's father is from the Kwale ethnic group in the Niger Delta. His mother is Yoruba, from Ògbómòsó. He has a good ear for languages and speaks a wide variety of them: Edo, Ishan, Tshekiri, Igbo, Isoko in addition to his Kwale and Yoruba. He joined the freedom fighters soon after dropping out of the University of Port Harcourt. He had been rusticated by the university authorities for participating in banned cult activities on campus. In one of the cult initiation ceremonies, a freshman had died of alcohol overdose. One of the students involved was the only son of an influential judge in Lagos, so the police could not press murder charges on the students. A prosecutor had suggested that they could heap all the blame on Sergeant given his poor background. Nobody would defend him and he could take the punishment for the murder on behalf of the rest. In the end though, they decided not to prosecute anyone. It was too risky; the press might complicate things by raising issues of preferential treatment and partiality.

The university was not so lenient or scared. All the twenty-six members of the cult were expelled from the University.

Sergeant soon learned that many of his cult colleagues expelled from the school with him were very soon attending foreign Universities, sponsored to travel abroad by their wealthy parents. He realized how unfair life could be. He had nowhere, no home to which to return. His father, a fisherman, had died in a canoe accident when he was only three. His mother ran a small vegetables and fruits stall in the market to struggle to give him an education. She invested everything she had on him, all her dreams, desires and energy, with the hope that he would complete his university education, get a great job, and make life a little better for her. She had been singing that song in his ears ever since he could understand language. She wanted him to be a lawyer.

He was only seventeen when he was admitted to the university to study law. During his first year in school, he began to develop a pessimistic attitude toward life. The lavish and corrupt lifestyle of the politicians, businessmen and other prominent people in public life gave him a revulsion against elite society. He realized that his mother's dream might not be realistic. Thousands of university graduates roamed the streets without employment. Thousands of lawyers were jobless. It was very difficult to succeed in the legal field in Nigeria without some law pedigree or

one form of connection or the other to privileged cambers. His father was not a lawyer and he knew nobody in the law world. His chances for success, he decided, were rather slim and grim.
He began to develop a deep resentment against his fellow law students whose parents were lawyers or who came from rich and prominent families with the proper connections. At some point, he hated them so much that in the attempt to avoid having contact with them, he began to avoid lectures. His GPA fell from 4.03 points to 2.42. This was when an acquaintance told him of the new fraternity that was suddenly on the verge of becoming the most powerful student underground cult on campus.

"The difference with us is that we are political," said his friend. "We are leftists who want to change the world for the better. The rich are getting richer and the poor are getting poorer. There is corruption in the heart of politicians. I don't have to go into details. You know what I mean. Our fraternity seeks social justice."

This cult was the perfect place for Sergeant, who was looking for something concrete and convincing like this underground association to attach himself to, something rebellious, energetic and articulate, a meeting point for like minds that wanted to change the world.
After he joined the cult, he soon discovered that most of what they did was mainly getting drunk on alcohol and getting high on marijuana. This lifestyle did not mix well with studying at the university. His GPA fell below 2:00, which was the probationary point. It was the semester in which he was trying to return to redeem his crashed GPA that the fraternity held an initiation party for a new set of freshmen recruits. It was during this initiation party that the fresh faced lanky and introverted new student died after consuming two fair-sized bottles of brandy, in a drinking competition. The poor boy went into a coma from which he never recovered. He expired from alcohol poisoning.

The university authorities immediately brought in the police; the party and the tragedy occurred on university premises. A separate body of inquiry of the university investigated the circumstances leading to the death. The recommendation of the body was that the fraternity be banned and all the executives of the fraternity be expelled from the university. As the assistant scribe of the fraternity, he was expelled.

He knew he could not return home to his mother and confront her with such a story. It would simply kill her. He left his hostel and moved into the streets, where he got himself involved with yet another group of drinkers and weed smokers. He found employment as a construction worker and shared a rented room in a "face-me-I-face-you" house with a colleague from the same construction company. It was a foreign oil subsidiary prospecting for crude oil and gas in the expansive fields of the Niger Delta.

His roommate, Godfrey, was born and raised in a fishing village that slowly succumbed to so much environmental oil pollution that all the marine life disappeared. He was also an agent that recruited into the anti-government organizations that were forming to bring attention to the plight of the people from the oil-producing regions of Nigeria.

Sergeant was an easy target for recruitment for Godfrey, who worked as a carpenter in the construction company, but who took serious his task as the recruitment captain of the underground group, Rivers Resistant Front. The construction company was a fertile ground for recruitment. It was packed with young and restless men, who felt somewhat excluded, dying unnoticed, screened-out at the edge of society, looking in from the outside, at the overflowing banquet tables of the rich; young men who could not envision themselves at these tables, workers who did physical labor on a daily basis and still lived below the poverty line, despite their unrelenting, back breaking, hard, manual, labor.
Every weekend, instead of going to church, Sergeant—who was at that time known as Chris—always sailed with Godfrey to isolated creeks in the Atlantic mangrove forests, for paramilitary training in insurgency. They knew the entire delta region like the back of their palms, as they sailed in and out of the waters in speedboats and canoes.

The underground organization mapped the entire space into military zones, each unit under different FMs or field marshals. Ten FMs came under the command of a commandant, all of whom were gathered under the control of the CG or commandant general. Nobody knew the CG nor many in the rest of the organization. One mostly knew only a couple of other people and one's own location in the general landscape of activities and structures.

The basic vision of the organization was to disrupt the effective function of the country, using any possible device or contraption. They usually attacked oil rigs, oil pipes and oil installations, but from time to time they kidnapped expatriate oil workers for ransom money to run their organization. His operations always took place at night and he often worked with six other young men, who like him, spoke a wide variety of languages from this region. The lingua franca was pidgin English.

Kidnapping was their most risky and sensitive activity; it was also the most lucrative aspect of their organization. They needed funds for ammunition, transportation, food, and allowances for the insurgents. The groups always planned meticulous kidnapping strategies, working hard on the details to ensure complete success. They gave training in discipline, endurance and ideology to new recruits, who rise from privates to the post of sergeant as NCO; and after commissioning, from the post of Lieutenant to FM. To be commissioned, a sergeant must lead a successful ransom operation to raise no less than fifty million naira.

That night, as he led his team of seven men, he was under consideration for a commission. If he could bring in seventy-five million naira at a swoop, he would be commissioned as a colonel. This Wewe matriarch might be the perfect opportunity for such a leap commission. He therefore picked his team carefully from the list of fighters in his zone.

Gideon was Sergeant's first pick. A twenty-three year-old welder, whose father, a former blacksmith, still lived in the creeks near Sapele, Gideon was built with a strange physique—his powerful arms were abnormally long, while his legs were non-proportionally short. He looked like a cross between a human and a gorilla. A stammerer, Gideon hardly talked to anyone. He was a dedicated metalworker, who had inherited his father's skills and his genes of passion, dedication and hard work. His handicapped father had been severely wounded during the Biafran war.

Popularly called Ogum, Gideon's father was one of the master craftsmen recruited by the Biafran army to develop weapons for the secessionist metals workshop in Awka. Ogum had a natural penchant for metals. He developed several automatic weapons, including a highly effective rapid-fire rifle that was cheap to construct, yet absolutely deadly. Ogum was working on an explosive device for use as a rocket launcher when the contraption accidentally detonated; blowing off both of his legs and his right hand. Everyone thought Ogum was as good as dead, especially given the scarcity of medical facilities and drugs in the experimental metals workshop during the war. Miraculously, Ogum survived, although he only received a shot of some painkiller and a couple of penicillin injections to prevent infection.

After the war, Ogum was pretty much useless at any job and totally dependent on his wife who fished in the creeks, and planted vegetables on a small piece of land. To subsidize the family income, Ogum began to peddle home-distilled liquor and weed among the young timber workers. These fellows were log fellers and laborers who migrated from camp to camp in pursuit of giant trees; they used the alcohol and the weed to steel themselves for the hard labor in the cold and treacherous waters, infested with crocodiles, and a limitless number of deadly water snakes.

Gideon's mother, a robust woman with an easy smile, had been dismissed as barren. Suddenly, after everyone had given up on her ability to bear a child, she became pregnant in her late forties. Gideon was the miracle child, staying an extra month in the womb. With the circumstances surrounding his birth, it was only natural that his parents would spoil him. His mother doted on him. He could hardly read or write. He had barely started primary school when his mother withdrew him, following an unfortunate incident: someone stole the teacher's wallet, and Gideon was the only suspect. Although no one could prove that he actually committed the offence, the headmaster of the local primary school proceeded to ruthlessly cane Gideon to extract a confession and accidentally injured him in the process. A piece of the cane broke and struck Gideon in the left eye, leaving him half-blind in that eye. His one good eye was as sharp as a hawk's talon though. He often shut the bad eye so he could focus properly with the good eye.

When Gideon left school, his father asked him what trade he would like to learn. Fishing was no longer viable in the creeks surrounding their village because of the oil spills from the crude oil extractions in the region. Gideon did not hesitate: he wanted to become a blacksmith. He had listened attentively several times as his father narrated stories about the joy of metalworking, especially of his experiments at Awka during the civil war. Gideon was also a natural with metals. He began to construct household utensils especially kerosene stoves, which he sold to clients in the village. He made perfect castings for forks, spoons, and knives, with decorative embellishments. He continued to do well with his metalwork until one fateful day when the only policeman in the village tarnished the honor of his family.

An alcoholic who drank for free from Gideon's father's liquor store and smoked free weed at his father's house, suddenly pounced on his mother and raped her in one of his drunken blank-outs. To make matters worse, Ogum witnessed the rape but could do nothing to stop it; the rogue cop had locked him up in the store behind the shop. Although everyone in the village knew that the rape occurred, no official charges were pressed against the cop, who was transferred to a neighboring village to prevent any further trouble.

After the rape, his father cried for several days. His mother could not be consoled. Every morning, she seemed unable to get up from bed to face the day. She first suffered a fever, then she developed rheumatism in every joint of her body; shortly thereafter, she began to hallucinate and finally completely lost her mind. Ogum, sitting helpless in his chair, suddenly looked twenty years older than his sixty-two years. He could not bring himself to look anyone in the eye; he felt so ashamed that he was unable to do anything to defend the honor of his wife. "If only I could get off the floor and rise to my feet, I'd strangle the creature with my five remaining fingers," Ogum kept repeating to everyone who came to console him after the rape.

Gideon was sixteen when the rape occurred. There was no doubt in his mind that he had to do something to restore the family honor.

One day, more than nine months after the rape, he took a canoe and rowed to Abiri, the village to which the authorities had transferred the rapist cop. It was easy to locate the cop's residence. The policeman had already gained notoriety as a drunk in his new station and had already raped a fourteen-year-old girl who hawked groundnuts in the village.

Gideon stayed in the canoe till dusk, and then made his way to the cop's house when it was dark. The stars twinkled as he walked briskly toward the cop's house. It was a one-bedroom house, with a dirty windowless sitting room. The only window, at the back of the house, was in the policeman's bedroom. It was open and the drunk cop fast asleep on a chair next to the bed; snoring. Gideon easily climbed into the room through the window and stood before the sleeping man, looking down on him. He decided to wake up the tiny man with a hard slap across the face.

Officer Terror – as he was known – woke up with a choking sound that brought an end to his loud snoring. He thought the young man in front of him was part of the nightmare that nightly tormented his sleep. He was so drunk that he did not know where he was. When a second stinging slap landed across his face, he began to recover his senses and tried to stand up. But he was too drunk, and fell back into the chair. Gideon hit him on the head with a kick that almost removed Terror's tiny head from the neck. Then one vicious kick followed another until Terror's face was completely covered with blood.

But Terror was just too drunk to defend himself, as he crawled around like a toddler on the dirty floor. Blinded by the blood oozing out of his eyes, Terror seemed to be groping for something just beyond his reach, on the only desk in the room. Gideon lifted up the desk with his powerful arms and threw it with all his might at Terror, who was still on his knees. The desk landed with a bone-crushing thud that split open Terror's skull. Terror passed out cold. A pistol hidden under the stack of old pornography magazines fell off the desk and landed on the floor.

Gideon took the gun and aimed it at Terror. He decided not to kill Terror with it. Gideon looked around the room and saw a long knife hanging from a hook on the wall. He seized the knife and grabbed Terror's trousers by the crotch. He was still out cold and did not stir. Gideon unzipped Terror's pants. He noticed that Terror's filthy underwear was soaked through with urine. "Bastard," Gideon hissed, before grabbing Terror's penis, and, with one stroke, severed it entirely. He opened Terror's broken jaw and stuffed the bleeding penis into the immobile cop's mouth.

A kerosene stove sat just outside the bedroom, in what served as Terror's sitting room and kitchen. Gideon grabbed the stove, and poured some of the fuel inside the stove on Terror's head. He doused the mattress on the bed with some more of the kerosene. Then he struck a matchstick that he found in a matchbox near the stove and set the cop's head on fire. He also lit the mattress, which immediately began to burn, giving off a sickly odor. Calmly, he opened the door from the inside and walked unhurriedly out. Everything happened within five minutes. He strolled back toward his canoe and waded into the water. Just before he stepped into his vessel, he heard an old woman who was returning from her fishing trip whisper, "You are coming from the devil's house." They stood together, silent. Almost immediately, as they both watched the shore from the sea, they saw a huge flame engulf Terror's house. "Did you kill him?" she asked. He did not reply, but heaved a sigh of relief and began to paddle his canoe toward his village.

When he arrived at his village, he went to his father. He was in the sitting room, staring vacantly at the wall. "Where is mama?" he asked.
His father gestured with his head to indicate that she was inside, on the bed.

"I have killed Terror," Gideon told Ogum. " I cut off his dick and stuffed it in his mouth."

His mother heard him from the bedroom. She immediately ran out and fell on her knees before him, holding him tight, sobbing.

"But I must go," Gideon continued. "A woman saw me do it. She is certain to tell the authorities and they would come after me."

"You are a man," Ogum said. "You have restored our honor. Do whatever you need to do."

XXX
Wewe woke up with a start. "I had a nightmare," he said. "Can you cancel my ticket, the one you just bought? I'm leaving tomorrow. I'm not waiting any longer."
"Why?"
"These nightmares," he said. "My mother is trying to reach me. I need to go and make some offerings to her."
"What sort of offering?"
"The *Babaláwo* will tell me."

Several months later, Wewe called me from Nigeria and announced to me that he had made the offerings.

"The *Babaláwo* asked me to do two paintings —one to Èsù and the other to herald the return of my mother to *Òrun*. Since I completed them, the nightmares have stopped."

"Excellent. I was worried when you

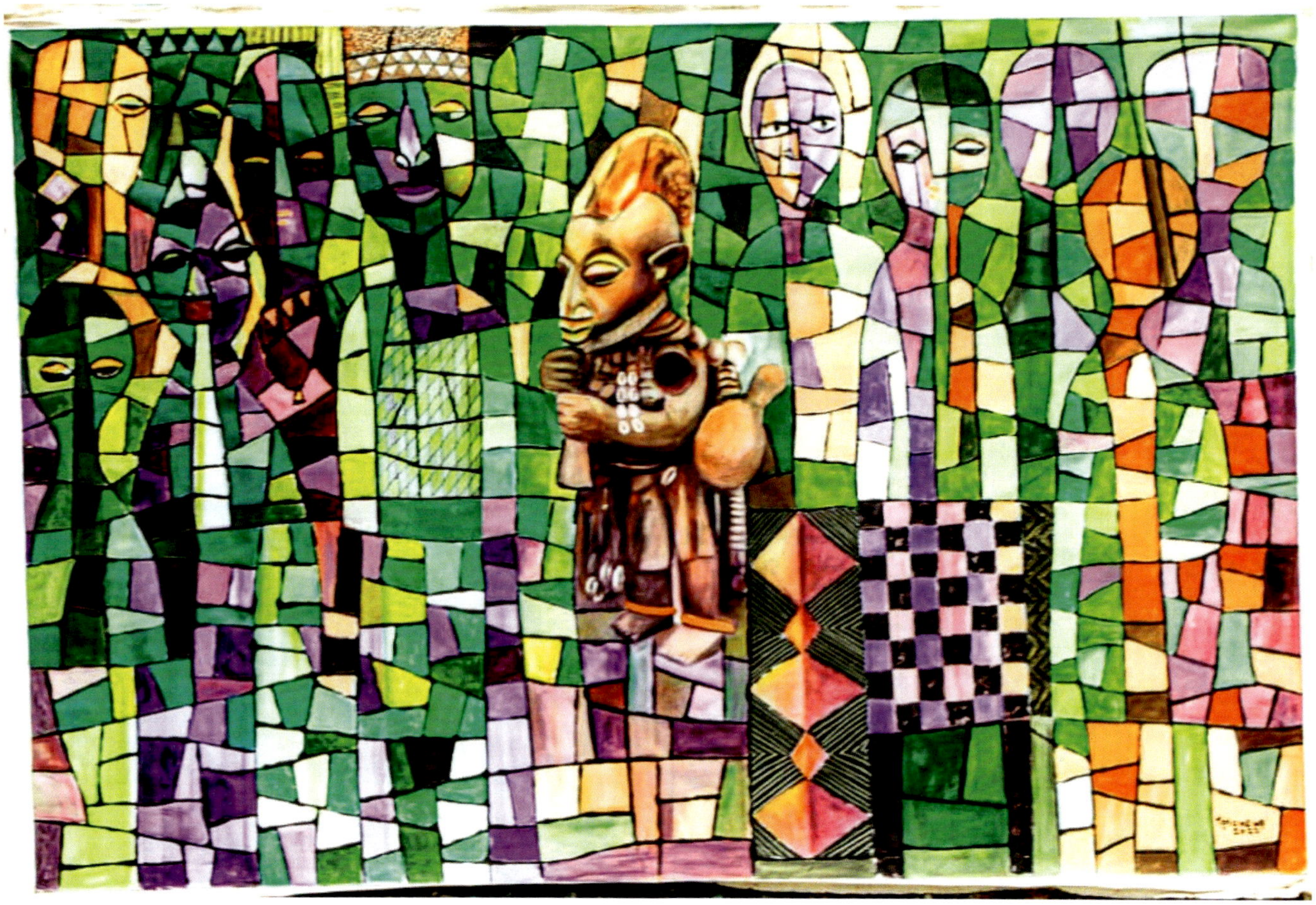

Figure 39: *Saint Èṣù at the Crossroads*, acrylic on canvas, 2022

narrated that last nightmare to me. I am glad they have stopped. Made fascinating story, though. Will you send me the images of the paintings?" I asked.
Moments later, he emailed me the pictures.

"The Èsù painting came to me before the image of my mother," Wewe said. "Èsù prepared the way at the crossroads between *ayé* (the world) and *ọrun* (the source) for Mama to row her canoe through to the other side of life."

In Yoruba metaphysics, Èṣù stands at the crossroads between intersections to bridge the divide or break the connection. Èṣù is predictably unpredictable in Yoruba philosophy; an idea that Wewe conveys in the painting by placing a representation of an Èsù image at the center of the composition. The predictability of Èsù lies in the capacity to support devotees and attack antagonists. When Wewe made the painting, he invited a *Babaláwo* who consulted Ifá to inquire about the challenges facing Wewe at that moment. It was the reference to Èsù that appeared. The Ifá priest chanted the following text of the *Ojú Odù* Ìrẹtẹ̀ Méjì that appeared for Wewe:

I   I
I   I
I I I I
I   I

Ìrẹtẹ̀ méjì.
Tí à n pe ni Èjì ẹlẹ́mẹ̀rẹ̀
Ó ní ká dijú dijú
Ká ṣe bí ẹni tó kú

Ká wẹni tí ó sunkún ẹni
Ká bùrìn, bùrìn, bùrìn
Ká fẹsẹ̀ kọ
Ká wẹni tí ó ṣe ni pẹ̀lẹ́
A dífá fún Ọ̀rúnmìlà
Níjọ́ tí baba ó fikú tan mọ̀lẹ́bí ẹ jẹ.
Ọ̀rúnmìlà òpìtàn, ó ní bí gbogbo ènìyàn ṣe
ń jó lé òun lọtǔn
Tí wọ́n ń yọ̀ mọ́ òun lósì
Òun fẹ́ mọ àwọn tó fẹ́ òun dénu nínú wọn
Òun fẹ́ mọ bí wọ́n ṣe fẹ́ òun dénú sí

Ọ̀rúnmìlà bá gbéra lọ́jọ́ kan
Babá lọ sí inú igbó
Ni ó wá lọ gbé igi arira
Ó gbẹ́ ẹ ní ère
Gẹ́gẹ́ bí èèyàn

Ó wá gbé e sínú ilé
Ó wá da aṣọ funfun bò ó
Ọ̀rúnmìlà wá pe Amósùn
Tí í ṣe ọmọ rẹ̀
Ó ní kó lọ kéde pé

Babá mà ti papòdà o
Sí gbogbo àwọn mọ̀lẹ́bí òun
Ọ̀rúnmìlà wá gun òkè àjà lọ
Láti lè mọ gbogbo ohun tó ń ṣẹlẹ̀.
Ni Amósùn bá dé ọ̀dọ̀ Ògún

Ó ní baba òun ló sùn ní àná
Tí kò jí ní àárọ̀ yǐ o
Ó ní kí Ògún wá bá àwọn mú aṣọ kúrò ní ojú u rẹ̀
Àti bí àwọn yíò ṣe ṣe ètò ilẹ̀ gbígbẹ́
Nítorí ìwọ Ògún

Ìwọ ni o nirin.
Ògún ní "Á à; Ọ̀rúnmìlà tí kú."
Ó ní Ọlọ́run ló mú u.
Ògún ní kí òun tó lè jáde nínú ilé
Ó ní òun yíò gba igba ajá

Ni Amósùn bá gbéra lọ sí ọ̀dọ̀ Ṣàngó.
Ó kó ẹjọ́ ó rò;
Gbogbo ohun tí ojú òún rí.
Sàngó ní kí òun tó lè jáde rárá
Òun ní láti gba igba àgbò

Ni Amósùn bá kúrò níbẹ̀
Ó gba ọ̀dọ̀ Ọ̀ṣun Oníbú ọlà lọ.
Amósùn dé ọ̀dọ̀ Ọ̀ṣun
Ó ní ohun báyìí, báyìí, báyìí,
Ni ó mà ṣe baba òun

Àsùnmọ̀jú òní ni babá mà papòdà o
Ó ku bí wọn ó ṣe wá palẹ̀ òkú mọ́.
Ọ̀ṣun ní igba àgbébọ̀ adìyẹ ni òún ó gbà
Bí wọ́n bá fẹ rí ẹsẹ̀ òun níta
Ó ní gàlè-gàlè Ọrúnmìla gan-an tiẹ̀ pọ̀

Yíò máa ṣe bí ẹni wípé
Òun nìkan ló wà nílé ayé.
Amósùn dọ̀dọ̀ Ọ̀sanyìn
Ọ̀sanyìn ná à sọ tiẹ̀
Amósùn gbéra ó dọ̀dọ̀ Ọbàtálá,

Ọbataàsà, Ọba takun-takun lóde Ọ̀rànjé
Amósùn kẹ́jọ́ ó rò fún un.
Ọbàtálá ní òun gan-an ni òún pa á!
Ó ní àkú-tún-kú ù rẹ lọ́nà ọrun.
Ó ní òun ti mọ̀ pé kò ní sàìkú láìpẹ́:

Ẹ̀dá ò lè má a ṣe gàlè-gàlè bẹ̀ẹ̀yẹn kó jayé pẹ́
Ó ní òun á gba igba ìgbín láì dín ẹyọ kan.
Ká mọ́ déènà penu
Amosùn tọ ọ̀dọ̀ gbogbo àwọn mọ̀lẹ́bí Ọ̀rúnmìlà lọ.
Gbogbo ohun tí kálukú sì ń sọ pátápátá

Gbogbo rẹ̀ ni Ọ̀rúnmìlà ń gbọ́ lókè àjà
Gbogbo ọ̀rọ̀ tí wọ́n sọ lókè odò
Letí ọmọ ẹyẹ ń gbọ́
Òhun ni Ọ̀rúnmila fi ọ̀rọ̀ náà ṣe.
Nígbàtí Amósùn wá fẹ́ má a bọ̀ padà wálé
Amósun wá ránti pé
Ó mà sì ku ẹnìkan tí wọ́n ń pè ní Èṣù u!
Àmọ́, ṣé ó yẹ kí òun tiẹ̀ yọjú sí Èṣù rárá?
Ẹni tí ó jẹ́ wípé ọ̀dájú ni.
Tí ó jẹ́ wípé ojú aláìda ni wọ́n fi ń wo Èṣù;

Ẹni tí gbogbo arayé kà sí ìkà.
Ó bá ni kí òun tiẹ̀ gbéra kí òun dé ọ̀dọ̀ Èṣù
Kí wọn má wípé òun ò ka Èṣù kún ǹkankan
Ìgbà tí yíò dé ọ̀dọ̀ Èṣù ńkọ́?
Iwájú ìta ló bá Èṣù

Bí ó ti rí Amósùn tí Amósùn ń bọ̀
Tí ó rí i wípé ojú Amósùn kọ́rẹ́ lọ́wọ́
Ó ní, "Amósùn ṣe kò sí ǹkan?
Kí ló ha dé?"
Mímú ẹnu tí Amósùn mú ẹnu lé ọ̀rọ̀

Wípé "Ọ̀rúnmìla ni...."
Èṣù ní kí ni ó ṣe é?
Amósùn ní "Baba ni ó sùn lánǎ
Tí kò jí, tó papòdà."
Kí Amósùn tó sọ ọ̀rọ̀ délẹ̀

Ni Èṣù ti gbé ara sókè bí ẹ̀ẹ̀mẹ́fà, bí ẹ̀ẹ̀meje
Tí Èṣù ti na ara rẹ̀ mọ́lẹ̀.
Bí Èṣù ti ń fi ojú ọ̀tún sunkún
Ni ó ń fi ti òsì sun ẹ̀jẹ̀
Kí á tó wí, kí á tó fọ̀

Kí Amósùn ó tó o délé
Èṣù ti ṣáájú Amósùn délé Ọ̀rúnmìlà.
Dídé tí Èṣù dé inú ilé Ọrúnmìlà
Ní gbàgede ni ó ti rí aṣọ funfun
Tí wọ́n dà bo ère mọ́lẹ̀

Èṣù rò pe òkú Ọ̀rúnmìlà ló wà níbẹ̀
Ó kérora, ó ní "Háà, ìwọ Ọ̀rúnmìlà tó ń tún ilé ayé ṣe
O ò gbọdọ̀ kú báyìí rárá
Bí ó ṣe gbé ara lẹ̀ sókè
Pé kó na ara rẹ̀ mọ́lẹ̀

Ni Ọ̀rúnmìlà bá sọ̀kálẹ̀ lókè àjà
Ni Èṣù bá ta kìjí
Ni Ọrúnmìlà bá gbá a mú
Ó ní kí ó fi ọkàn balẹ̀
Ọrúnmìlà ní òun ò kú.

Ó ní èése mọ̀ ó se
Ó ní ká dijú dijú
Ká ṣe bí ẹni tó kú
Ká wẹni tí ó sunkún ẹni
Ká bùrìn, bùrìn, bùrìn

Ká fẹsẹ̀ kọ
Ká wẹni tí ó ṣe ni pẹ̀lẹ́
A dífá fún Ọ̀rúnmìlà
Níjọ́ tí baba ó fikú tan mọ̀lẹ́bí ẹ jẹ.
Síbẹ̀ síbẹ̀, Èṣù ò gbàgbọ́ ná à

Ọ̀rúnmìlà wá á gbá a mú
Ó ní kí Èṣù sí aṣọ kúrò lóju ǹkan tí ḿ bẹ nílẹ̀.
Ṣíṣí tí Èṣù sí aṣọ
Ni ó rí i pé igi ni ó wà ḿbẹ̀
Ni Èṣù bá jókǒ kalẹ̀

Ọ̀rúnmìlà bá ṣàlàyé wípé òun ni òún dá ọgbọ́n bẹ́ ẹ̀
Pé bí gbogbo ayé ṣe ń yé òun sí lọ́tǔn
Tí wọ́n ń yé òun sí lósì
Òun fẹ́ mọ ẹni tó fẹ́ òun dénú
Ni òun ṣe wípé kí wọn lọ kéde òkú òun
Ìwọ Èṣù tí a kà sí ẹni ibi tẹ́lẹ̀
Àṣé o kì í ṣẹni ibi
Àṣe ìwọ gan an ni o fẹ́ òun dénú dénú
Ọ̀rúnmìlà wá ní láti òní lọ
Ó ní òkèlè àkọ́bù omo awo

Ni wọ́n gbọ́dọ̀ kọ́kọ́ fún ìwọ Èṣù
Ó ní ẹlẹ̀ẹkejì
Ibi tí òun Ọ̀rúnmìlà bá ti wà nínú ilé
Kí ìwọ Èṣù má a wà ní ẹ̀hìnkùnlé
Kí o má jìnnà sí òun.

Òkèlè àkọ́bù awo
Kí wọn ó má a fi ti Èṣù fún Èṣù
Kí ó tó di pé awo tó lè ṣe ǹkankan o
Kí wọn ó má a fi ìbà fún Èṣù
Kí ìwọ Èṣù kọ́kọ́ má a jẹun.

Kí o kọ́kọ́ má a yó
Kí ó tó di pé òún jẹun
Kí ó tó di pé òun mu
Ni Èṣù bá bẹ̀rẹ̀ sí ní dúpẹ́
Ni Ọ̀rúnmìlà bá ṣí aṣọ kúrò lórí ère

Ni wọ́n rí i wípé igi arira ni
Ijó ní ń jo
Ayọ̀ ní ń yọ̀.
Ó fohùn sókè ó fi dígbe
Ó ń kọrin bí ẹní kIfá

Ó ń kIfá bí ẹni ń kọrin
Ó ń ṣe:
"Ẹkún igi arira lẹ̀ ń sun ò
Ẹkún igi arira lè ń sun;
Ọ̀rúnmìlà òpìtàn tẹ̀ ló kú
Kò mà tiẹ̀ kú mọ́
Ẹkún igi arira lẹ̀ ń sun.

Irete Meji
Also known as Eji elemere
It says we should close our eyes
And pretend to be dead

To see who will mourn our death
We should keep walking
And dash our toes against a rock
To see who cares we got hurt
They cast Ifá for Ọ̀rúnmìlà

When the patriarch pretended to his relatives that he was dead
Òrúnmìlà, storyteller, noticed that multitudes of people celebrated him on the right
And numerous others hailed him on the left
Yet he wanted to know those who truly loved him among them
He wanted to know the depth of their love for him.

Òrúnmìlà got up one day
And headed for deep in the forest
Located the Arira tree
And sculpted it
Into a human form

And placed it in his house
Then covered it with a white cloth.
Òrúnmìlà then called Amosun
Who was his son
And asked him to announced publicly

That he was dead
Ensuring all his friends heard the message.
Òrúnmìlà then climbed up the rafters
To see how people would react to the announcement.
Amosun went to Ògún

Told him that his father went to bed last night
But didn't wake up the following morning.
He asked Ògún to help them to uncover the deceased's face

And assist with the burial processes
Especially because it was Ògún's prerogative

As the divinity who handles metals for digging.
Ògún exclaimed, "Òrúnmìlà is dead."
He said it was divine retribution.
Ògún said before he could as much as step out of his house
He would take an offering of two hundred dogs.

Amosun then went to see Sàngó
And narrated the entire story
Detailing what he was going through.
Sàngó said if they wanted him to leave his abode
He wanted an offering of two hundred rams.

Amosun left the place
And proceed to Òsun Oníbú-olá's home.
When Amosun reached Òsun's place
He said this tragedy happened
To his father

Overnight, his father died
And they now needed to plan for the funeral ceremony.
Òsun demanded an offering of two hundred large hens
If they wanted her to lift a finger to assist them.
She added that Òrúnmìlà was such an arrogant person

Who loved to lord it over everybody.
Amosun then proceeded to Òsanyìn
Òsanyìn offered excuses and pretenses.
Amosun moved on to Obàtálá
Obàtálá, the great one with a mansion at the source.

Amosun fully explained the situation to him.
Obàtálá explained that he was in fact the one who murdered Òrúnmìlà
And wished Òrúnmìlà even greater misfortunes than death.
Obàtálá said he knew Òrúnmìlà's death was imminent
Because nobody as arrogant as Òrúnmìlà was could live long.
He demanded an offering of nothing less than two hundred giant snails.
To cut a long story short
Amosun visited all of Òrúnmìlà's relatives
But Òrúnmìlà heard the excuses of every one of them
From the rafters where he hid himself.

Every word that people utter upstream of the river
Is audible to the bird
Just as Òrúnmìlà heard what was going on around him.
When Amosun turned back to return home
He suddenly remembered that

There was still one fellow called Èsù he had not called upon.
But should he even bother telling Èsù?
This was a fellow notorious for being heartless.

A fellow well known as a callous character
Someone considered as pitiless.

He decided to visit Èsù for the sake of it
Otherwise, it might appear he didn't accord Èsù any respect.
What happened when he got to Èsù's house?
Èsù was outside his house.
As soon as he saw Amosun approaching him,

And noticed that Amosun wore a frown
He asked, "Amosun, what is the matter?
Hope there is no problem"
Amosun opened his mouth
And said, "Òrúnmìlà is the matter".

Èsù asked what the matter was with Òrúnmìlà.
Amosun said, "My father went to bed last night
But failed to wake up this morning, totally dead."
Before Amosun even completed his words
Èsù jumped up high into the air six or seven times

Dashing his body on the ground viciously.
Èsù wept tears in the right eye
And blood in the left.
In a matter of moments
Before Amosun got home

Èsù was already in Òrúnmìlà's house.
As soon as Èsù entered the house
He saw the white pall in the corridor,
The shroud placed on the wooden sculpture.
Ese instantly assumed Òrúnmìlà's body was under the shroud

And cried out in agony, "Woe! You Òrúnmìlà who repairs the world
You cannot perish like this!"
He jumped up again
To dash his body against the floor
But Òrúnmìlà came down from the rafters.

Èsù was startled.
But Òrúnmìlà held him
And assured him that all was well.
Òrúnmìlà told Èsù that he Òrúnmìlà did not die
He said he was just pretending to be dead.

He said we should close our eyes
And pretend to be dead
To see who will mourn our death
We should keep walking
And dash our toes against a rock
To see who cares we got hurt
They cast Ifá divination for Òrúnmìlà
When the patriarch pretended to his relatives that he was dead.
But Èsù was still not convinced it was just acting.
Òrúnmìlà held Èsù again

And asked him to remove the shroud from the object on the floor.
Once Èsù removed the shroud
And saw that it was just a carving under the

"He revealed that people do not die in Yoruba philosophy. This is why, for instance, when a monarch passes away, people say the *Ọbá wàjà*, meaning the monarch has climbed up the rafters"

pall
Èsù immediately sat down on the floor, relieved.
Òrúnmìlà explained that it was all his ploy
As people were hailing him on the right
And greeting him on the left
He wanted to find out who truly loved him
Leading him to ask them to announce his obituary.
And you, Èsù, who everybody assumed was a bad person,

It turns out you are not bad in any way.
You were the only person who truly loved him.
Òrúnmìlà then said that as from that moment
The first morsel of food of all Ifá devotees

Must first be offered to Èsù.
Secondly, he said,
In any house in which he Òrúnmìlà is present within the house
You Èsù must be placed at the back of the house
So you are never far from him.
The first morsel of all diviners when they eat
Should be given as offering to Èsù.
And before diviners make any pronouncement
They must first pay homage to Èsù.
You Èsù must always be well fed

You Èsù must always be fed to satisfaction
Before he Òrúnmìlà even touches any meal
Or touches any drink.
Èsù began to offer thanks
As Òrúnmìlà fully removes the shroud from the carving

To reveal that it was sculpted from the Arira tree.
Èsù began to dance
And began to celebrate.
He raised his voice lyrically
And began to sing like they chant Ifá verses,

Chanting Ifá verses, like they croon songs,
He began to sing:
"It is for the Arira tree that you are crying
It is the Arira tree you are mourning
Òrúnmìlà, the storyteller, whose obituary you announced

Is far from deceased
It is for the Arira tree that you are crying."

The *Babaláwo* explained the divination by highlighting the role of Èṣù as the divinity that stands at the intersection between life and death, good and bad, health and disease, fortune and misfortune. This is why people say:
Èṣù má ṣe mí
Ọmọ ẹlòmíràn ni kó o ṣe.
Èsù do not wreck me

Find someone else to ruin.
The *Babaláwo* made the connection between the Ìrẹtẹ̀ Méjì verse and transition of Wewe's mother. He revealed that people do not die in Yoruba philosophy. This is why, for instance, when a monarch passes away, people say the *Ọbá wàjà*, meaning the monarch has climbed up the rafters. When monarchs climb up the rafters, they are feigning death, to see how people would react to the announcement of their obituary.

It is same with all Yoruba people: same as Òrúnmìlà, they go to *Ọ̀run*, the source, and watch the reaction to the news of their death.

In other words, the *Babaláwo* said that Wewe's mother, like all mothers, did not die. "Mothers never die or tarnish," the *Babaláwo* confirmed, "because mothers are gold."

What Wewe must do, the *Babaláwo* said, was to make a painting to assure his mother that he was aware that she was alive. Òrúnmìlà produced a sculpture, the *Babaláwo* said, but a painting is what Wewe's mother required, painted in her semblance. It will become the surrogate for Wewe's mother, and a visual assertion of his love for her.

In response to the *Babaláwo*, Wewe completed the painting titled *The Return of Our Mother II*. Several years earlier, when he was searching for her after she was kidnaped, he did the first one. For the second version, he locates his mother at the intersection between *Ayé* (the world) and *Ọ̀run* (the source).

Dressed in white *ìró* and *bùbá*, the mode of attire associated with Yoruba women, Wewe's mother sits in the middle of a canoe used among her people, in the dense network of creeks of the Atlantic Ocean.

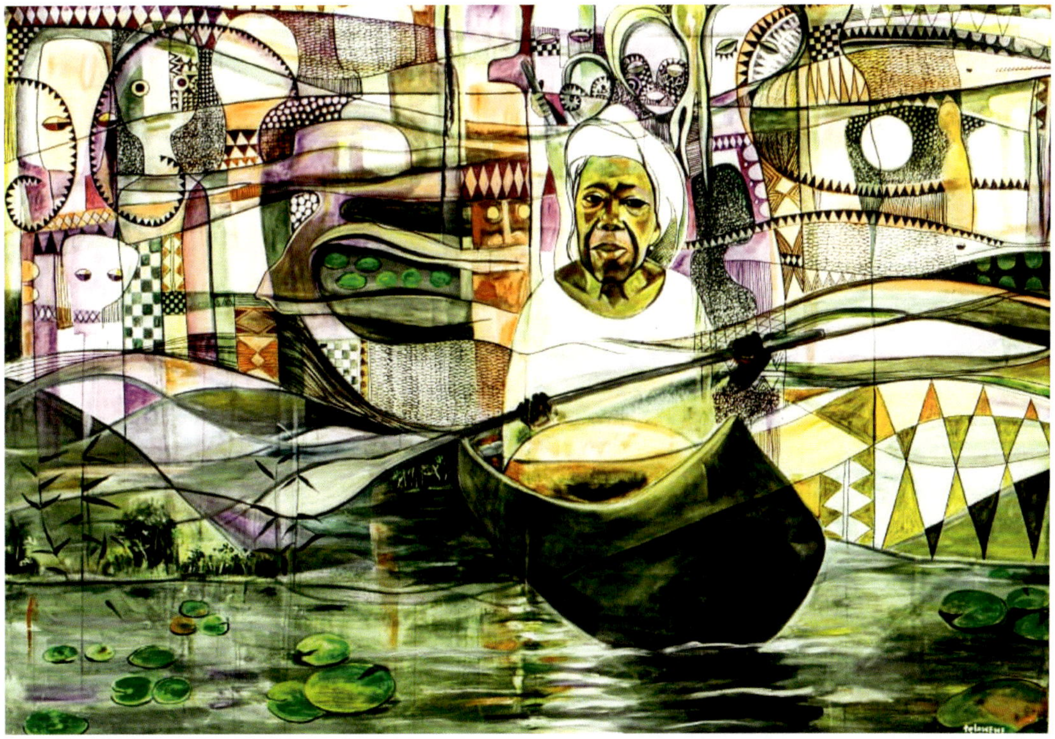

Figure 40: *The Return of Our Mother II*, acrylic on canvas, 2022.

She holds the *òbèlè*, the paddle, with which she navigates her way forward toward the viewer, who occupies the position of the painter, Wewe, as he works on the canvas. The water is calm, rich with green seaweeds that colors the tranquil surface green.

The calmness on her face reflects the serenity of the waterway along which she is paddling. She appears to be returning from the land of the Irúnmolè, the divine forces of *Ọ̀run*, whose appearances have a touch of human configuration, yet transcend the imitation of the individual natural figure. The realism with which Wewe portrays his mother makes her body distinct from the other figures in the composition. She is one of them clearly, and she is returning from their abode, moving toward her son, the painter.

"Olókun (the divinity of the oceans) has taken her daughter," Wewe says in reference to his mother, "and brought her back from the other world. Shame to the kidnappers! Shame to our security system! Shame to those who wished her dead!"

BIOGRAPHY

Tola Wewe

Born on the 19th of November, 1959, in Shabomi – an incredibly heterogeneous community in the western delta of the Niger River, in present Ondo State, Nigeria, Adetola Wewe studied at the Government Teachers College, Ikorodu from 1975 to 1978.

In 1979, he gained admission into the University of Ifè, (now Obafemi Awolowo University, Ilé Ifè) to study his first love, Fine Arts, in which subject he obtained a Bachelor's degree in 1983.

Not done with the pursuit of the academic study of Art, he proceeded to the University of Ìbàdàn to pursue a Master's degree program in African Visual Arts, which he obtained in 1983.

Thereafter, he shared his acquired knowledge with upcoming students, first, as a Fine Arts teacher back at home at the Teacher's College, Igboegunrin in Ondo State from 1984 to 1985, after which he moved to the Adeyemi College Education in Ondo town (an affiliate of his alma mater, the University of Ifè) as a lecturer from 1987 to 1991.

In 1991, he moved to Lagos where he joined the Daily Times Newspapers as Senior Artist. Barely a year into this, already getting tired of the very fast pace of life in the commercial heartbeat of Nigeria, he did brief stints as the Art Editor of the Exchequer Goose Communication and – as an opportunity to experience the Arts Market – as General Manager of Signature Art Gallery, Lagos, between 1992 and 1995.

In 1995, he packed up his paint brushes, easels and his family and moved back to his home state, Ondo, to fully devote himself to his life's mission – creating art. This he has done with tremendous and phenomenal success, with successful exhibitions both home and abroad (see below).

In 2009, he was appointed as the Honorable Commissioner for Culture and Tourism in Ondo State (2009 -2011) as an acknowledgement of his vast experience and stellar reputation as an artist. It was during his time as Hon. Commissioner that the Mare Festival – an annual festival to celebrate the international heritage site of Ìdànrè and its hills – in which mountain climbers from all over the world gather to test their skills on the hills was conceived and inaugurated.

Tola Wewe has garnered awards both at home and internationally, in recognition of his passionate devotion to and celebration of his African culture and tradition.
At home, he has been honored and celebrated in his traditional culture. In 2005, he was doubly honored with two chieftaincy titles from two different kingdoms in his home state of Ondo: as the Obagbemigun of Ìdóàní Land, a chieftaincy title bestowed on him by HRM Oba Aderemi B. Atewogboye II, the Alaani of Ìdóàní, and as Bobagunwa of Odòwó, Ondo Kingdom. In 2014, in the neighboring Osun State, he was installed as the Oluaye Agbasaga by HRM Oba Abdulwahab Oyedotun, Bibire I, Òràngún of the ancient Ìgbómìnà kingdom of Ìlá Òràngún.
In 2005, the Department of Fine Arts of His Alma mater, Obafemi Awolowo University, Ilé Ifè, rewarded him with an "Outstanding Alumnus Award".

In 2003, The Culture and Creativity Art Forum (CCAF) honored Wewe with a "Merit for Creativity" award, for his outstanding contribution to the arts.

Internationally, Wewe was honored as an "Artist Honoree" by the county of Los Angeles, USA in 2004.

At 2012 Olympic Games in London, he was awarded an "Olympic Gold Medal" by the International Olympic Committee/

Ministry of Culture of the People's Republic of China.

Married with four children, Wewe enjoys babysitting his grandchildren.
Selected Exhibitions
1988 Exhibition of Ondo State Professional Artists, Ministry of Information, Youth and Social Welfare, Akure.
1989 Ona 1, Ibadan.
1989 "Multiplex Realitie", O.A.U, Ife, Ilé Ifè.
1989 "Pushing the Limits of Vision", Lagos
1989 "Exhibition of contemporary Life Art", Ilé Ifè.
1990 "Beyond Visual Beauty", National Museum, Lagos
1990 "Ona 2", National Museum, Lagos
1991 "Provincial Monuments", Ondo
1992 "Our Own", National Museum, Lagos
1993 "The Best of Ife", Lagos
1993 "Styles", Lagos
1993 "Just Before Christmas", Lagos
1996 Russian Cultural Centre, Lagos
1997 Lola Gallery, Lagos
1998 Nimbus Art Centre, Lagos
1999 Alliance Francais, Lagos
1999 Elf Village, Port – Harcourt
2000 Lola Gallery, Lagos
2000 Centre Culturel Francais, Cotonou, Rep. of Benin
2001 Parish Gallery, Washington DC. USE
2002 Bettendorffsche Galerie Im Schlossgarten Gauangelloch/Liemen, Germany
2003 Elf Village, Port-Harcourt
2003 Bettendorfsche Galerie Im Schlossgarten, Gauangelloch/Liemen, Germany
2003 Kunst Forum Das Carre, Heidelberg, Germany
2004 Nicon Hilton, Abuja, Nigeria
2004 12th Pan African Film/Art Festival, Los Angeles, U.S.A
2004 Nimbus Art Centre, Lagos
2004 Espace Alberica, Paris, France
2004 Bettendorfsche Galerie Im Schlossgarten, Gauangelloch/Liemen, Germany
2004 Platterforum, Denver, Colorado, USA
2005 Nimbus Art Centre, Lagos
2005 Neo Art Gallery, Denver, Colorado, USA
2005 Conningsby Gallery, London
2006 Bettendorfsche Galerie Im Schlossgarten, Gauangelloch/Liemen, Germany
2006 Galerie des Beauxarts, Heeze, Netherland
2007 The Civic Centre, Lagos
2008 Galerie 23, Amsterdam, Netherland
2010 "The return of Our Mother", Lagos
2010 The Mojo Gallery, Dubai, UAE
2011 "Footnotes", Etisalat sponsored, Lagos
2012 Olympic Exhibition, London
2013 Nike Art Centre, Lagos
2014 Red Door Gallery, Lagos
2014 Ashanti Gallery, Abuja
2015 Galerie Duvivier, Paris, France
2015 Alliance Francaise and the Moorhouse, Ikoyi, Lagos
2016 BeHendorffsce Galerie, Im Schlossgarten, Gauangelloch/Liemen, German

2016 Gallery of African Arts, London
Numerous shows between 2016 and 2022.

Gallery

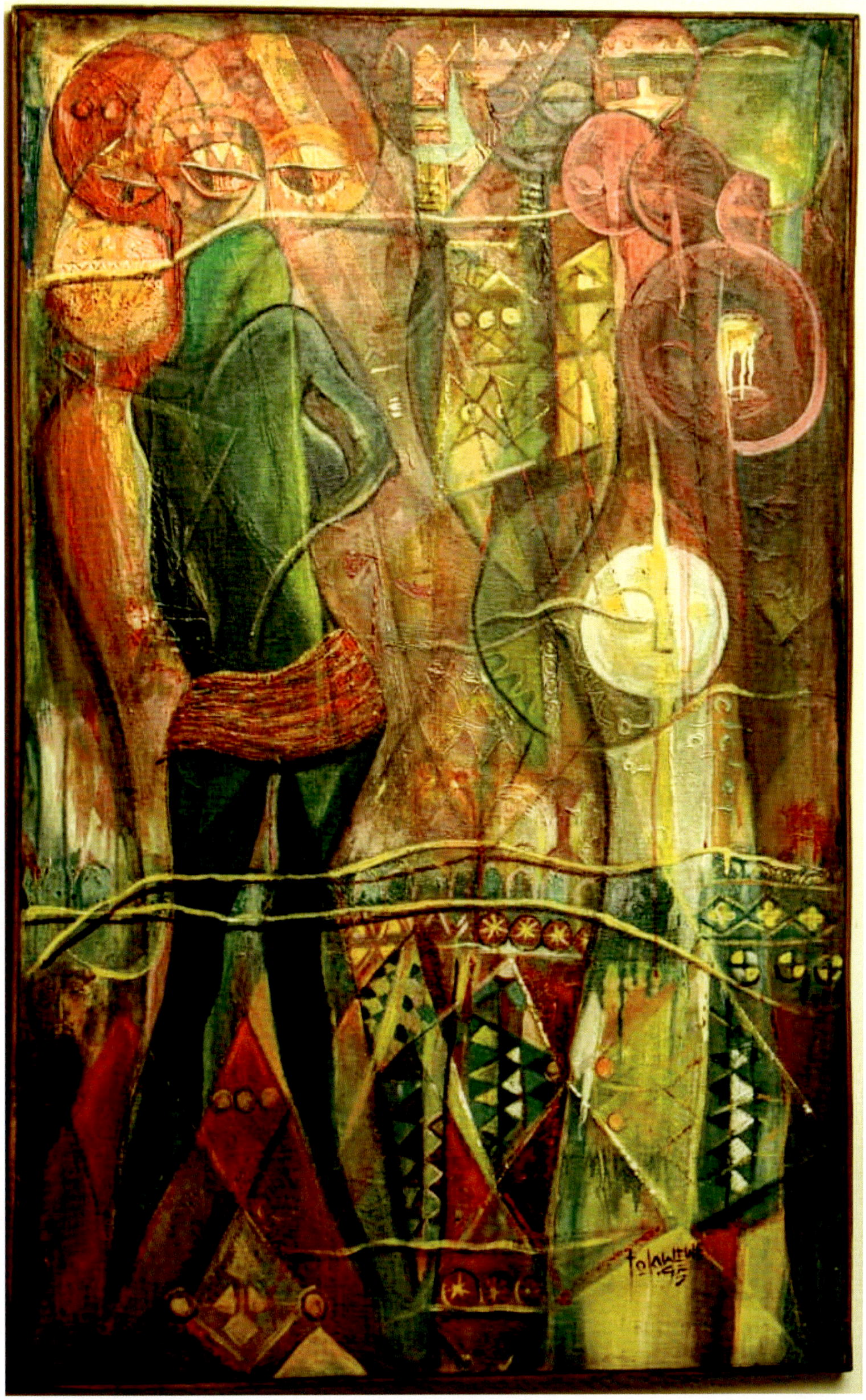

Fig. 41: Urban Migrants Have No Family Names, acrylic on canvas, 1995.

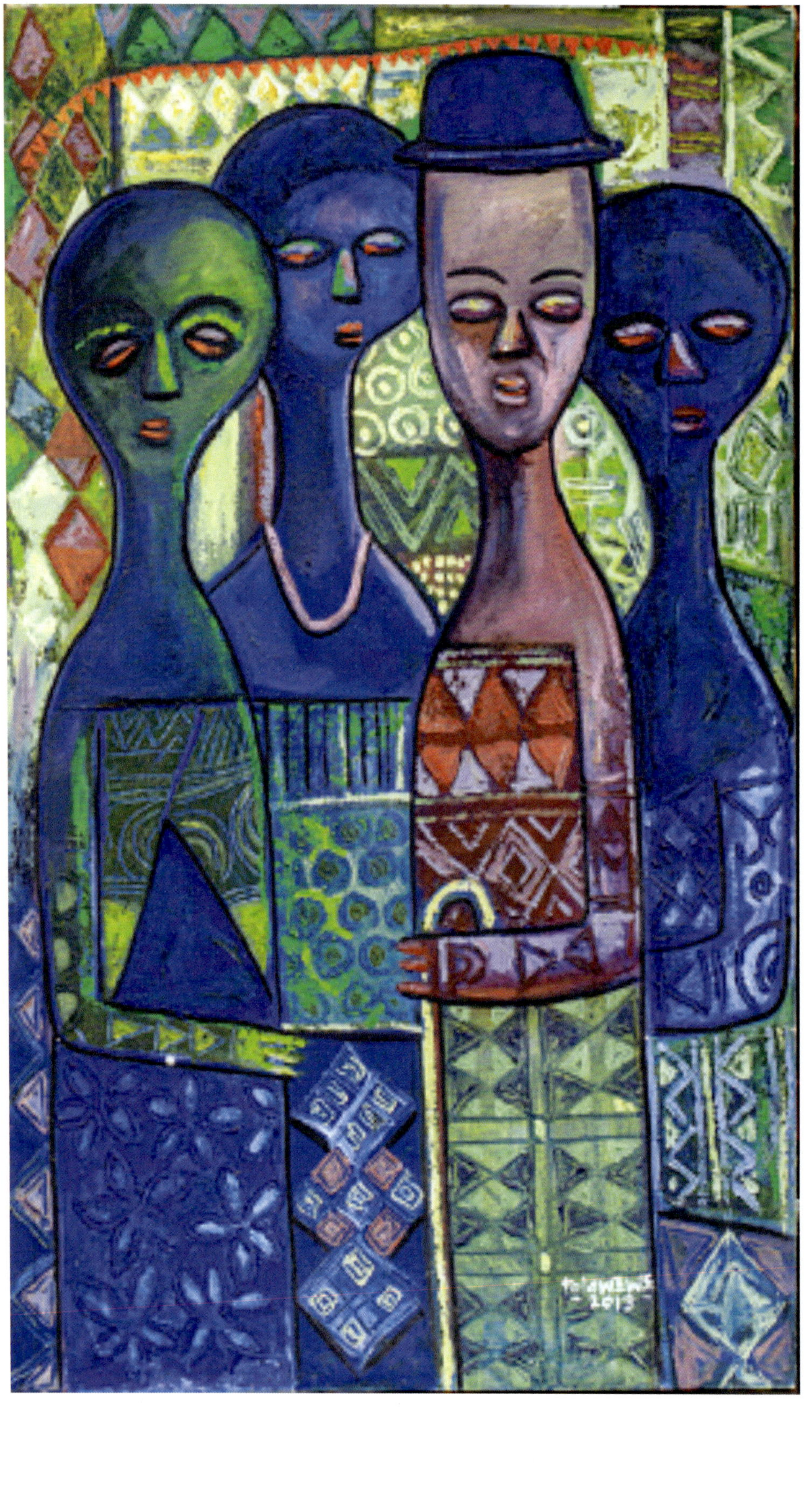

Fig. 42: The Regent and Her Three Wives, acrylic on canvas, 2013

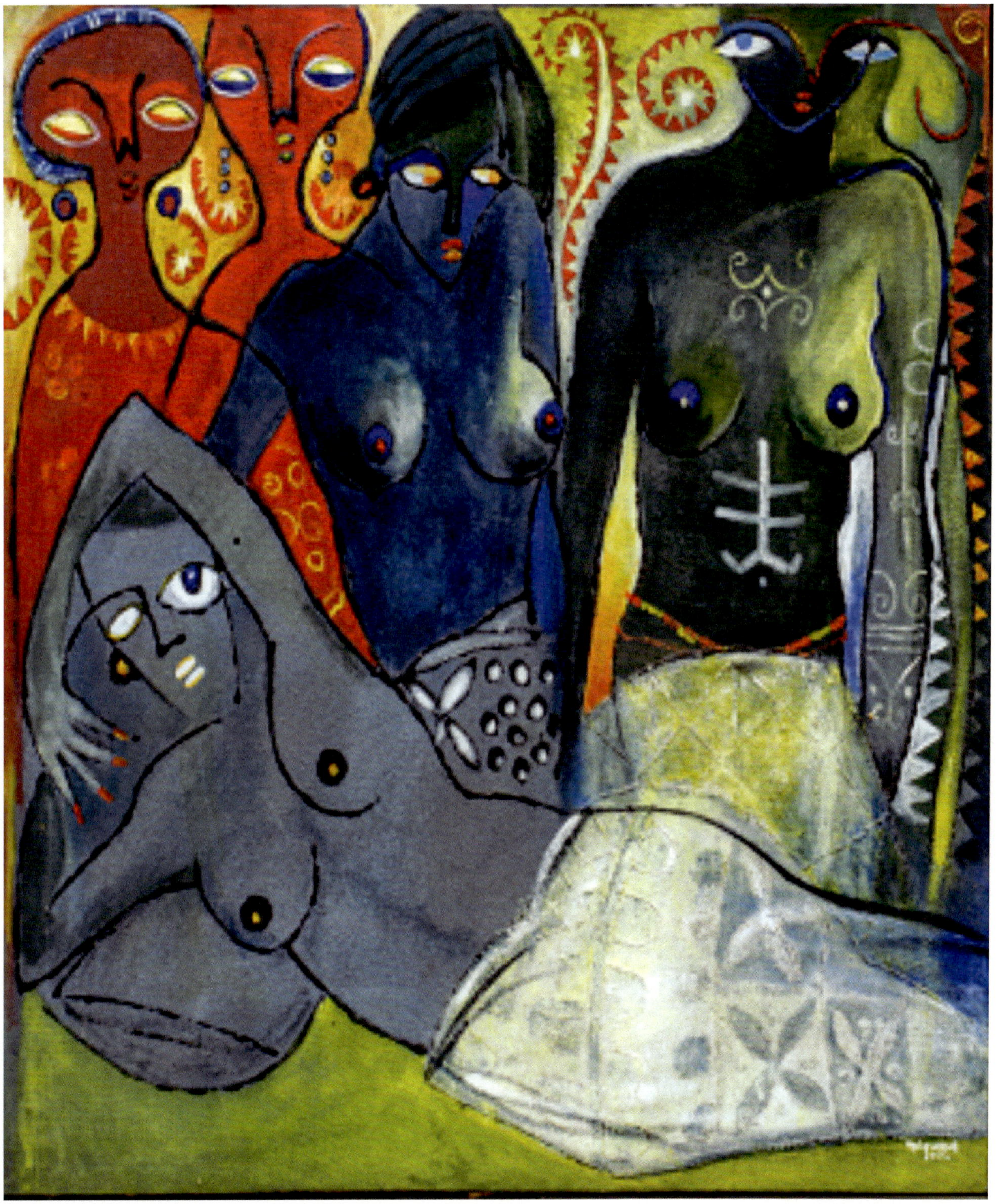

Fig. 43: Algerian Postcard, acrylic on canvas, 2002.

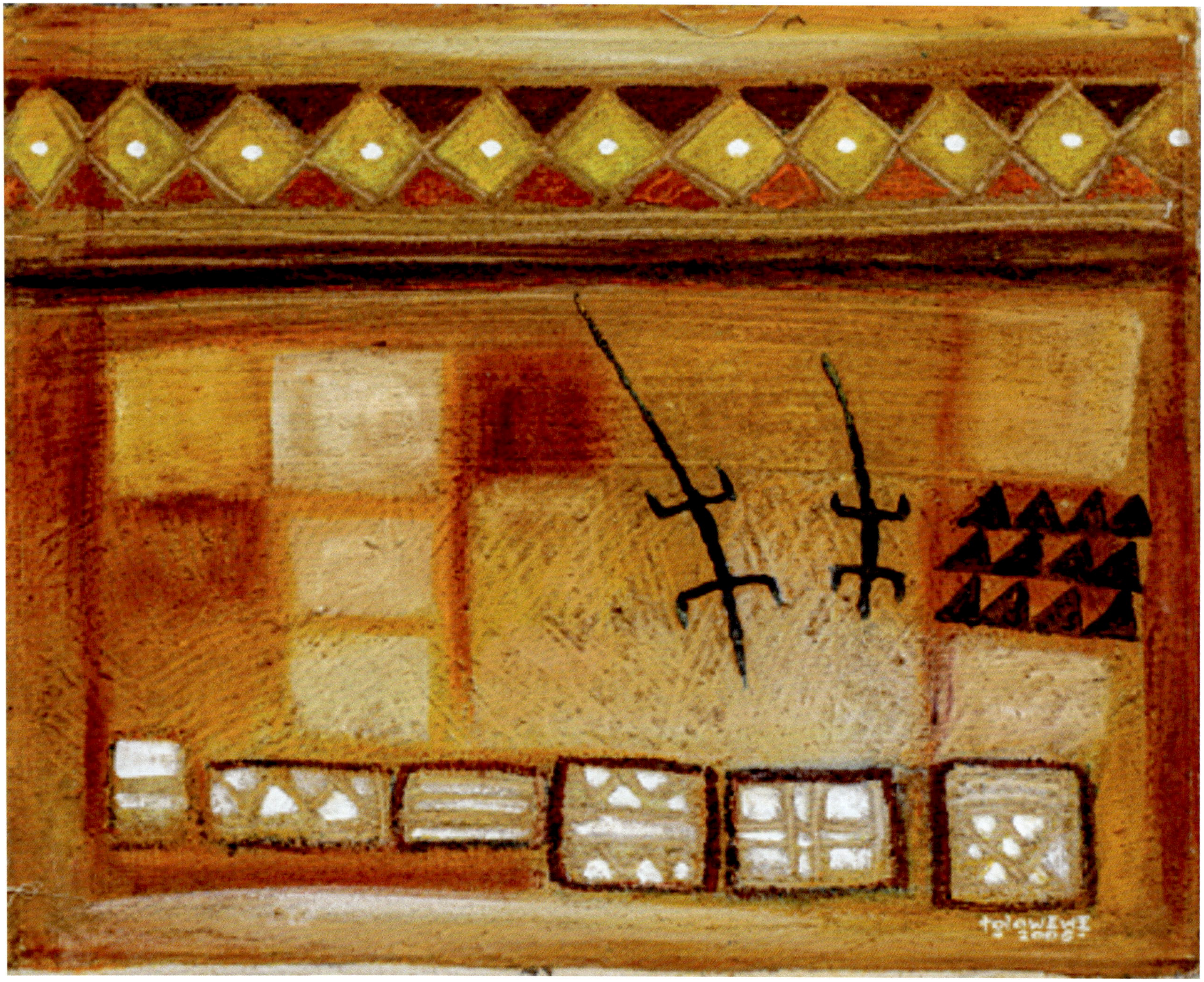

Fig. 44: All Lizards Lie Prostrate, We Know Not Those With Belly Aches, acrylic on canvas, 2006.

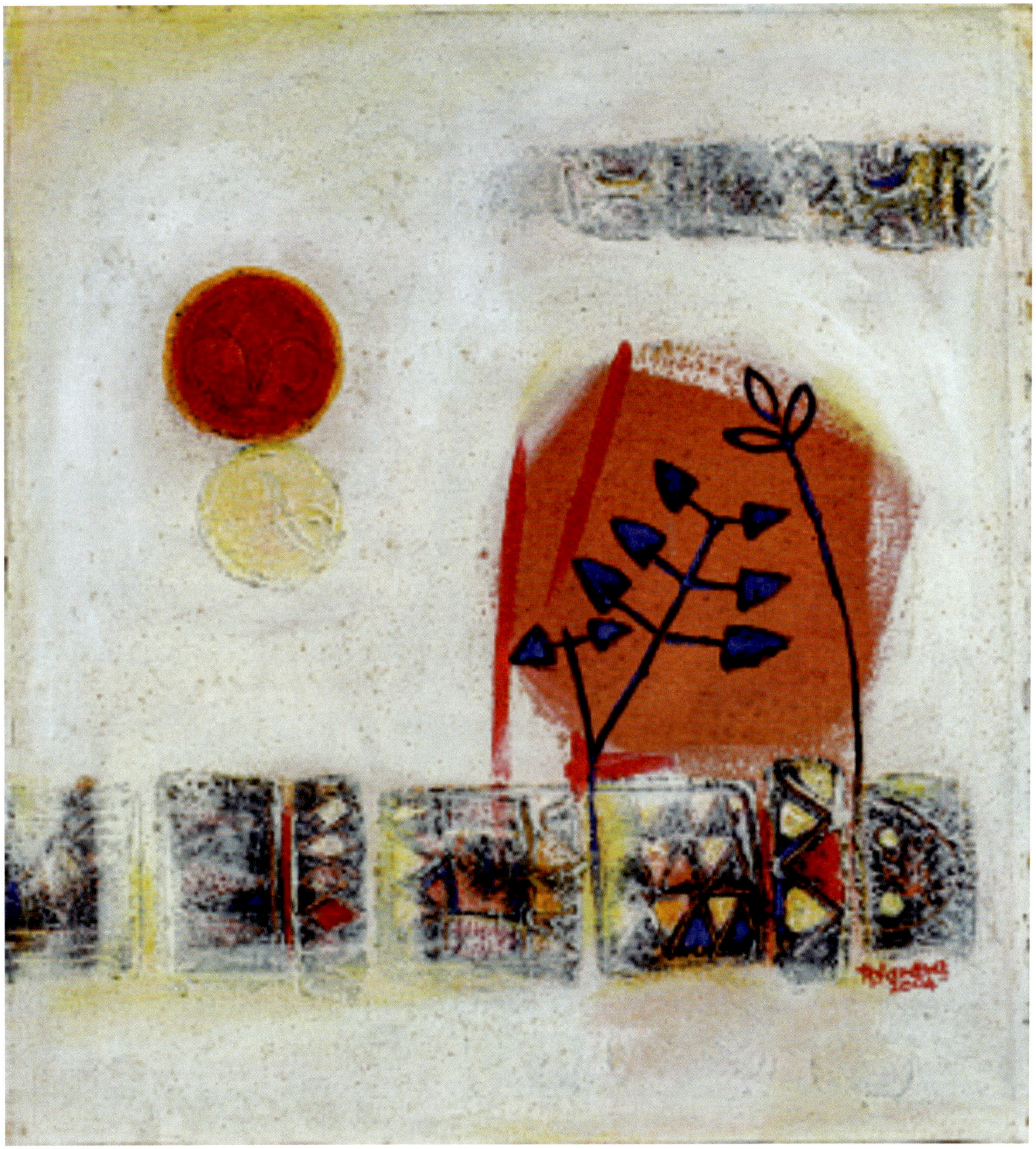

Fig. 45: Flowers Blooming on the Rocks, acrylic on canvas, 2004

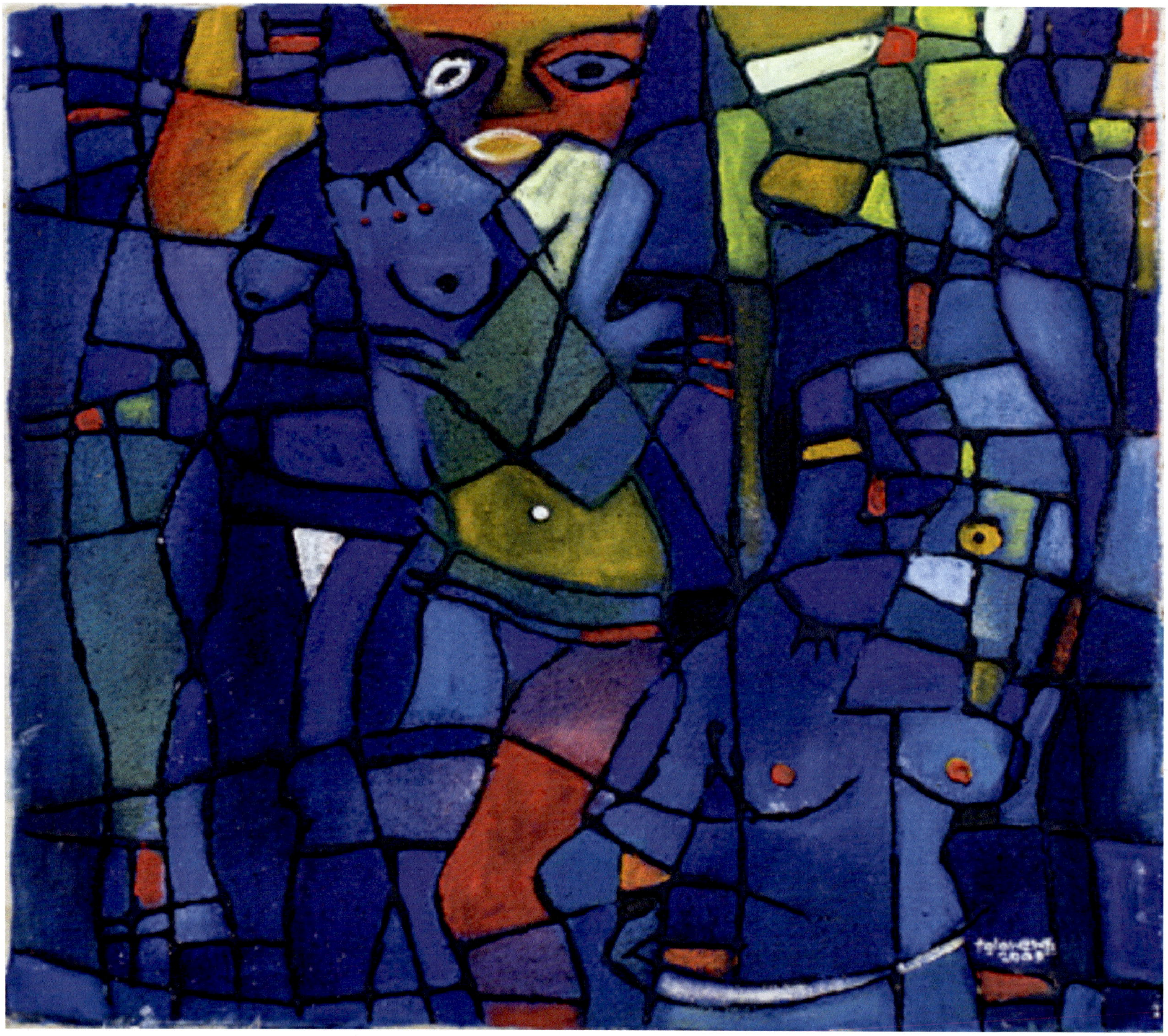

Figure 46: Daughters of the Indigo Dyer, acrylic on canvas, 2005

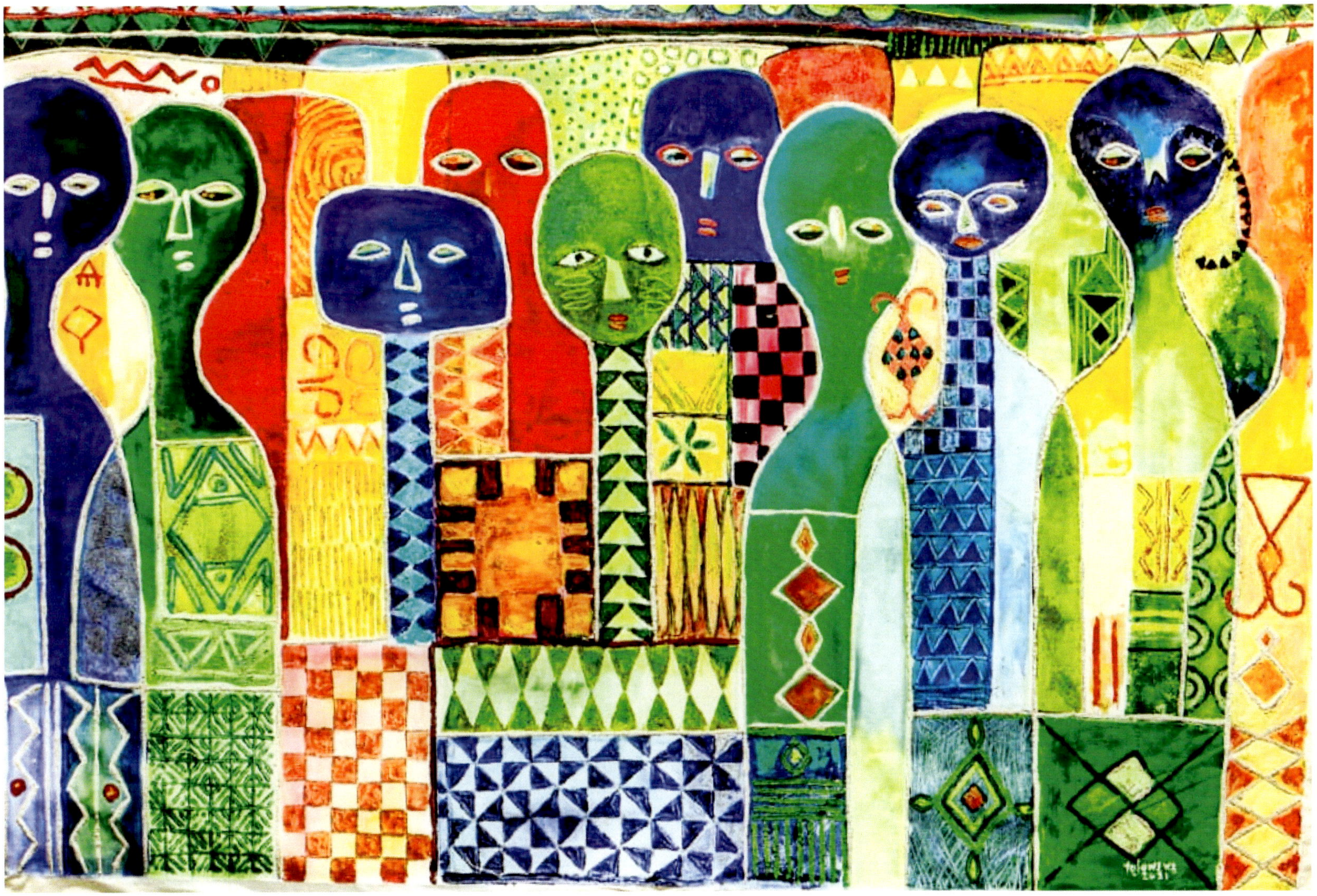

Figure 47: The Tree Does Not Make a Forest, acrylic on canvas, 2021

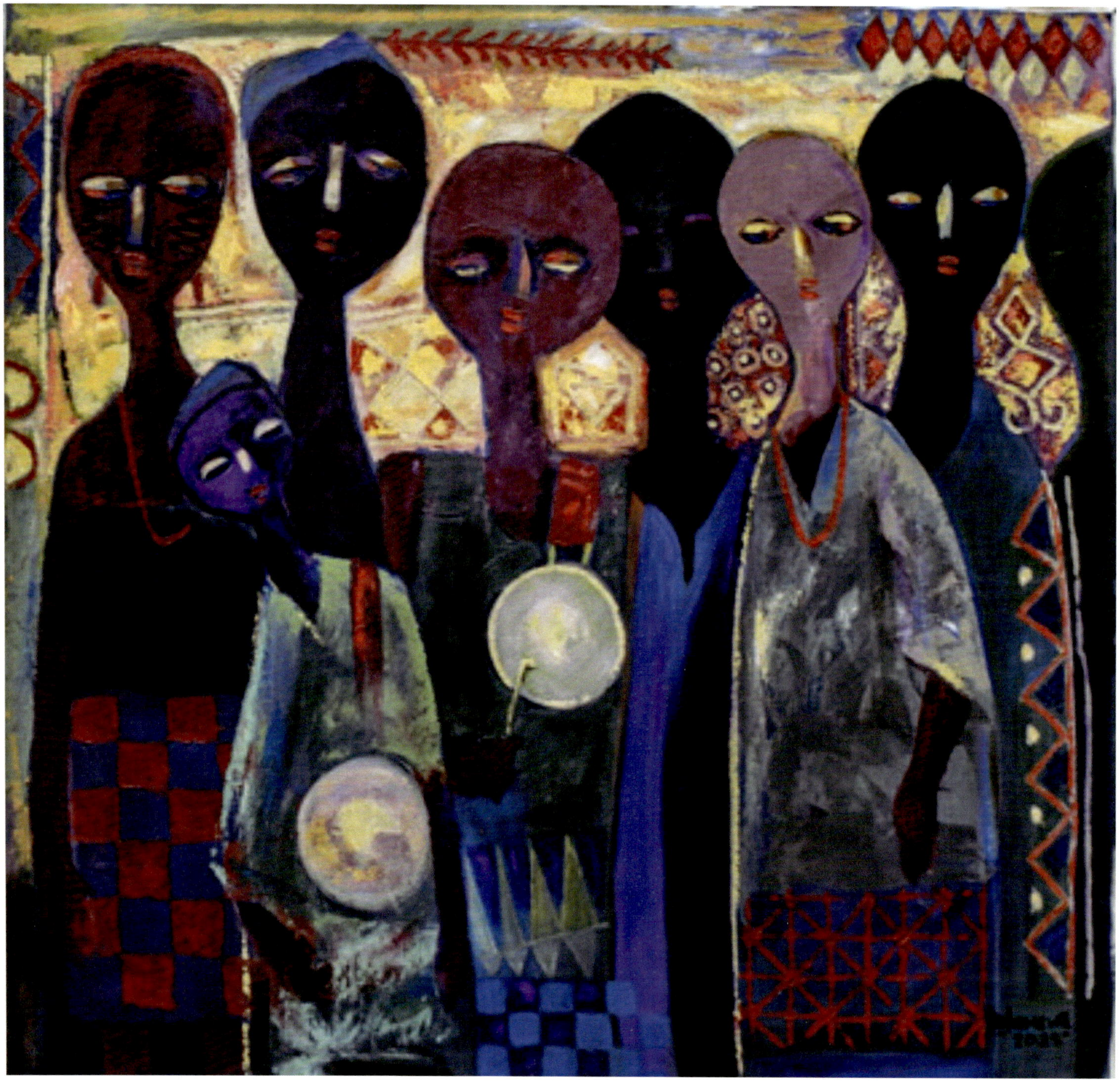

Figure 48: The Wedding Party, acrylic on canvas, 2022.

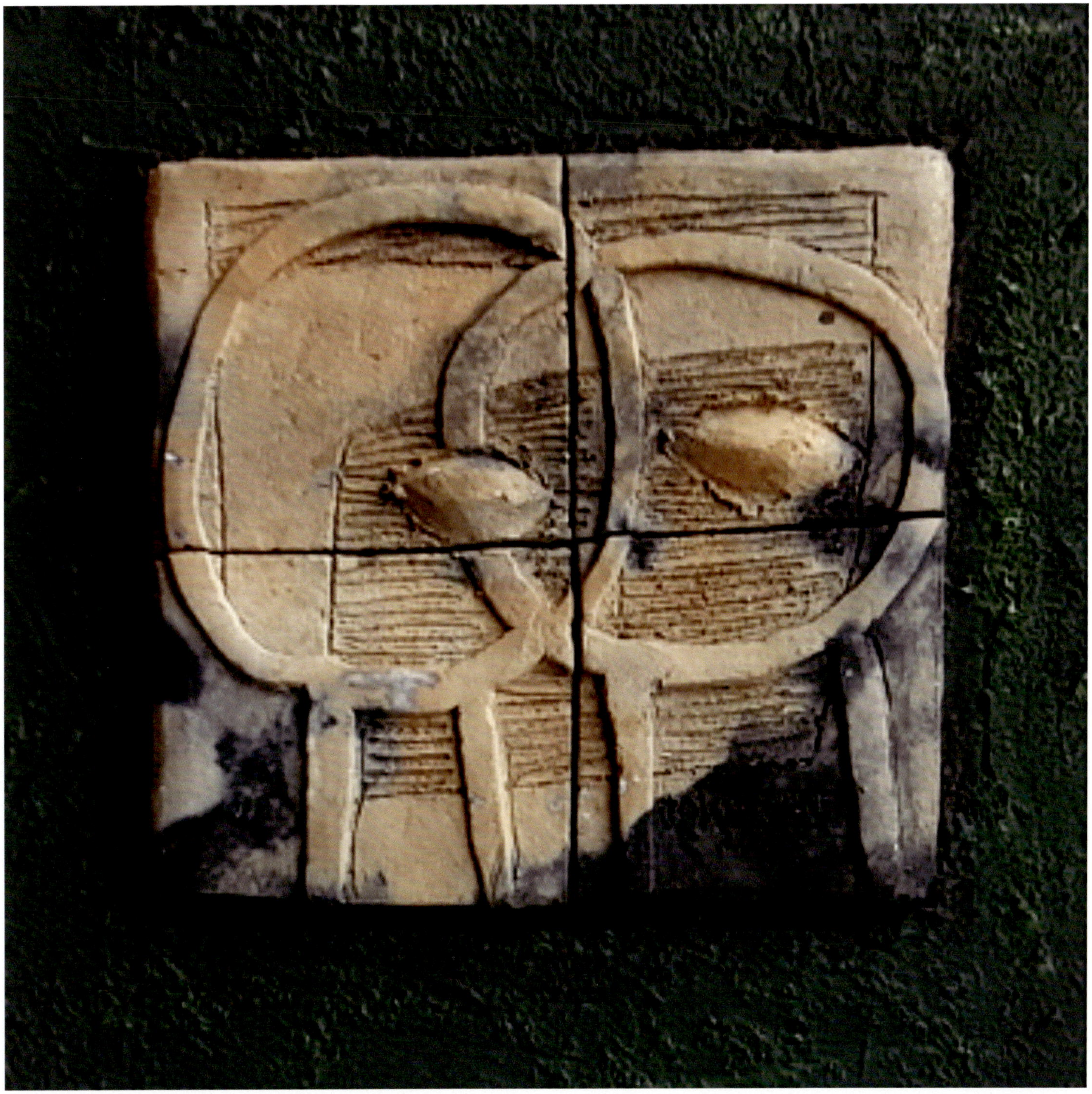

Figure 49: Eye to Eye, terra cotta on canvas, 2022

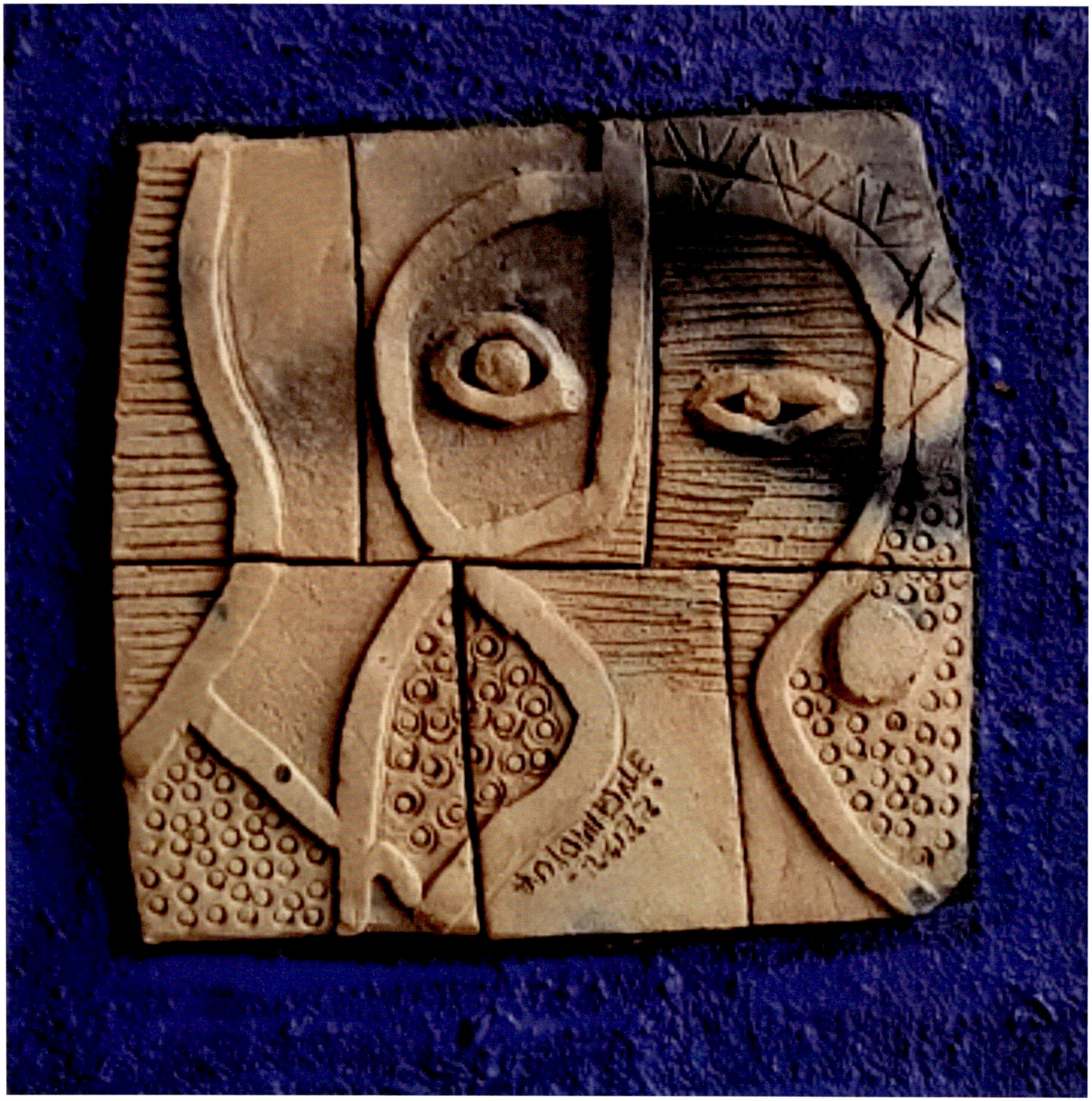

Figure 50: Intimacy, terra cotta on canvas, 2022.

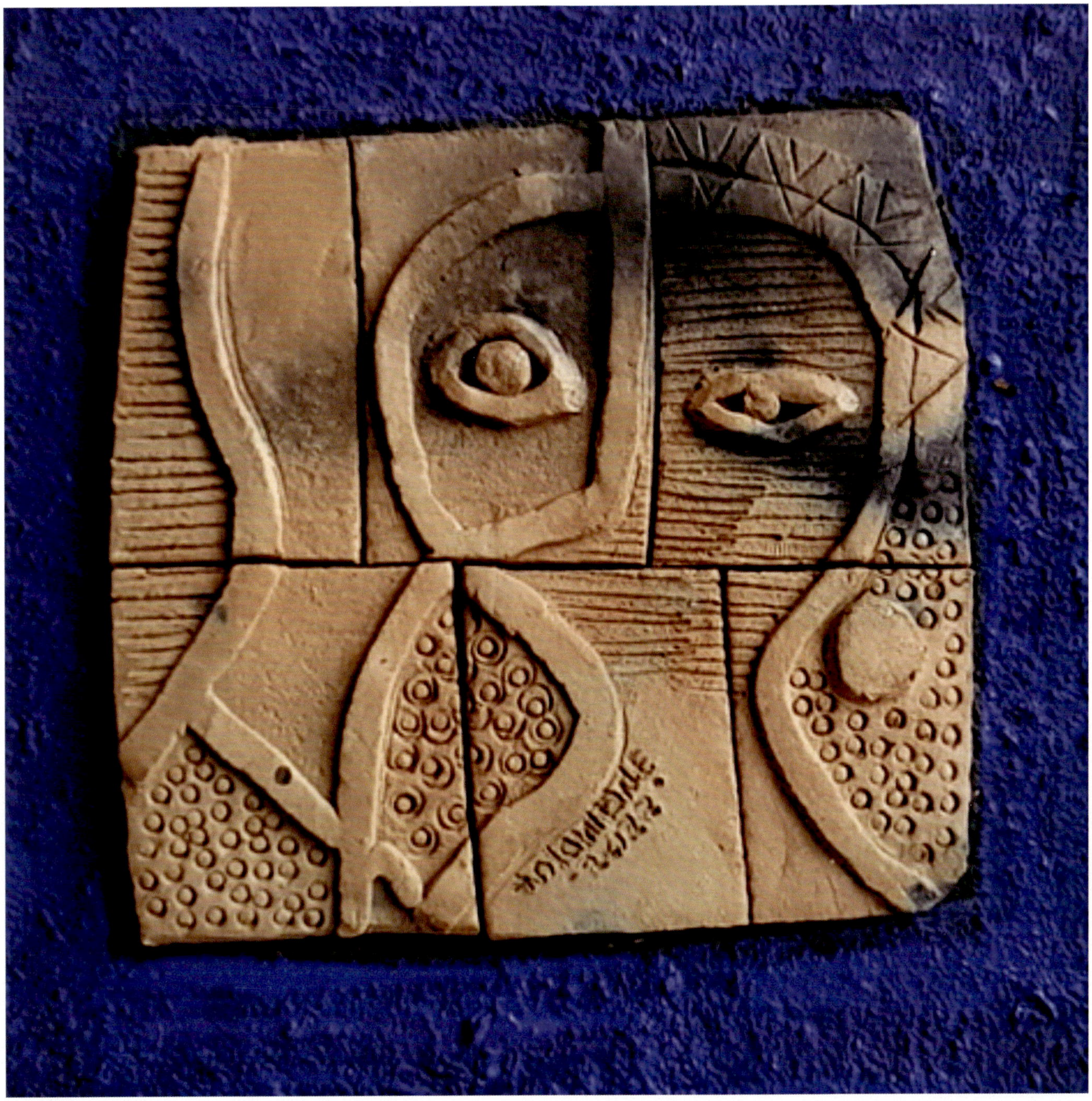

Figure 51: The Third Eye, acrylic on canvas, 2022.

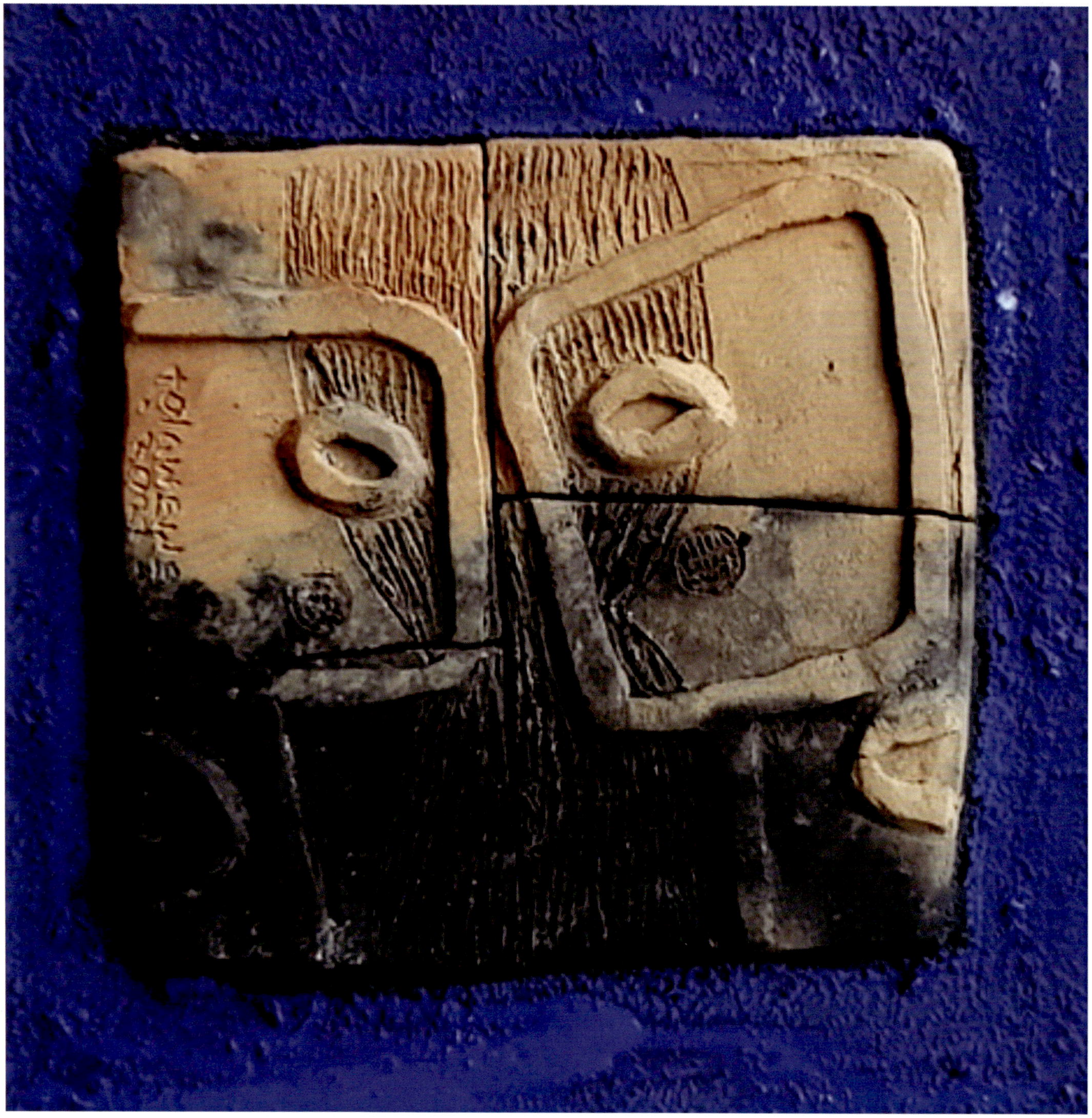

Figure 52: Third Party, terra cotta on canvas, 2022

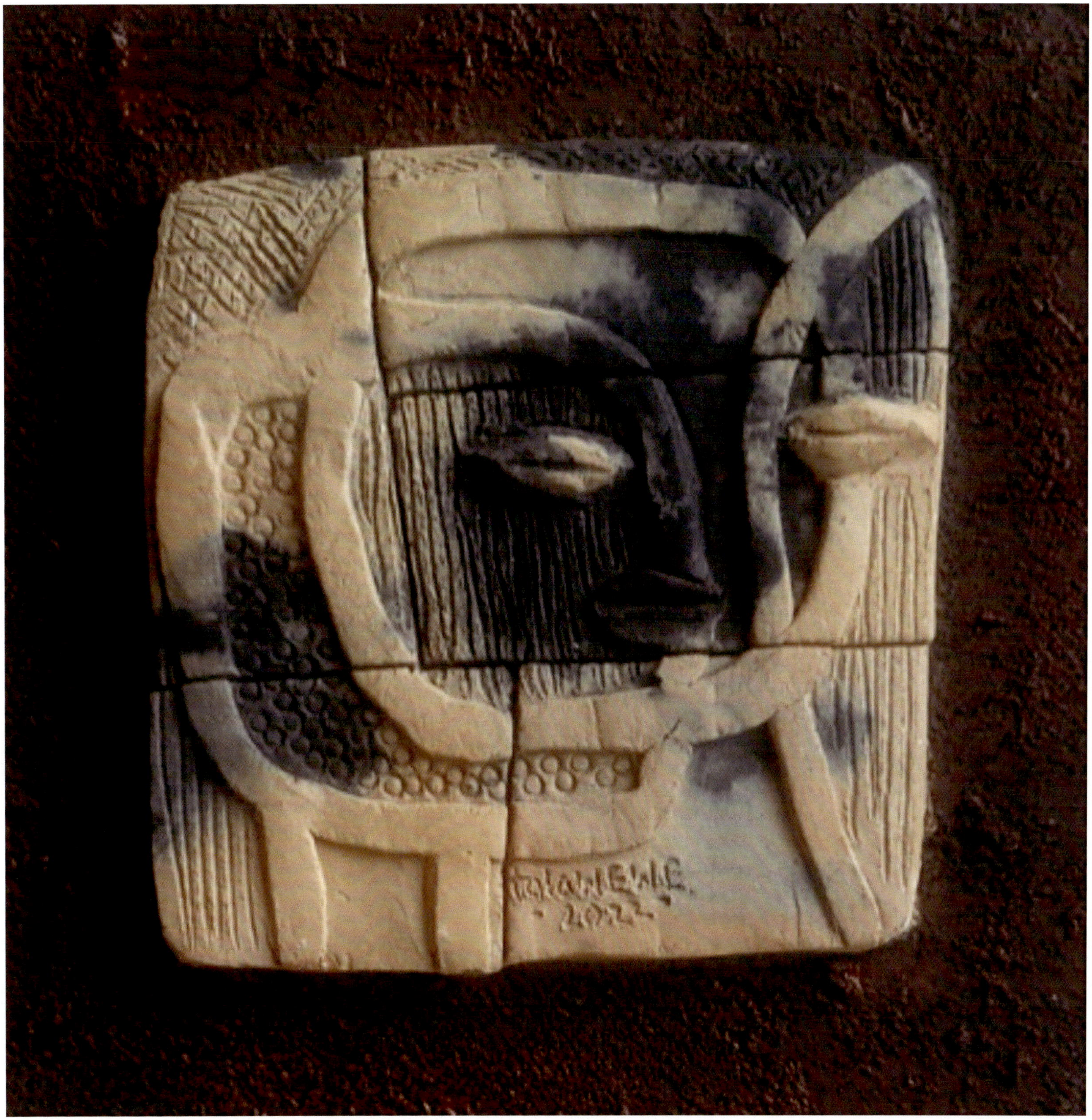

Figure 53: Second Generation, acrylic on canvas, 2022.

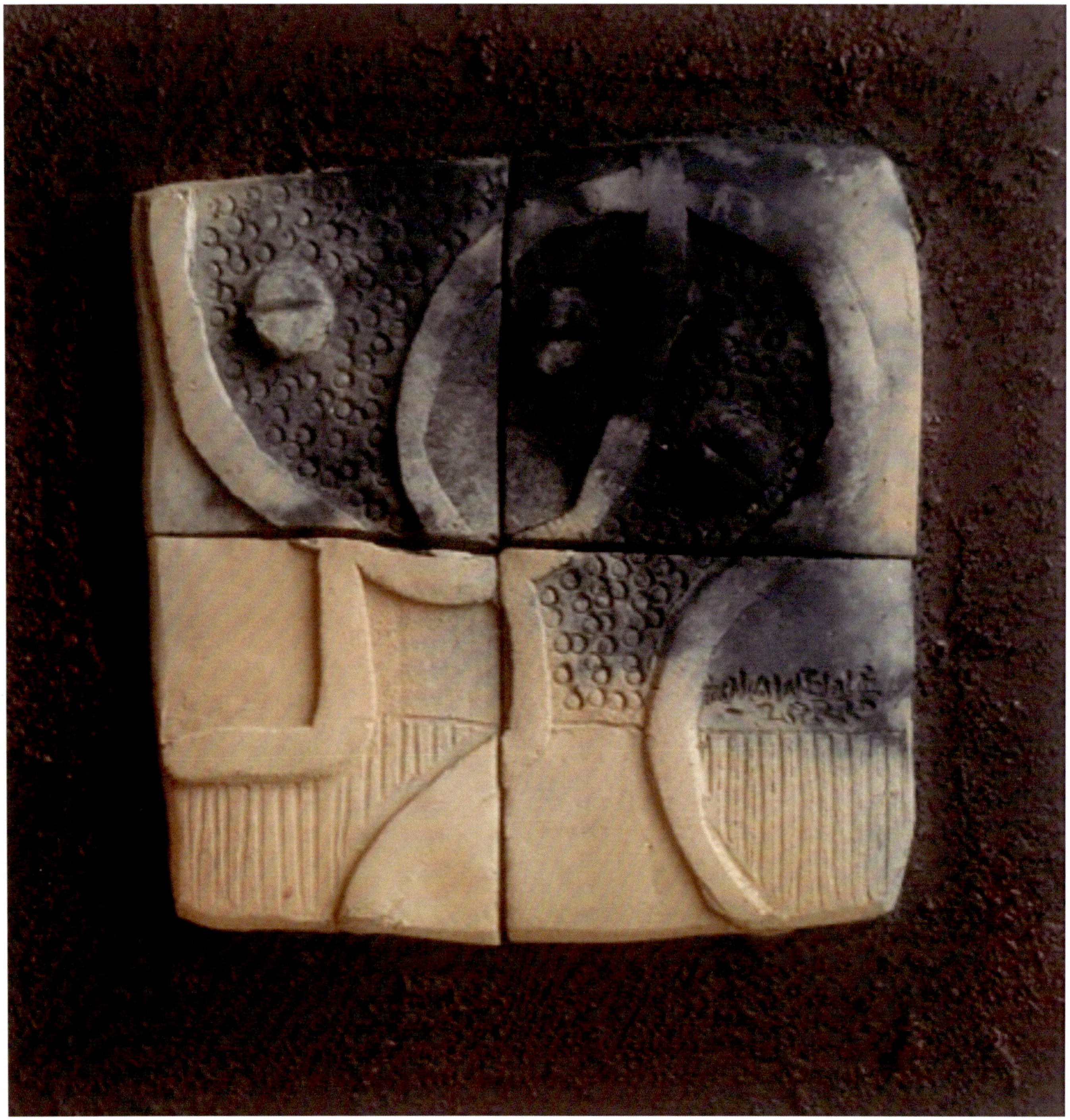

Figure 54: Things Fall Apart, acrylic on canvas, 2022

Endnotes

1 This figure, which is in Naira the Nigerian currency, is equivalent to one million US dollars.
2 "It was just a deceitful promise."
3 https://www.moma.org/learn/moma_learning/joseph-kosuth-one-and-three-chairs-1965/, accessed July 23, 2022.
4 Phone communication with Tola Wewe, January 4, 2022.
5 Sandra M. Grayson, *Symbolizing the Past: Reading Sankofa, Daughter of the Dust and Eve's Bayou*, (Lanham, New York, Oxford: University Press of America, 2000), p.19.
6 Yambo Ouloguem, *Bound to Violence*, pp. 14-16.
7 Henry Drewal, "Beauty and Being: Aesthetics and Ontology of Yoruba Body Art," in *Marks of Civilization*, ed. Arnold Rubin, (Los Angeles: Museum of Cultural History, 1987), pp. 83-96.
8 Cornelius Adepegba, *A Survey of Nigerian Body Markings and their Relationship to other Nigerian Arts*, (Ann Harbor, MI: Doctoral dissertation, Department of Fine Arts, Indiana University, Bloomington. University Microfilms International) 1976.
9 Audre Lorde, "From the House of Yemanja," *The Black Unicorn: Poems*, (New York: Norton, 1978).
10 Audre Lorde, "Uses of the Erotic: The Erotic As Power," in *Sister Outsiders*, pp. 53-59
11 See Ulli Beier, *Contemporary Art in Africa*, Frederick A. Praeger, 1968).
12 Ulli Beier, *Contemporary Art in Africa*, Frederick A. Praeger, 1968).
13 See Marshall Mount, *African Art: The Years since 1920*, (New York: Indiana University Press, 1989).
14 Phone interview conducted with Chike Nwagbogu, January 2020.
15 Michael Fajuyigbe, *Ife Art School in the History of Modern Nigerian Art,* (Ile-Ife: Department of Fine and Applied Arts, Obafemi Awolowo University, Ph.D. Thesis, 2018).
16 Wole Soyinka, *The Lion and the Jewel*, (Oxford: Oxford University Press, 1963).
17 These writers are famous for their innovative use of the English language.
18 *Iwin* means mysterious being.
19
20 Michael Fajuyigbe, *Ife Art School in the History of Modern Nigerian Art.*
21 Gerald Moore and Uli Beier,eds., *Modern Poetry From Africa*, (Harmondsworth, Middlesex: Penguins Books Ltd, 1963), p.44.
22 Orhan Pamuk, *My Name is Red*, (Vintage, 2006).
23 The mythologies of hunters who went hunting to provide sustenance for family only to return and find them dead are replete in Yoruba folkloric traditions.
24 Karen Chernick, "When Duchamp Agreed to Forge One of His Most Famous Works," https://www.artsy.net/article/artsy-editorial-duchamp-agreed-forge-one-famous-works, accessed August 21, 2022.
25 *Gàrí* and *ègúsi* are dishes Yoruba people relish with meat or fish.
26 See Danto, *After the End of Art*, (Princeton University Press, 1998).
27 The idea of "washing your eyes" is called *Ìwejú* among the Yoruba.
It is a mythical procedure that is supposed to enable you to see things hidden from others.
28 See Danto, *After the End of Art*, (Princeton University Press, 1998).
29 Fela Kuti, *Alagbon Close*, "Why Black Man Dey Suffer," (Lagos: FAK, 2007).

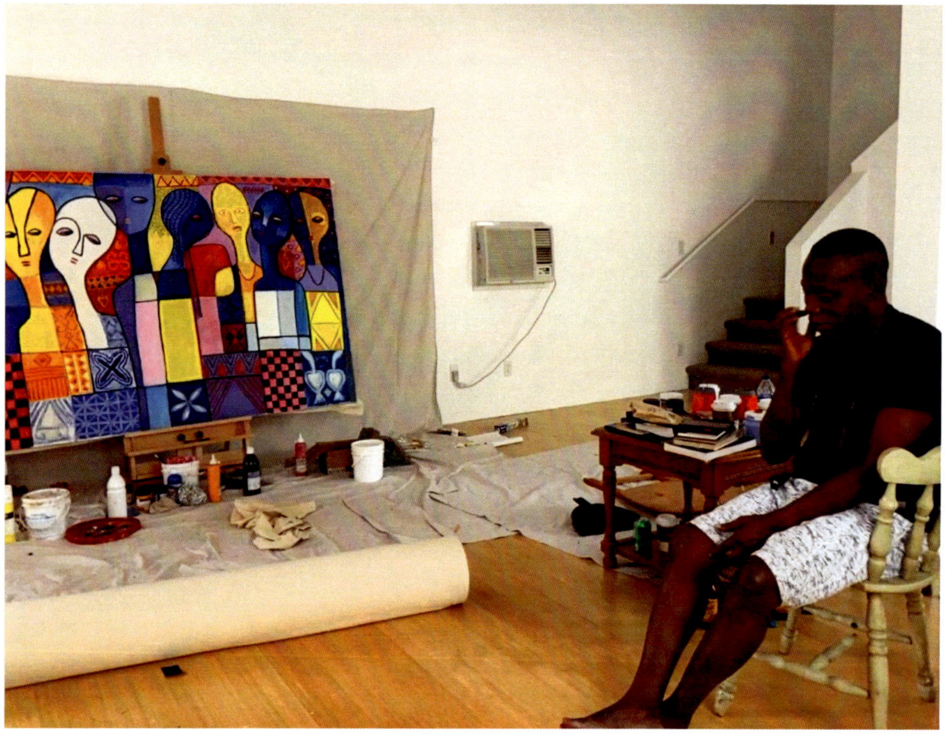

Tola Wewe in Austin, Texas